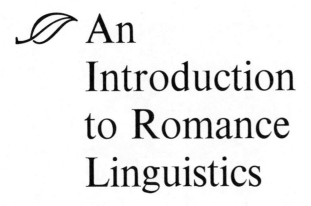

An Introduction to Romance Linguistics

D. Lincoln Canfield
J. Cary Davis

SOUTHERN ILLINOIS UNIVERSITY PRESS
Carbondale and Edwardsville

Feffer & Simons, Inc.
London and Amsterdam

Library of Congress Cataloging in Publication Data

Canfield, Delos Lincoln
    An introduction to Romance linguistics.

    Bibliography: p.
    Includes index.
    1. Romance languages.   I. Davis, John Cary,
joint author.   II. Title.
PC43.C3   440   74-34260
ISBN 0-8093-0677-8

To our beloved maestros

Ralph Hayward Keniston
and
Tomás Navarro Tomás

Contents

Maps

Figures

Preface

This book is the result of many years of teaching Romance philology and linguistics. It should fill a gap which has long existed, and one even more critical with the loss of such out-of-print references as *The Romance Languages* (Posner), *From Latin to Romance in Sound Charts* (Boyd-Bowman), and *Manuel d'ancien français* (Paton) (see Bibliography). The authors are indebted to many sources and kind friends, of whom the following deserve special mention: Miss Maria Ibba, Prof. Clement F. Heverly, La Lia Rumantscha (Ligia Romontscha), the U.S. Library of Congress, Miss M. MacLeod of the British and Foreign Bible Society, Prof. Thomas Bledsoe, Prof. John Fisher, Dr. Mario A. Pei, Prof. Massimo Pittau of the Università di Sassari.

In such a complex undertaking as this, errors are bound to occur. We can only beg the reader's indulgence and hope they have been kept to a minimum. One takes comfort in the well-known phrase, "even Homer nods," while keeping in mind Voltaire's dictum to the effect that "philology is that science in which consonants count for very little and vowels for nothing."

We have tried to incorporate in this text all the features found useful in our own classes. As the title indicates, this is only an "Introduction" to a field of study which has infinite possibilities and offers continually exciting challenges to the researcher. One of the least familiar areas is that of Rhaeto-Romance.[1] For this reason, samples of several of these dialects are included in the Appendix, along with selections from other Romance languages for comparison. We trust the student will find them of value. In most cases English translations are not given, with the feeling that this would be cheating the reader of the fun of personal discovery. One very badly needed item is a grammar of Sardo, plus any kind of reading material in the dialects of that highly important but neglected language. The Bibliography has purposely been made rather extensive, in the hope that the interested student will be lured into further study in what has been for many of us the "Best of All Possible Worlds."

Carbondale, Illinois　　　　　　　　　　　　　　D. Lincoln Canfield
September 1973　　　　　　　　　　　　　　　　J. Cary Davis

1. In this text the English spelling Rhaeto-Romance has been chosen as standard, although variant dialectal spellings may occur in the appropriate context.

Signs and Symbols

Italics are used for the orthographic representation of words: *moi;* but capitals are used for the original Classical Latin forms: LÉGE.

Brackets are used for phonetic transcription: [mwa].

Slashes (parallel diagonal lines) are used for phonemic representation: /mwa/.

> means "becomes" or "goes to": LÉGE > Sp. *ley* [lej].

< means "comes from" or "is derived from": *ley* < LÉGE.

The subscript (.) is used under *l*, *n*, *m*, and other consonants to indicate syllabic value for that consonant: for example, English *cotton* [kaʔṇ], *maple* [mɛjpl̩].

\ "falls" or "disappears." The same meaning can be indicated by the zero symbol [∅], not to be confused with the IPA vowel symbol [ø].

An asterisk indicates that the form following it is postulated, but unattested: *VÉCLU (< VÉTULU).

· indicates hiatus, as in *sea* [sé·a], or Rm. *foa·ie.*

// word division, pause.

‿ or ⁀ a tie, as in Sp. *lee* [lée].

’ aspiration, usually of a consonant: *time* [t'ajm].

× crossing or contamination of one word by another.

~ indicates nasal quality.

′ is used to show palatalization or fronting: k > k′.

: is used to indicate unusual vowel length: Fr. *rose* [ro:z].

No attempt has been made to list regional etyma as such (as Meyer-Lübke does) where they diverge from Classical or Vulgar Latin. In the case of the Latin words, a generalized oblique form, without the accusative *-m* ending once regularly listed, is given as the etymon except where a special derivative from the Latin nominative or other cases exists: for example, Spanish *hombre* < L. HÓMINE(M), but It. *uomo* and Sp. *Dios* from the Latin nominatives HÓMO and DÉUS. Stress accents are usually given for (Vulgar) Latin etyma.

In his listing of many derivative forms, such as Sardinian (Logudorese) and Rhetian words, Meyer-Lübke prefers to show phonetic values through the use of *k*, *k'*, *l'*, and so on, although the languages involved may employ *c* (Sard. *crobu*) and varied other spellings, as in Engad. *chavagl* (instead of Meyer-Lübke's *k'aval'*), and Engad. *chasa* (*chesa*), Surmiran *tgesa* (< CÁSA).

Some Romanian dictionaries use a stress accent on infinitive forms, others do not, for example, *cântà* or *cânta*. Many Romanian words with *-ân-* have an older form with *-în-* now considered dialectal, poetic, or archaic, such as *vînt* (= wind), today generally spelled *vânt*. *Cânta* used to be *cînta*. A "learned" restoration of the Latin vowel?

The listing of derivatives from the Latin normally occurs in the phonological section of this text in the order (1) Italian, (2) Sardinian,[1] (3) Romanian, (4) Spanish, (5) Portuguese, (6) Catalan, (7) Provençal, (8) French, and (9) Rhetian[2] (except where identical forms or some other factor seems to call for a different order). These are usually abbreviated as *It., Sard., Rm., Sp., P., C., Pr., Fr., Rh.*, with Engadinian, Friulian, and Vegliot as *Engad., Friul., Vegl.* Other abbreviations occasionally used include *Gal.* (Galician), *Pied.* (Piedmontese), *Venez.* (Venetian), *Lomb.* (Lombard), *Gasc.* (Gascon), and so on. Most other abbreviations should be self-explanatory.

1. See Posner 259–60, 261–62 and Elcock 478–81, 473–78 for capsule histories of Rhetian and Sardinian.
2. See note 1 above.

Definitions

ACCENT. 1. Relative intensity of a syllable based on volume of air. 2. Relative prominence through pitch or length. 3. Dialectal trait; a characteristic pronunciation.

ACCRETION. "Growth" — the addition of an element to a basic form, usually a syllable from wrong division between words, as LA VESPA > *L'AVIESPA > Sp. *la//avispa.* Compare Apheresis.

ACOUSTIC. Of or pertaining to sound, the sense of hearing or the science of sound. (Acoustic phonetics).

ACUTE ACCENT. A symbol used in printing and writing to indicate principal stress.

AFFIX. A word element that is attached to a base or stem such as a prefix or suffix.

ALLOPHONE. Any of the variant forms of a phoneme: the aspirated /p/ of *pit* and the unaspirated of *spit* are allophones.

ALTAIC. A language family of Europe and Asia, including Turkic and Mongolian.

ALVEOLAR. Formed with the tip of the tongue touching or near the upper gums.

ANALOGY. The alteration of form or structure to accommodate to a paradigm. The creation of forms on the basis of a proportion a:b = c:x (*sing, sang, sung* leads to *bring, brang, brung*).

ANALYTIC (ANALYTICAL). Expressing a grammatical category by using two or more words instead of an inflected form. In languages, the use of independent morphemes for grammatical functions.

ANDALUCISM. Linguistic trait of Andalusian origin.

ANGLICISM. A word or phrase of English origin or inspiration.

ANTEPENULT. The syllable before the last two in a word, as *-bi-* in *ability.*

ANTICIPATION. The tendency to assimilate one sound to a following one in some degree. Compare Assimilation and Umlaut.

APHERESIS. The omission of an unstressed syllable or sound at the beginning of a word. Compare Accretion.

APICAL. The articulation involving the apex (tip) of the tongue ([t], [d], [s]).

APOCOPE. A cutting off or omitting of the last sound or syllable of a word (*primero-primer*).

ARCHAISM. A construction or form that is antiquated with respect to a particular time. No longer current.

ARTICULATION. The movements of speech organs used in producing a speech sound. Any speech sound.

ASPIRATION. The pronunciation of a consonant followed by a puff of air (English [th], [ph], [kh]).

ASSIBILATE. To produce with a hissing sound. To convert to a sibilant.

ASSIMILATION. Alteration of a sound or form by making it similar to another, usually preceding or following.

ATONIC. Without accent; not stressed (atonic vowel).

AUGMENTATIVE. A suffix added to the basic root to form a new word indicating largeness, and sometimes awkwardness or unattractiveness, as Sp. *casucha* (< *casa*). See Diminutive.

BALTIC. A group of languages of the Indo-European family on the eastern coast of the Baltic Sea.

BERBER. Of or pertaining to the Afro-Asiatic languages of tribes of Northwest Africa.

BILABIAL. Pronounced with both lips ([m], [p], [b]).

BILINGUAL. Able to speak two languages.

CACUMINAL. Pronounced with the tip of the tongue turned back and up toward the roof of the mouth.

CASTILIAN. The Romance dialect of Castile, now the standard language of Spain and Spanish America; Spanish.

CATALAN. The Romance language spoken in Catalonia. Not a dialect of Spanish.

CELTIC. A group of languages of the Indo-European family (Gaelic, Welsh, Breton).

CENTUM. Of or pertaining to the group of Indo-European languages that retained the velar [K] of primitive Indo-European. Compare Satem.

CHECKED VOWEL. A vowel in a closed syllable (= one ending in a consonant). Compare Free (vowel).

CIRCUMFLEX. A mark (ˆ) used to indicate a quality of pronunciation (P. *côr;* Fr. *rôle*), or loss of a following *s* (Fr. *bâton*).

CLICK. An implosive sound produced by drawing air into the mouth and clicking the tongue. Common to certain African languages.

CLOSE(D). Said of vowels pronounced with relatively small aperture above the tongue, for example *i, u*. Compare Open (vowel).

CLOSED SYLLABLE. A checked syllable, one ending in a consonant.

CODA. The terminal consonant in a closed (checked) syllable.

COMPARATIVE PHILOLOGY. A diachronic (historical) study of a language as it evolves and develops into several variants (Latin into the Romance languages).

CONJUGATION. The inflection of a particular verb.

CONSONANT. A speech sound produced by a partial or complete obstruction of the air stream by any constriction of the speech organs.

CONTAMINATION. The alteration of a form through misunderstood association with another (Sp. *estrella* from *stella* contaminated by *astro*).

CONTINUANT. A consonant, such as *f* or *m*, which may be prolonged without change of quality.

CREOLIZED. In language development, the incorporation of the basic elements of a dominant language with the structure or vocabulary of a subordinate language (French Creole of Haiti).

CROSSING. See Contamination.

DALMATIAN. A Romance language once spoken along the eastern coast of the Adriatic Sea.

DIACHRONIC. Pertaining to language phenomena as they change with time.

DIALECT. A regional or social variety of a language.

DIERESIS. A mark (..) placed over one of two adjacent vowels to indicate that two separate sounds are involved.

DIGRAPH. A group of two letters representing a single speech sound, as *ea* in *meat*, or *th* in *path*.

DIMINUTIVE. A word that is characterized by a suffix that denotes smallness, familiarity, or affection; the suffix itself.

DIPHTHONG. A complex speech sound made up of a vowel and a semivowel pronounced as one syllable.

DIPHTHONGIZE. To pronounce as a diphthong. To become a diphthong.

DISSIMILATION. The process by which one of two similar phones in a single word is changed to become unlike the other.

DISTINCTIVE. Characteristic of distinctive features. Phonemically relevant features.

DOUBLET. One of two (or more) words within a language derived from the same source by different routes of transmission (Sp. *minuto-menudo;* Fr. *minute-menu*).

ELISION. The omission of an unstressed vowel or syllable in pronunciation, as Engl. *'tis* (= *it is*).

ELLIPSIS. The omission of a word or words necessary for complete syntactical construction but not necessary for understanding. Adj. *elliptic(al)*.

ENCLITIC. A word or particle having no independent accent in a sentence and forming an accentual unit with the preceding word (L. *populusque;* Sp. *dígame*).

ENGADINE, ENGADINIAN. A dialect of Rhaetian or Romansch, spoken in eastern Switzerland.

ENGENDERED. See Transitional.

EPENTHESIS. The insertion of an *excrescent* phoneme into a word ([fɪləm] for *film*).

EPIGLOTTIS. An elastic cartilage located at the root of the tongue that folds over the glottis during the act of swallowing.

ESOPHAGUS. The tube connecting the mouth and pharynx with the stomach.

ETYMOLOGY. The origin and historical development of a word as evidenced by study of its basic elements; the branch of linguistics that studies the derivation of words.

ETYMON. An earlier form of a word from which the later ones derive.

EUPHEMISM. The substitution of an inoffensive term for one considered offensively explicit.

EXPLOSIVE. A plosive consonant; more commonly called an *occlusive* or *stop*.

FREE. Designating a vowel in an open syllable, one not ending in a consonant (a syllable without a coda).

FREE VARIATION. Occurring without a set pattern.

FRICATIVE. A consonant produced by the forcing of breath through a constricted passage. Also called a *spirant* or *continuant* ([š], [f], [ɫ]).

FRIULIAN. The Rhaetian dialect of Friuli in northeastern Italy.

FRONTED. Said of a sound pulled forward in the mouth, as Latin [u] > French [y], or [k] of CÁTTU > [š] of Fr. *chat*.

GALICIAN. *Gallego*, the Romance dialect of Spanish Galicia and actually a variety of Portuguese.

GALLICISM. A French word or idiom appearing in another language.

GALLO-ROMANCE. The Romance language that developed out of Vulgar Latin in what is now France.

GEMINATE. To occur in pairs.

GLOTTAL. Articulated in the glottis.

GLOTTAL STOP. A speech sound produced by a momentary complete closure of the glottis, followed by an explosive release.

GLOTTIS. The vocal structures of the larynx.

GRAMMAR. The study of the structure of languages; the phenomena with which this study deals; a normative set of rules of standard usage; the "natural" structure for the native speaker.

GRAMMATICAL. Conforming to the rules of grammar, either normative or as a determined usage.

GRIMM'S LAW. A formula describing the regular changes undergone by Indo-European stop consonants represented in Germanic.

HIATUS. The immediate sequence of two vowel sounds, each of which constitutes a separate syllable.

HYBRID. A word whose elements are derived from different languages.

HYPERBOLE. An exaggeration or extravagant statement used as a figure of speech.

HYPERCORRECTION. A change in a speech habit on the basis of incorrect analogy with the intention of improving structure (*for you and I; he excaped; they attacted*).

HOMOPHONE. A word having the same sound as another word but differing from it in spelling, origin and meaning (*sum* and *some*).

IBERIAN. Of or pertaining to the Iberian Peninsula (Modern Spain and Portugal).

ILLYRIAN. The Indo-European language of the Illyrians.

IMPLOSION. The stopping of the breath in the articulation of a stop consonant.

INDO-EUROPEAN. Belonging to or constituting a family of languages that includes the Germanic, Celtic, Italic, Baltic, Slavic, Greek, Armenian, Hittite, Tocharian, Iranian, and Indic groups.

INFIX. An inflectional or derivational element inserted into the body of a word.

INFLECTION. A change in the form of a word to indicate a change of meaning or relationship, such as the -*s* to indicate a plural (Sp. *mano, manos;* Fr. *main, mains*) or verb endings in conjugations (Sp. *llamo, llamas, llama,* etc.).

INTENSITY. Stress; comparative volume of air in articulation.

INTERDENTAL. Pronounced with the tip of the tongue protruding between the teeth; a consonant articulated in this manner ([θ], [đ]).

INTERVOCALIC. Immediately followed and immediately preceded by a vowel.

INTONATION.   Pitch, musical tone.

ISOGLOSS.   A geographical boundary line delimiting the area in which a given linguistic feature occurs.

ITALIC.   The Italic branch of the Indo-European family of languages.

JUDEO-SPANISH.   Also called *ladino*. Spanish of the Jewish people who were expelled from Spain in 1492.

KINESICS.   The study or science of gestures and body motion for communication.

LABIAL.   Formed mainly by closing or partly closing the lips ([b], [m]).

LABIODENTAL.   Articulated with the lip or lips and teeth.

LABIOVELAR.   With simultaneous bilabial and velar articulations, such as [w].

LADIN.   Term used in Switzerland for the Engadine dialects of Rhaeto-Romance (q.v.). Sometimes refers to Dolomite Ladin in north Italy.

LANGUE D'OC.   The form of Romance surviving in southern France in Provençal. Its word for "yes" was *oc* (< L. HOC).

LANGUE D'OÏL.   The Romance language of Gaul north of the Loire that formed the base of modern French. Its word for "yes" was *oïl* (modern *oui*) (< L. HOC ÍLLE).

LARYNGEAL.   Produced by or with the larynx. Glottal.

LATERAL.   A sound produced by breath passing along one or both sides of the tongue.

LATIN.   The ancient Italic dialect of Latium. Of or related to Latium, its people or its culture.

LATINISM.   An idiom structure or word derived from or in imitation of Latin.

LENGTH.   The quantity of a vowel. Duration of articulation.

LEXICAL.   Of or pertaining to vocabulary.

LEXICOGRAPHY.   The writing or compilation of a dictionary.

LEXICOLOGY.   The study of the lexical (vocabulary) component of a language.

LEXICON.   A vocabulary; a dictionary; the stock of words of a particular profession.

LIAISON.   The pronunciation of a previously lost final consonant of a word followed by another word beginning with a vowel.

LIGURIAN.   Of or pertaining to Liguria (capital, Genoa). The language of the area.

LINGUA FRANCA.   A mixture of Italian with French, Spanish, Arabic, Greek, and Turkish, spoken in the Mediterranean, especially in the Levant.

LINGUISTICS. The science of language; the study of the nature and structure of human speech.

LIQUIDS. A popular designation of the sounds [l] and [r].

MEDIAL. A sound syllable or letter occurring between the initial and final positions of a word or morpheme.

MONOSYLLABIC. Having only one syllable.

MORPHEME. A minimum unit of form-meaning distinction: *raincoats* /rein-kot-s/ (using phonemic, not phonetic symbols).

MORPHOLOGY. The patterns of word formation in a particular language, including inflection, derivation, and so on, and the study and description of same.

MUTATION. The change that is caused in one vowel by its assimilation to another vowel.

NASAL. A nasal sound. Formed by lowering the soft palate so that most of the air is exhaled through the nose: [n], [m], [ŋ], [ã].

NASALIZE. To pronounce as a nasal sound by allowing some of the outgoing voice to issue through the nose.

OBSOLESCENT. In the process of passing out of use.

OCCLUSIVE. A stop consonant, explosive, plosive. Occluding or tending to occlude.

ONOMASTIC. Of or pertaining to a name or names.

ONOMATOPOEIA. The phonological formation of a word to sound like its referent: *buzz, hiss, crack*.

OPEN. Relative degree of vowel opening, based on oral angle of articulation.

ORTHOGRAPHY. Spelling. The aspect of language study concerned with letters and their sequences.

OXYTONE. A word stressed on the last syllable. Compare Paroxytone and proparoxytone.

PALATAL. Produced with the front of the tongue against or near the hard palate: [j], [č], [š].

PALATALIZE. To produce with a palatal quality.

PALATE. The roof of the mouth, consisting of the bony front, the *hard palate*, backed by the fleshy *soft palate*.

PARADIGM. A list of inflectional forms used as an example of a declension or conjugation.

PARALINGUISTICS. The study of nonverbal communicative behavior; more specifically, the study of peculiar suprasegmental speech effects.

PAROXYTONE. Having principal stress on the penultimate (next to the last) syllable.

PARTICLE. One of a class of forms that are not inflected: prepositions, conjunctions.

PARTITIVE. Serving to divide into parts; some of.

PASSIVE. A form or construction indicating that the grammatical subject is the object of the action.

PENULT. The next to last syllable of a word.

PHARYNX. The cavity to the rear of the tongue which connects the oral and nasal cavities with the esophagus and larynx.

PHARYNGEAL. Pertaining to or coming from the pharynx.

PHILOLOGY. Historical linguistics. The diachronic study of language.

PHONE. An individual speech sound.

PHONEME. A minimum unit of sound-meaning distinction. One of the set of the smallest units of speech that distinguish one utterance or word from another in a given language; the [m] of *mat* and the [b] of *bat* are English phonemes.

PHONETICS. The branch of linguistics dealing with the study of the sounds of speech. Articulatory phonetics deals with the description of speech production, acoustic phonetics, with reception.

PHONOLOGY. The science of speech sounds. The sound system of a particular language or its evolution.

PITCH. Relative intonation or musical tone as determined by frequency of vibrations.

PLOSIVE. A stop consonant, an explosive, an occlusive. Complete closure of the passage at some stage of articulation.

POPULAR. Standard development of words from the mother tongue through the different stages of vulgar use, subject to the phonological and morphological changes peculiar to the language, as opposed to learned and semilearned developments.

POPULAR ETYMOLOGY. The deformation of a word due to its fancied relationship to some other word, for example, L. MELAN-CHÓLIA > It. *mal-in-cuore.*

POSTDENTAL. Articulated with the tip of the tongue behind the teeth.

POSTTONIC. Coming after the stressed syllable.

PREDORSAL. Articulated with the front part of the dorsum (back) of the tongue against or near the palate.

PREFIX. An affix put before a word, changing its meaning.

PRETONIC. Coming before the stressed syllable.

PRIMARY STRESS. The principal or strongest stress of a word.

PROCLITIC. Said of a short word having no stress of its own, pronounced and sometimes spelled as part of the following word, as in the popular Spanish phrase ¿*Qué hubo*? [kjuƀo].

PRONUNCIATION. The act or manner of articulating speech.

PROPAROXYTONE. Having principal stress on the antepenult (two syllables from the end).

PRO(S)THETIC. Said of a phoneme or syllable added at the beginning of a word, as in Sp. *escala* from Latin SCÁLA.

PROVENÇAL. The Romance language of Provence (Southern France), especially the literary language of the troubadours. (See Langue d'oc.)

QUALITY. The timbre of tonal color which distinguishes one speech sound from another.

QUANTITY. The duration in time of an uttered sound.

RADICAL. Of or designating a word root.

REFLEXIVE. Designating a verb having an identical subject and direct object: *She dressed herself.*

REGRESSIVE. Tending to return or revert: regressive assimilation.

RETROFLEX. Pronounced with the tip of the tongue turned back against the roof of the mouth.

RHOTACISM. The substitution of an *r* for another consonant sound, usually an *l*: L. CAPÍT(U)LU > Fr. *chapitre.*

ROMANCE. (Romanic) designating, or belonging to any of the languages that developed from Vulgar Latin.

ROMANIAN. Variant of Rumanian.

ROOT. A word or word element from which other words are formed.

SARDINIAN. The Romance tongue spoken on the island of Sardinia.

SATEM. Designating those Indo-European languages, including Indo-Iranian, Armenian, Albanian, and Balto-Slavic groups, in which original velar stops became fricatives ([k] > [s], [š]) and labiovelar stops became velars ([kw] > [k]). Compare Centum.

SCHWA. A symbol ([ə]) for a neutral (central) vowel sound; also the sound itself.

SECONDARY STRESS. A stress accent weaker than primary accent but stronger than lack of stress.

SEGMENTAL. Applied to the vowel and consonant phonemes.

SEMANTICS. The study or science of meaning and meaning change in language forms.

SEMICONSONANT. A vocal sound of vowel character, but used as a consonant preceding other vowels, such as the *w* and *y* of *we* and *you.* In positions following other (stressed) vowels, as in *bow* and *boy,* these are generally called semivowels. In both cases they are part of a diphthong and are represented by the symbols [w], [j].

SEMILEARNED. Said of a word whose popular (standard) development has been checked or restrained by scholarly, legal, or ecclesiastical influence, as Sp. *siglo* (< L. SAÉCULU). The learned form would have been *seculo*, the popular one *sejo*.

SEMIOTICS. Now used for nonverbal communication, including paralinguistics and kinesics.

SEMIVOWEL. A vocal sound of vowel character but used as the latter element of a diphthong with partial consonantal quality, as the *i* and *u* of P. *oiro*, *ouro* [ɔ́jru, ɔ́wru]. Similar to, but with less strong articulation than semiconsonants (q.v., for distinction).

SIBILANT. A speech sound that suggests hissing or whistling: [s], [š], [z], [ž].

SONANT. A voiced speech sound.

STEM. The elements common to all the forms of an inflectional paradigm, usually more than a root.

STOP. See Occlusive.

STRESS. Relative loudness resulting from special effort of emphasis in utterance. What most persons mean by "accent" in a word (q.v.).

SUBSTRATUM. An underlying layer of language influence on an imposed language.

SUPRASEGMENTAL. Phonological traits beyond the segmental: stress, pitch, length.

SUPERSTRATUM. A layer of language influence superimposed on an existing language.

SURD. A voiceless sound.

SYNCOPE. The shortening of a word by the omission of a sound, letter or syllable.

SYNERESIS. The drawing together into one syllable of two consecutive vowels ordinarily pronounced separately.

SYNONYM. A word having the same, or nearly the same, meaning as another in the language.

SYNTACTIC. Related to syntax.

SYNTAX. The way in which words are related to each other in the formation of utterances, chiefly with respect to order and agreement. In combination with morphology it is referred to as "grammar" (q.v.).

SYNTHESIS. The combining or compounding of words and elements to produce a new and longer word: DE-ÚNDE > Sp. *donde;* cf. Engl. *cutthroat.* A synthetic language is one that combines elements to produce other forms, such as *like + ly = likely, + hood = likelihood.*

TABOO. A ban or inhibition attached to a word or usage by social custom or emotional aversion, usually regional.

TENSE. Enunciated with taut articulatory muscles (the Spanish vowels are more tense than the English; Romance /p/, /t/, /k/, are usually more tense than the corresponding Germanic phonemes).

TILDE. A diacritical mark (~) placed over a letter, as over the letter *n* in Spanish to indicate a palatal nasal sound, and over a vowel in Portuguese to indicate nasality (*são, Camões*).

TONE. Relative pitch. In "tone" languages (like Chinese) this quality may be not only phonemic but syntactic and/or semantic.

TONIC. Stressed, especially with tonic stress. Compare Atonic.

TRANSITIONAL. A transitional sound is an extra one "engendered" (= produced) rather automatically in the transition from one sound to another, for example, L. TÉN(E)RU > Fr. *tendre* (Engl. *tender*).

TRILL. To pronounce with a vibrating articulation, as the *rr* in Sp. *carro;* a trilled articulation. Compare Vibrant.

TRIPHTHONG. A unit of three vowel sounds pronounced in one syllable as in Sp. *buey, principiáis.*

ULTRA CORRECTION. A change in a speech habit on the basis of incorrect analogy. Also called hypercorrection.

UMLAUT. A change in a vowel sound caused by partial assimilation to a vowel or semivowel, originally occurring in the following syllable, now often lost. The diacritical mark placed over a vowel to indicate an umlaut: (ö, ä, ü).

UNVOICED. Voiceless: pronounced without vibration of the vocal cords.

URAL-ALTAIC. A hypothetical family of languages including the Uralic and Altaic families.

UVULA. The small fleshy mass of tissue suspended from the back of the soft palate.

UVULAR. Articulated by vibration of the uvula or by friction between the back of the tongue and the uvula.

VEGLIOT. Dalmatian (q.v.).

VELAR. Formed with the back of the tongue on or near the soft palate: [g], [k].

VIBRANT. A trilled sound; usually produced by vibration of tip of tongue, uvula, or lips.

VOCAL CORDS. Folds of mucous membrane projecting into the cavity of the larynx, the edges of which can be drawn taut and made to vibrate by the passage of air from the lungs, thus producing vocal sound.

VOCALIC.   Pertaining to or having the nature of a vowel.

VOCALIZE.   To change a consonant into a vowel during articulation.

VOICED.   A sound uttered with voice (accompanied by vibration of the vocal cords): [d], [b], [m].

VOICELESS.   Uttered without vibration of the vocal cords: [t], [p], [s].

VOWEL.   As opposed to a consonant (q.v.), a speech sound, usually voiced, but sometimes whispered, that is not characterized by audible friction of air in the oral passage, but rather by a coupled-cavity resonance varied by the position of the tongue in the mouth cavity.

VULGAR LATIN.   The common speech of ancient Rome, the basis for the development of the Romance languages.

WAU.   A name sometimes given to the sound of the semiconsonantal *u* [w], as in L. ÁQUA, Sp. *manual*.

YOD.   The tenth letter of the Hebrew alphabet. Term used in historical linguistics for a "y" sound [j] which by assimilation may exert a heightening influence on a vowel of the preceding syllable.

An Introduction to Romance Linguistics

Crobu cun crobu non si tirad ogu
Un sombrero no tapa dos cabezas

Chapter 1

Introduction

Language and Culture

Although we all use language, few of us realize what a marvelous skill we possess. The human baby is the only young of any species that has an inclination to babble, and it is now thought that by a process of elimination he finally selects from a very large repertoire the sounds and structure patterns that he hears in his environment. This selection is made for the most part long before he goes to school and his guidelines are fixed by the home first, then by the "street," and in the long run his principal teacher may very well be the "kid across the street."

This language that he has learned quite well, in sound, form, and pattern, by the age of six is only one part of a vast culture that his society presents to him already made through centuries of interaction, and his very nature and way of life will be determined in large measure by this culture. Throughout life the language that he learned will be the key to the rest of his societal behavior, which includes attitudes, concepts, reactions, ways that have been learned in a climate of unawareness and that will be very tenacious in his adult life. These ways of doing things fall into several social categories: association, interaction, play, bisexuality, temporality, territoriality, defense, subsistence, exploitation, etc. One of the best examples of a system of informal culture is the pattern of gestures that a given culture uses. Spanish, for instance, has at least a hundred fairly standardized gestures that are used among 200 million people, and yet few of these *hispanos* remember having learned them and would have difficulty in describing them. Most of our language, too, has been given to us in a climate of unawareness.

Given the fact that we learn most of the structure of our "native" language without realizing what is going on, and also the fact that this structure tends to be tenacious over the years and even centuries, it is not surprising to note that although vocabulary changes constantly (university campuses demonstrate this), one's pronunciation and grammar change

1

very little after adulthood, and it is difficult for the adult to assume the language posture of another culture, just as it is difficult for him to assume the attitudes and ways of another culture.

Language and Writing

Although all people of the earth speak languages, some of the "primitive" ones being more complicated than the "civilized," less than half of human beings read and write.

Writing is not the same as language. It is a system of graphic symbols that may represent sounds, syllables, or even ideas. Systems of graphic symbols become so fixed that although the language they represent may change, they remain constant and thus misrepresent speech. English speakers normally have numerous and serious misconceptions about English and about language in general, because our school systems still use a normative approach, based on the written letter, to teach the alphabet, the sound system (which the child already knows), and spelling.

Most of us were taught, as our grandchildren are being taught, that English has five vowels: *a*, *e*, *i*, *o*, *u*, and that these are long and short, that the long vowels "say their own name." The marks to indicate long and short are the marks used to indicate length or lack of it in Latin: ‾ and ˘. What is called *long* in this way of doing things is actually a diphthong that does not correspond to the written symbol. The word *name*, for instance, was written as it is because the Latin letters involved represented quite phonetically the spoken word [name]. In the meantime the spoken word has gradually changed and is [nɛjm]. English has developed through the centuries a system of nine to twelve vowels, depending on dialect, but the child is not told this, in spite of the fact that he uses them. He could be taught to analyze what he actually does and then shown how he must represent this behavior by an antiquated system of spelling. As it is, the speaker of English usually carries misconceptions about letters, spelling, sounds, and so on, throughout his life. As an example of how far astray English has gone from the path of "phonetic" spelling, consider this anonymous poem illustrating the difficulties of a foreigner learning English:

TRY'N TO LARN ENG-LEESH

Ima tol' p-l-o-u-g-h
   She'sa pronon-ced "plow."
'Atsa no so very hard,
   I tink zeez inglese I get t'rough.

But zen la professora she say
    Een 'at case, o-u-g-h eez "oo."
I laugh, "Ha-ha, you don' say so!
    Zeez eng-leesh mak' me cough."

"Not coo," she say, "for een 'at wo-ord
    O-u-g-h eez 'off'."
"Ah, mama mia! Socha strange-a sounds
    Een wo-ords mak' me hiccough."

"Not so, not so, you're wrong again,
    O-u-g-h eez 'up'
Een hiccough." Zen I cry "Enough, enough!
    You mak' my t'roat feel rough."

"Een bot' doze wo-ords o-u-g-h
    eez 'uff': *enuff*, and *ruff*."
"Oh no," I say, "I try to spik —
    No can pronounce zem though."

"Perhaps een time you'll larn, but now
    'At wo-ord, she'sa sound like 'owe'."
"Ay, San Giuseppe — help me, please —
    Zeez inglese sure air tough."

"Again, that's 'uff'," to me she say,
    "You know, like *muff* and *cuff*."
"I cang go on, I mus' geev up,
    I'll drown me een a lough."

"That you may do, if you insist,
    But here o-u-g-h eez 'ock'."

Zen I get mad, I tak eet from her desk,
    And heet her wiz her clough.

Syntax and Language

Most linguists now regard the phonemes (basic sounds) and the morphemes (basic forms) of a language as finite, while the syntax (grammar) is more than a collection of morphemes, and we do not need attestation to certify that a sentence is grammatical. The fact that syntax is so closely linked to meaning and semantic change means that it is practically infinite in possibilities, and yet the "native" speaker of a language can certify grammaticality, although the number of possible sentences is infinite and the expressive power of the language is infinite. Though the matter is very complex, the speaker of the language has a unique "feel" for the possibilities. Many now believe that the human being has an implicit, inborn knowledge of the nature of language.

The application of this inborn knowledge, if there be such, to "dead" languages implies a thorough conditioning process in the distinctive features of that language to the extent that one has a "feel" for its structure, both surface and deep, and for the possibilities of expression.

Linguistics and Philology

One who speaks many languages is not necessarily a linguist, and a linguist does not always speak many languages. A polyglot is one who speaks many languages. In the modern sense, a linguist is one who analyzes and describes aspects of language. Many linguists speak only their own first language. Many polyglots know very little about the phonology, morphology, and syntax of the languages that they speak and still less about the notation systems that might be used to describe them.

The general study of linguistics is divided on the basis of temporal factors into diachronic studies and synchronic studies. Diachronic implies that the examination of features is to be made on a continuum, from one time in history to another, for example, Latin to French. In this type of study it is evident that change may be an important element and that the major consideration, in any case, is development. Synchronic linguistic studies consider features present at one time, usually the present, and change and development are replaced by geographical and social distinctions. As might be surmised, it is difficult to separate completely these two approaches in a thorough examination of phenomena. In the examination of the Latin-to-Romance continuum, for instance, one is struck by the conservative development of Italian on the one hand, and the very considerable change in French. In the synchronic comparison of these two languages one could not avoid the consideration of diachronic elements. In the same Latin-to-Romance continuum a synchronic study of Spanish would show generally a later diachronic stage than Italian.

The term *philology* as used in the United States is essentially diachronic linguistics or historical linguistics. These latter terms have been preferred in recent years to *philology* because the latter word, as used in Europe, indicates both literary and linguistic scholarship. A good example of this is the vast recorded scholarship of the *Zeitschrift für Romanische Philologie*.

The Elements of Language

Linguists generally divide their consideration of language into phonology (the sounds); morphology (the forms, especially the grammatical inflexions); and syntax (the arrangement and agreement of forms as related to meaning). As has been pointed out, the expressive power of both the phonology and morphology of a given language is finite, while the number of possibilities of syntactic expression is infinite. Lexical studies such as etymology (origins of words) and semantics (meaning changes) are considered by many as a part of linguistics, while others limit linguistics to the consideration of structural features.

Phonology

Phonology deals with the phonemes (minimum units of sound-meaning distinction) of a language and the variants of these (allophones) according to situation as they constitute a system. Phonetics, on the other hand, is the scientific study of the sound features of a language. Articulatory phonetics is a branch of physiology, in a sense, and examines the production of sounds in the speech apparatus of the human being. Acoustic phonetics studies sounds as they are heard, using many recording devices to this end, and is a branch of physics.

Phonology may also deal with the suprasegmental aspects of a language (sound features that are not consonants or vowels): intonation (musical pitch); stress (volume of air); length (relative time for articulation); juncture (open or closed transition). Beyond this, phonology may even consider paralinguistic devices (modifications of the normal segmental or suprasegmental features for the purpose of obtaining "effects" in speech), for example, coughing on purpose or lowering the voice, whistling as a signal, grunting, snorting, using the Bronx cheer, and so on.

Segmental Features

Human speech sounds are made up of vowels and consonants, embellished by the traits just described. The combinations of vowels and consonants are spoken of as the segmental features of a language. All humans use combinations of vowels and consonants for communication, but the arrangements vary a great deal from language pattern to language pattern. Some behavior patterns tolerate complicated clusters of consonants (the Slavic languages), others have developed a CVCV system (Japanese, Italian), others tolerate only certain final consonants in the syllable (Spanish). The key to the vowel-consonant combinations and arrangements is the syllable, which can be described in terms of onsets, nuclei, and codas: that is, initial consonant or cluster, if any; vowel or vowel combination; terminal consonant if any.

A vowel is voice (that is, vibration of the vocal cords) modified by some definite configuration of the superglottal passages and without audible friction. Some languages have only three basic vowel sounds (Quechua, Tagalog, Arabic, for example). Others have fifteen or more (French, Portuguese). Vowel systems are often shown on a "vowel triangle," which is a schematic device for indicating roughly the position of the tongue with relation to the palate during the production of the sound, as well as the width of the opening of the jaws. The basic triangle which we shall need for Vulgar Latin or early Romance is shown in figure *1*.

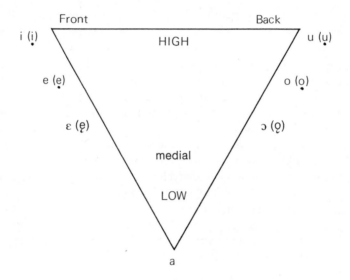

1. *Vowel triangle for Vulgar Latin*

The symbols in parentheses are those used by the Spanish linguists (Menéndez Pidal and Tomás Navarro), the others by the International Phonetic Alphabet.

A consonant, on the other hand, is speech sound characterized by audible friction, occlusion, vibration, or other impediment to the free passage of air from the lungs. Consonants are either voiced or voiceless, depending on whether the vocal chords vibrate during the passage or not. [t] and [d] are alike except that the vocal cords vibrate in the case of [d], not in the case of [t].

The borderline between vowel and consonant is sometimes a thin one, and [w] and [j] are called semiconsonants or semivowels, depending on their position with relation to other vowels. In some languages these take on audible friction. In the English of today, both British and American, certain consonants, notably [l] and [r] have lost their friction or vibration and have moved into the realm of the vowel, although the configuration may vary dialectally. Such borderline sounds often assimilate contiguous vowels or are assimilated by the vowels, leaving a single sonant where both consonant and vowel had existed.

Certain symbols have been developed by descriptive linguists to represent phonemes, phones, morphemes, and so on. For several years, too, consonants have been described on the basis of point of articulation, type of obstruction to the passage of air, namely, fricative, occlusive, vibrant; and whether the vocal cords vibrate or not. Thus a bilabial voiced occlusive could be only [b]; a bilabial voiceless occlusive would be [p].

The symbol generally agreed upon for the phoneme is the letter enclosed in slashes: /t/. Brackets are used to indicate phonetic value: [t]. The phoneme /t/ in the English of the United States, for instance, has several phonetic manifestations (allophones): [tʰ] (*two times two*); [r] (*Betty, butter, water*);[1] [t] (*step, stop, spent*); [ʔ] (*button, button, who's got the button*). The sound-meaning unit understood by an American in all these cases is /t/. As an illustration of a finite system of phonemes in a Romance Language, the following are those of Spanish, showing distinctions that exist. A phonemic transcription of the sentence, *Las damas de la Habana, Cuba* would be /las dámas de la abána, kúba/. A phonetic transcription would be [laz đámaz đe la aƀána kúƀa]. In the first case the elements are abstract symbols that indicate minimum units in the system. In the second case, the actual sounds are depicted as they occur under the circumstances of the utterance.

The symbol generally employed to indicate the morpheme is the brace { }. The morpheme, like the phoneme, is an abstract entity that is used to represent a whole class of forms that have the same function. The morpheme for the plural in English is {z}. Its allomorphs can be represented with phonemic notation: /-s; -z; -ız; -en; ∅ (zero)/, as in *hits; boys; bushes; oxen; sheep.*

The Classification of Languages

Many of the more than two thousand languages of the world have been classified on several bases. Two of the most common ways of putting languages into classes or groups are the typological and the generic. The former lists languages by tendencies in structure: those that tend to be

---

1. Some equate this /t/ allophone with [d], not [r].

analytical in syntax formation, as opposed to those that tend to be synthetic or agglutinative, for instance. The second means of classification puts together languages that are demonstrably related, having descended from a common ancestor. Today the second method is generally used, and we speak of families of languages, which in turn are divided into groups, the groups into languages and the languages in many cases into dialects of geographical or social designation.

Chapter 2

The Romance Languages Today

The most widely spoken of the Romance languages today is Spanish, both in terms of the number of speakers (about 200 million) and in terms of the number of political units in which it is the first language. It is the official language of Spain; the eighteen republics of Spanish America, Puerto Rico, Spanish Morocco in Africa; and it competes with English and Tagalog in some parts of the Philippine Islands. Heavy concentrations of Spanish speakers are to be found in New York City, Miami, Chicago, Los Angeles, and vast areas of the American Southwest, where in some regions it enjoys official status with English. Since World War II it is one of the five official languages of the United Nations, along with English, Russian, French, and Chinese.

French is not only the daily speech of the inhabitants of France, but is also spoken as one of the standard tongues in Belgium, Switzerland, Luxembourg, French Canada; the present and former colonial holdings in Africa, Asia, the South Seas, and the West Indies, such as Algeria, Tahiti, Zaire (the former Congo), Niger, French Guiana (Cayenne); Vietnam, Cambodia, and other parts of former French Indo-China. In Haiti it is spoken principally in a creolized form. It is the literary language of cultured persons, and along with English, the international language of travelers, used and understood in many parts of the world. It is one of the five official languages of the United Nations. As a first language, French is spoken by about 80 million and it is the auxiliary language of millions more.

Portuguese, as everyone knows, is spoken in Portugal and the Azores, but many people do not realize that it is the language of the largest nation of South America, namely Brazil. The port city of Macao across the bay from Hong Kong, Madagascar (now part of Tanzania), Goa in India, are examples of the once widely-flung empire of Portugal where Portuguese is still spoken, or was spoken until recently. There are over 100 million speakers of Portuguese.

Italian is largely confined to Italy, Sicily, and Sardinia — where it competes with the native Sardinian dialects. It was at one time the official language in Eritrea, Libya, and other former colonies of Italy in Africa. Before World War II it was also spoken in Trieste and other localities along the Dalmatian coastline, today parts of Austria and Yugoslavia. At one time Italian was spoken by more people than English. Today they number about 60 million.

Provençal is still current in some towns of southern France, in the vicinity of Marseilles, but is not officially sanctioned or promoted, and its speakers seem ashamed of its use. There has been no significant literary output in Provençal since the attempt to "revive" the language a century or so ago. During the Middle Ages and the Renaissance, it was highly important and very influential upon its neighbor languages, lending many words to all of them and initiating many literary movements and genres adopted by them. It was the first of the Romance languages studied by Friedrich Diez.

On the other hand, Catalan, which often resembles Provençal and is considered by some scholars to be an offshoot or variety of the latter, is very much alive. It is the daily speech of Catalonia (Cataluña, Catalunya) and Valencia in eastern Spain, and the Balearic Islands, although officially subservient to Spanish and frowned upon by Madrid. The two chief centers, Barcelona and Valencia, were the first cities in the Iberian peninsula to have their own printing presses and a publishing tradition pridefully upheld today. There are many volumes printed in Catalan, including children's books, in spite of the fact that Castilian is the language of instruction in the public schools, and there is a professorial chair in Catalan, at the University of Madrid.[1]

Romania was the most eastern outpost of the Roman Empire to maintain the Latin language brought by its conquerors. In spite of successive invasions by Magyar, Slav, and Turk, the country has kept its ancient name and the language many of the characteristics of the Roman tongue, although Romanian is heavily infiltrated by Slavic words and features. It still has a vestige of Latin cases (see chap. 3, sec. 7). Romanian has a very respectable literary output, formerly greatly influenced by French writers.

Rhetian

Under the term Rhetian (Rhaeto-Romance, Raeto-Romansch, etc. — various forms and spellings) are included many dialects and subdialects of this branch of Romance spoken in the Grisons of eastern Switzerland,

---

1. An archaic form of Catalan is still spoken in the city of Alghero (Alguer, Alguero) in Northwest Sardinia. There are also large concentrations of Catalan speakers in parts of Argentina, as evidenced by the celebrated Jocs Florals in Mendoza in that country.

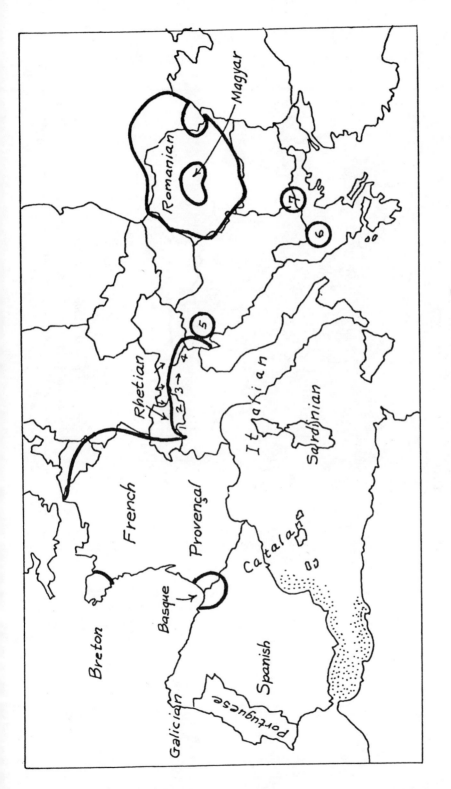

The Distribution of Romance Languages in Europe

Rhetian Dialects: 1, 2, Swiss Rumantsch: Engadinian, Sursilvan, Sutsilvan, Surmiran; 3, Dolomite Ladin; 4, Friulian

Others: 5, *Vegliot (Dalmatian)*; 6, 7, *Scattered Romanian Dialects*

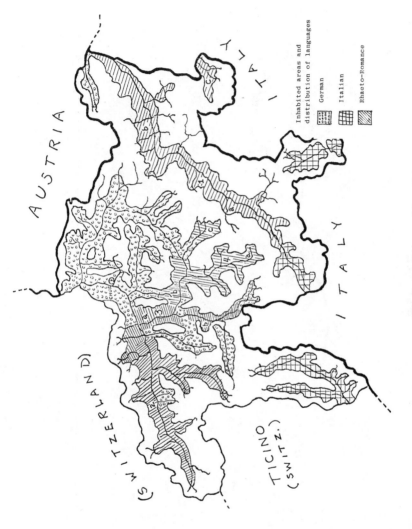

The Swiss Canton of Les Grisons

1, *Ladin* (a, *Haute-Engadine*; b, *Basse-Engadine*; c, *Val Müstair*); 2, *Sursilvan*; 3, *Sursilvan* (a, *Schams*; b, *Domleschg*); 4, *Surmiran* (a, *Oberhalbstein*; b, *Unterhalbstein*; c, *Bergün-Filisur*) northeastern Italy, and parts of Austria. Each group has been greatly influenced by neighboring languages (especially Italian and German) in vocabulary, spellings, syntax, and the like, but all have their own distinctive characteristics and linguistic developments. Authorities list at least three divisions: (1) a western group (Romansch), composed of Sursilvanian (or *Sursilvan*), near the sources of the Rhine, Subsilvanian (*Sutsilvan*) and Surmeirian (*Surmiran*) in the Central Grison, and Engadinian (Upper and Lower) in the forty-five-mile-long Engadine Valley; (2) a central group in the Italian sections, sometimes referred to as Dolomite Ladin; (3) an eastern group, Friulian, spoken in Friuli, a former duchy now mostly in Venezia and Venezia Giulia. (See maps, the Distribution of Romance Languages in Europe and the Swiss Canton of Les Grisons.)

The original population of these mountainous valleys spoke Rhetian, a language some think akin to Etruscan, perhaps related to the Illyrian branch of Indo-European (see fig. 5). The conquering Roman legions brought Latin, which in time developed into the various dialects of Rhaeto-Romance. Spoken formerly over a much wider area, they are still today the regular idiom of more than fifty thousand Swiss, in addition to those speakers outside the Swiss borders. The dialects are very much alive: more than five thousand works have been published in Rhaeto-Romance since 1552, and there are many classroom texts used regularly in the primary and secondary schools. In 1938 Rumantsch or Romanche was officially declared a fourth national language of Switzerland.

Meyer-Lübke's *REW* (*Romanisches etymologisches Wörterbuch*) has been used as the source for many Rhetian words and spellings. He regularly lists only Engadinian and Friulian, plus the Dalmatian Vegliot, with an occasional entry for Ladin. The word *Rumantsch* or *Romansch* (various spellings) is often used to indicate the entire group of Rhetian dialects spoken in Switzerland, just as certain scholars have used *Ladin* (< LATÍNU) as an overall word for the whole Rhaeto-Romance branch. In Switzerland, however, the latter term (*Ladin*) is usually applied only to Engadinian, which is considered by some linguists as the chief dialect of Rhaeto-Romance. Samples of several of the Rhetian dialects are included in the Appendix of this text.[2]

Dalmatian, as its name suggests, was formerly spoken over a wide area along the eastern shore of the Adriatic. (See map, Linguistic Areas of

---

2. See Posner 259–60 and Elcock 478–81 for capsule histories of Rhetian. Meyer-Lübke (*REW*) has his own phonetic system of spellings which usually differ from the orthography actually used in the various dialects (e.g., *k'aval'* for Eng. *chavagl*). Where the correct forms are known, they are regularly given in preference to those of the *REW*.

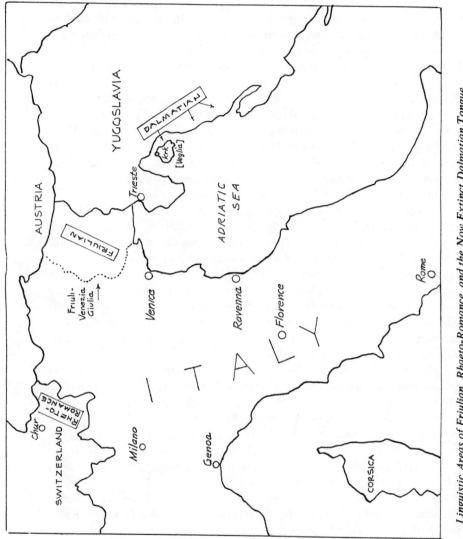

Linguistic Areas of Friulian, Rhaeto-Romance, and the Now Extinct Dalmatian Tongue

Friulian, Rhaeto-Romance, and the Now Extinct Dalmatian Tongue.) It finally died out on the island of Veglia in the last century, hence the name Vegliot generally applied to it by such authorities as Meyer-Lübke.

Sardinian is composed of four very similar dialects: Cagliaitan or Campidanese (Campidanian) in the South, Sassarese and Tempiese (Gallurese) in the North, and Logudorese in the center of the island. (See map, Sardinia and Its Four Principal Dialects.) This last is considered by some linguists as the most important, and is the one regularly listed in Meyer-Lübke's *REW*. As in the case of Rhaeto-Romance, he regularly uses phonetic spellings, such as the letter *k* for the "hard" sound of *c*, in his word samples. The northern dialects have been somewhat more affected by Italian than the others.[3] One of the most striking distinctions between the northern and southern dialects is the use by the former of derivatives from ILLE rather then IPSE for the definite article. This feature and other peculiarities of the separate dialects are well illustrated in the Biblical reading selections in the Appendix. See Posner (261–63) and Elcock (473–78) for short historical summaries.

3. La lingua sarda si divide in due varietà dialettali principali: 1) Logudorese; 2) Campidanese. A sua volta il logudorese si divide in tre suddialetti: a) Logudorese comune; b) Logudorese settentrionale; c) Logudorese centrale o nuorese. Quest' ultimo ha la caratteristica di essere il più arcaico e genuino.

Il dialetto campidanese si divide in due suddialetti principali: a) Campidanese cittadino; b) Campidanese rustico o campagnolo. Il campidanese è molto meno genuino ed arcaico del logudorese in generale. Il dialetto cagliaritano non è altro che il *campidanese cittadino*.

Il dialetto gallurese è un dialetto corso, importato nella Sardegna settentrionale da Corsi immigrati in Sardegna.

Il dialetto sassarese da alcuni autori è considerato *non sardo*, da altri sì. I primi sostengono che il sassarese è un dialetto italiano fortemente sardizzato; i secondi invertono i termini: un dialetto sardo fortemente italianizzato. Io sono di questa seconda opinione (Massimo Pittau).

Sardinia and Its Four Principal Dialects

Chapter 3

The Phonology of Romance

§1. The Syllable

The unit of utterance known as the syllable is normally a vocalic core separated from other nuclei of speech by consonants or clusters of consonants of some sort. The syllable is in a sense the pulse of speech and in its maximum extent will consist of an initial consonant (*onset*), a vocalic core (*nucleus*), and a consonantal termination (*coda*). The syllable of a monosyllabic utterance may be onset + nucleus, coda or onset + nucleus, or nucleus + coda, or simply nucleus alone. The English words *pan*, *pa*, *an*, *a* illustrate these types. In the development of languages, vowels have been known to slough off leaving a *syllabic consonant: n* [n̩] for *and*.

All languages have their own syllabic features and limitations. Just as they have certain phonemes and allophones, they have limited arrangements and characteristic of these elements. As an example, Spanish tolerates as onset any of the consonants of its system, but the only clusters it allows are those of consonant plus /l/ or consonant plus /r/, and its only codas are /l/, /d/, /r/, /n/, /s/, /θ/. English, in turn, has a long list of initial clusters and many possible codas.

The Consonants

There are two principal ways of describing speech sounds: (1) in terms of articulation and (2) in terms of perception as revealed by spectrographic analysis. In this text, sounds are described in terms of articulation, which means that the principal factors are point of production in the speech apparatus, manner of articulation, and whether the sound has voice (the vocal cords vibrate) or not.

With respect to the place of articulation, the points involved include bilabial, labiodental, interdental, dental, alveolar, palatal, velar, uvular, and glottal (laryngeal). See Definitions for specific details of articulation.

17

As far as manner of production is concerned, the principal ways are these: occlusives (stops, explosives), affricates, fricatives, nasals, laterals, vibrants (flaps, trills), semiconsonants.

Consonants are also either voiced or voiceless (surd).

By combining these three factors, a fairly accurate description can be made of the consonants, usually with three words, for example, voiceless bilabial occlusive ([p]).

The following chart (fig. 2) shows the place of articulation, the manner of articulation, and the presence or absence of voice, of the majority of the consonants that occur in the Romance languages. The symbols employed represent modifications that have been made in recent years of the International Phonetic Alphabet. The main reason for many of these changes has been to facilitate the typing and printing of phonetic symbols.

CONSONANT SYMBOLS

Stops
- p   Voiceless bilabial occlusive: Fr. *pain*; Sp. *pan*
- b   Voiced bilabial occlusive: Fr. *bon*; It. *bagno*
- t   Voiceless dental occlusive: Fr. *ton*; Sp. *tanto*
- d   Voiced dental occlusive: It. *dente*; Sp. *dámelo*
- k   Voiceless velar occlusive: Sp. *cal*; Fr. *qui*
- g   Voiced velar occlusive: Fr. *gai*; It. *gatto*

Affricates
- ts   Voiceless dental affricate: It. *zingaro*
- č   Voiceless palatal affricate: Sp. *chico*; It. *cinque*
- ŷ   Voiced alveolopalatal affricate: Sp. *yo, un yugo*
- ĝ   Voiced palatal affricate: It. *Giorgio, gemma*

Fricatives
- φ   Voiceless bilabial fricative: Sp. (dialectal) *fuego*
- ƀ   Voiced bilabial fricative: Sp. *haba, la barca*
- f   Voiceless labiodental fricative: Fr. *feu*; It. *franco*
- v   Voiced labiodental fricative: Fr. *rêve*; It. *avete*
- θ   Voiceless interdental fricative: Sp. (Spain) *cinco, luz*
- đ   Voiced interdental fricative: Sp. *nada, verdad*
- s   Voiceless dental fricative: Fr. *laisser*; Sp. (L.A.) *rosa*; It. *passo*
- z   Voiced dental fricative: Fr. *rose*; P. *rosa*
- ś   Voiceless alveolar fricative: Sp. (Spain) *rosa, oso*
- ż   Voiced alveolar fricative: Sp. (Spain) *desde, los dos*
- š   Voiceless palatal fricative: Fr. *cher*; P. *chave*, It. *pesce*
- ž   Voiced palatal fricative: Fr. *jeter*; P. *jôgo*
- x   Voiceless velar fricative: Sp. *jamón, gente*
- ǥ   Voiced velar fricative: Sp. *hago la guerra*
- h   Voiceless glottal (laryngeal) fricative: Sp. (dialectal) *majo*

Vibrants
- r   Voiced alveolar single flap: It. Sp. *caro*
- r̄   Voiced alveolar multiple vibrant: Sp. *carro*; It. *guerra*

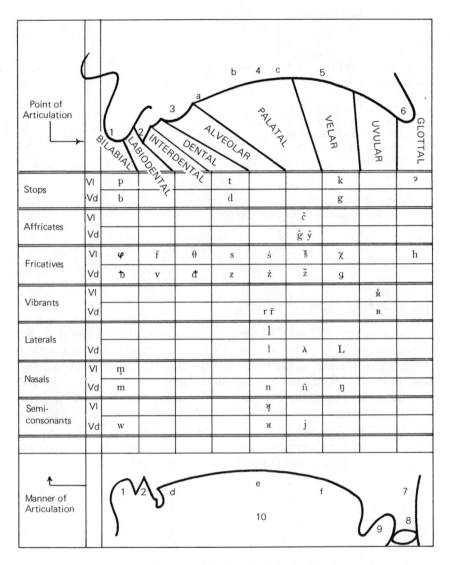

Point of Articulation →		BILABIAL	LABIODENTAL	INTERDENTAL	DENTAL	ALVEOLAR	PALATAL	VELAR	UVULAR	GLOTTAL
Stops	Vl	p				t		k		ʔ
	Vd	b				d		g		
Affricates	Vl						č			
	Vd						ĝ ŷ			
Fricatives	Vl	φ	f	θ	s	ṡ	š	χ		h
	Vd	ƀ	v	đ	z	ż	ž	ɡ		
Vibrants	Vl								R̥	
	Vd						r r̄		ʀ	
Laterals	Vl						l̥			
	Vd						l	λ	L	
Nasals	Vl	m̥								
	Vd	m					n	ñ	ŋ	
Semi-consonants	Vl						ɹ̥			
	Vd	w					ɹ	j		

Manner of Articulation ↑

2. Articulatory organs and phonetic chart: 1. lips; 2. teeth; 3. alveolar ridge; 4. palate (a. prepalate; b. midpalate; c. postpalate); 5. velum; 6. uvula; 7. pharynx; 8. vocal cords; 9. epiglottis; 10. tongue (d. predorsum; e. mid-dorsum; f. postdorsum); Vl. voiceless; Vd. voiced

R Voiced uvular vibrant: Fr. *Paris, rose*
R̥ Voiceless uvular vibrant; P. *carro*; Sp. (Puerto Rico) *perro*
Laterals
   l Voiced alveolar lateral: Fr. *elle,* Sp. *él,* It. *il*
   λ Voiced palatal lateral: Sp. (Spain) *ella*; It. *sbaglio*; P. *ôlho*
   L Voiced velar lateral: P. *mal*
Nasals
   m Voiced bilabial nasal: Fr. *mon*; It. Sp. *mano*
   n Voiced alveolar nasal: Fr. *non*; Sp. *no*; It. *non*
   ñ Voiced palatal nasal: Fr. *baigner*; Sp. *baño*; It. *bagno*; P. *banho*
   ŋ Voiced velar nasal: Sp. *cinco, tengo*; It. *banco*
Semiconsonants
  Sonants
   w Voiced bilabial-velar sonant: Fr. *moi*; Sp. *agua*; P. *eu*
   j Voiced palatal sonant: Fr. *hier*; *travail*
   ɥ Voiced bilabial-palatal sonant: Fr. *lui*

§2. The Evolution of Vowels

Most scholars of the Classics are convinced that Latin had only five basic vowels: /i/, /e/, /a/, /o/, /u/, all of which could occur long or short in the temporal sense, as has been described: ā [aa], a [a]. Certain combinations of these occurred in one syllable as diphthongs: /ae/ [aj]; /oe/ [oj]; /au/ [aw]. Spoken Latin (Vulgar Latin) gradually replaced the quantity of Classical Latin with quality, as far as the vowels are concerned, and what had been long became closed in articulation, and the short tended to become open. Stress took the place of length as far as the syllable is concerned. Figure 3 illustrates the correspondences.

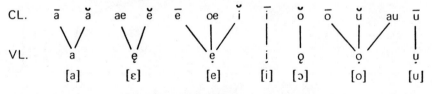

3. *Vowel development from Classical to Vulgar Latin*

Beyond Vulgar Latin the stressed vowels had a tendency to become diphthongs in some of the Romance languages, notably French, Spanish, and Italian. Later evolution of the French vowels brought the diphthongs back to single vowels, but not the original ones, as we shall see.

Tonic or stressed vowels evolve somewhat differently from atonic (unstressed) ones. The general development of tonic vowels for Spanish and Old French, for example, is shown in figure *4*.

VL.	a	ẹ	e̦	i̦	ǫ	o̦	au	u
Sp.	a	ie̦	e̦	i̦	ue̦	o̦		u̦
OFr.	a(e)	ẹ(ie)	e̦(ei)	i̦	ue̦	o̦(o̦u)		[y]¹

4. Tonic-vowel development from Vulgar Latin to Spanish and Old French

As a result of the shift from the factor of length to that of quality with stress, the stress on the penultimate syllable became the usual thing, and many words that had in the process developed stress on the antepenultimate syllable (proparoxytones) tended to eliminate the unstressed syllable, thus becoming paroxytones. This development continued in most of the Romance languages except Italian and Romanian. Classical Latin had already made PÓSTU out of PÓSITU, and ÁLTU ("tall, high") from ÁLITU ("well-nourished"!). FÁBULA becomes Spanish *habla*.

Other examples of this general tendency are the following:

L. TÁBULA > Sp. *tabla*, Fr. *table*, C. Pr. *taula;* but It. *tavola*, P. *tabua* (Rm. *masă* < MÉNSA)

L. DUÓDECIM > Sp. *doce*, Fr. *douze*, P. *doze*, Pr. C. *dotze;* but It. *dodici* (Rm. *doisprezece* = a different development)

L. PÉDICA > Sp. *piezgo*, Fr. *piège*, C. Pr. *petge;* but It. *piedica*, Rm. *piedică*

L. FRÁXINU > Sp. *fresno*, Fr. *frêne*, C. *freixe*, P. *freix*, Pr. *fraisse;* but It. *frassino*, Rm. *frasine*

Vowels preceding the stressed syllable, unless protected by a consonant cluster, tended to fall:²

L. BONITÁTE > Sp. *bondad*, P. *bondade*, Fr. *bonté*, It. *bontà*, C. *bondat*.

---

1. Spelled *u* but pronounced like the German umlauted *ü*. Modern French shows a still further development of some of these vowel sounds.
2. In initial position, initial attack in itself tends to preserve the vowel.

L. RADICÍNA > Fr. *racine,* Sard. *raigina,* Pr. *razina;* but Rm. *rădăcină*

L. *BLASTIMÁRE > Fr. *blâmer,* Pr. *blasmar,* Rm. *blama;* but It. *biasimare,* Sp. P. *lastimar,* C. *llastimar*

L. MATUTÍNU > Fr. *matin,* It. *mattino,* C. *matí,* Pr. *mat(t)in*

L. VERECÚNDIA > Fr. *vergogne,* It. *vergogna,* Sp. *vergüenza,* P. Pr. *vergonha,* C. *vergonya*

L. ALICÚNU > Fr. *aucun,* It. *alcuno,* Sp. *alguno,* P. *algum,* Pr. *alcun,* C. *algú(n)*

Protected by a cluster:

L. GUBERNÁRE > Sp. *gobernar,* Fr. *gouverner,* P. C. Pr. *governar,* It. *governare,* Rm. *guverna*

L. ORNAMÉNTU > Fr. *ornement,* Pr. *ornamen,* It. P. Sp. *ornamento,* C. Rm. *ornament*

A shift in stress accent naturally had its effect on any possible absorption or suppression of what had been an unstressed vowel, or which became an unstressed vowel:

L. (Grk.) SYMPHONÍA > It. *simfonia,* Sp. *sinfonía* or *zanfonía* (= hurdy-gurdy)

(but) VL. *SIMFÓNIA > It. *zampogna,* Sp. *zampoña* (= shepherd's pipe)

The same syllable, in tonic (stressed) and atonic (unstressed) position, developed differently, as illustrated by the pronoun ILLA in the following examples:

CL. ILLA VIDET ILLAM LUNAM   (That [girl] sees that moon)
VL. élla védẹt (el) là lúna

It.	*ella vede*	*la luna*	
Sp.	*ella ve*	*la luna*	(She sees the moon)
P.	*ela vê*	*a lua*	
Fr.	*elle voit*	*la lune*	

Some modern Romance languages — especially Spanish and Portuguese — regularly shifted the stress accent of certain -ERE Latin verbs, while others like Italian (and often French) preserved the original stress. Examples are: PÉRDERE > It. *perdere,* Fr. *perdre,* (stress on first syllable), but Sp. P. *perder* (stress on last); MÓLERE > It. *molere*, Fr. *moudre* (stress on first syllable), but Sp. *moler*, P. *moer* (stress on last); SÁPERE > It. *sapere* (stress on first syllable), but Fr. *savoir*, Sp. P. *saber* (stress on last). Catalan has *perdre*, *moldre*, but *saber*.

VOWEL SYMBOLS (See Figure 1)

i As in French, Spanish, Italian *si*, Rm. *și*
e (ẹ) As in Fr. *quai*, Sp. *te*
ɛ (ę) As in Fr. *nette, naître*
a As in Fr. *salle*, Sp. *pata*
ɑ As in Fr. *pas*
ɔ (ǫ) As in Fr. *porte*, It. P. *porta*
o (ọ) As in Fr. *eau*, Sp. *tono*
u As in Fr. *bout*, Sp. *tu*
y (ü) As in Fr. *lune*
φ (ö) As in Fr. *feu*
œ (ö) As in Fr. *neuf*
ə As in Fr. *cheval* (often called "neutral vowel" or *schwa*)
ɐ Occasionally used to indicate the slurred *a* in P. *para* (pɐrɐ)
ɪ Occasionally used to indicate the open *i* in Portuguese: *cidade* [sidáĝɪ]

The comparison of languages over the years has led to the assumption that some are related and come from a common source. Many assumptions of this type have been confirmed after study and investigation and so many similarities have been found in phonology, in syntax and, above all, in lexicon, that geneological classifications have evolved gradually. The divisions have become family for the largest or gross classification, and the family may be divided into groups usually identified regionally or politically and having more identifiable similarities. The group, in turn, may have languages that are very definitely related and the languages may have several dialects. These last units are usually mutually intelligible.

The principal families of the world are the Indo-European, the Afro-Asiatic, also known as the Hamito-Semitic, the Sino-Tibetan, the Altaic, the Dravidian, the Malayo-Polynesian and the Finno-Ugric. Beyond these better-known families, there are hundreds of units that are families by the same geneological standards, and yet they are represented by only a few people or have not been studied to any extent. The Basque of northern Spain and southwest France is an example. It has no known relative.

The Indo-European family is the largest and the best known and takes in about half the population of the world, including nearly all of Europe, most of the Western Hemisphere and a large section of India. It has many groups or branches, including Indic, Iranian, Albanian, Baltic, Slavic,

Greek or Hellenic, Italic or Romance, Celtic and Germanic. New members of the family are discovered from time to time (see fig. 5).

The Italic or Romance group of the Indo-European family represents the expansion of a language unit once centered in Rome, and the derivation of the Romance languages from Latin has been recognized for centuries. They represent the uninterrupted historical continuation of the spoken rather than literary variety of Latin.

The spoken variety of Latin traditionally goes by the name of *Vulgar Latin*, but because of the connotation of *vulgar*, some scholars prefer the adjectives *popular* or *spoken*. Evidence indicates that Vulgar Latin existed side by side with Classical Latin and was spoken by all strata of Roman society, and as a matter of fact, the term *vulgar*[3] was also applied by writers and the clergy to the nascent Romance languages to distinguish these from the Latin of scholarship. Naturally the spoken and the literary influenced each other to the extent that normative influences of the Classical have at times weighed heavily on the Vulgar, giving us "learned" terms and usage.

The political and social upheavals of the fourth century and the barbarian invasions after the fall of the empire loosened the bonds between the literary and the spoken varieties of Latin and furthered the cause of the latter. Gradually, too, the Vulgar Latin of what sometimes is called Romania[4] showed regional differentiation, some of it undoubtedly due to loss of the common empire but much of it substratum influence from pre-Latin languages.

Romance historical linguists have often accounted for the separate developments of Spanish, French, and other Vulgar Latin dialects by assuming articulatory modifications carried over by speakers who adopted Latin as their second language. Such influences are referred to as substratum. Celtic influence on the Vulgar Latin of Gaul is cited as the cause for the development of [y] (*lune*) in the French system, and Basque influence during the formation of Castilian from Vulgar Latin may be the cause for the conversion of Vulgar Latin intial [f] to [h]: FŎLIA > *foja* > Sp. *hoja*.

Superstratum influences occur when speakers of an established language are overrun or conquered by people who speak a different language but may not succeed in converting the original settlers totally. The Vulgar Latin of northern Gaul was demonstrably affected by Germanic

3. < VÚLGUS, "the common people."
4. The entire region of Roman Conquest in contradistinction to the present-day country of Romania (Rumania).

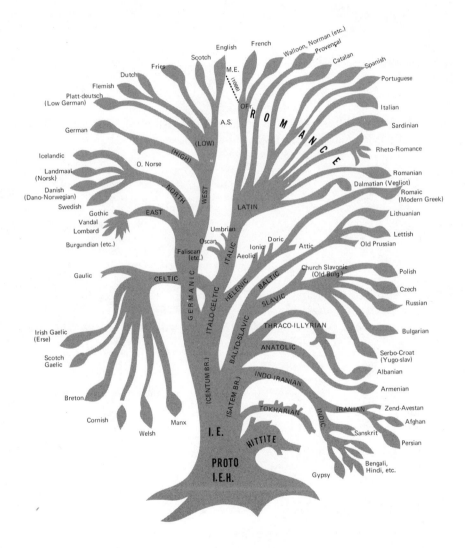

5. *Indo-European-Hittite language tree*

languages, notably Frankish, while southern France and Iberia show little
that can be referred to as Germanic, except in lexicon. Old French diphthongization and the neutralization of unstressed vowels, especially finals,
is undoubtedly a Germanic trait.

§3. Tonic or Stressed Vowels

Tonic /á/

In free syllables (syllables without coda) stressed /a/ remained in
most of the Romance territory, as shown below:

L.	CANTÁRE /kan-ta-re/	PRÁTU /pra-tu/	CÁPRA /ka-pra/
Sard.	cant*a*re	pr*a*du	cr*a*ba
It.	cant*a*re	pr*a*to	c*a*pra
Rm.	cânt*a*	pr*a*t	c*a*pră
Sp.	cant*a*r	pr*a*do	c*a*bra
P.	cant*a*r	pr*a*do	c*a*bra
C.	cant*a*r	pr*a*t	c*a*bra
Pr.	cant*a*r	pr*a*t	c*a*bra

But in northern Gaul (i.e. "France"), /a/ > /e/ [a > aj > e] (later opened
in some cases): Fr. *chanter*, *pré*, OFr. *chievre* (MFr. *chèvre*).

In a checked stressed syllable (a syllable with a coda) /a/ continues
unchanged, even in northern Gaul:

L.	ÁR·CU	CABÁL·LU	PÁR·TE
It.	*arco*	*cavallo*	*parte*
Sard.	*arcu*	*caddu*	*parte*
Rm.	*arc*	*cal* (< *caal*)	*parte*
Sp.	*arco*	*caballo*	*parte*
P.	*arco*	*cavalo*	*parte*
C.	*arc*	*cavall*	*part*
Pr.	*arc*	*caval*	*part*
Fr.	*arc*	*cheval*	*part*

Influence of a Palatal Element

A semiconsonantal *i* or *y* (sometimes called a *yod*, from a letter in the
Hebrew alphabet) usually exerted a lifting influence, so that an *á* plus
y [j] was raised to [e].

Process: $á + y$ (= [aj]) > éi [ɛj] > ẹ [e].

This is a process of assimilation in which the lower element [a] is pulled to a higher position in the mouth, then in turn pulls the higher (palatal) element ([j] or yod) to meet it and the two may then become one (fig. 6).

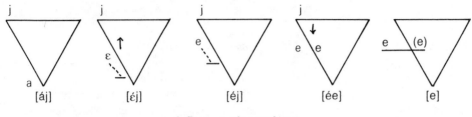

6. *Process of assimilation*

This process is not complete in all languages, but the lifting power of a yod (or similar palatal element in a consonant) was especially strong in the West, namely, in Gaul and the Iberian Peninsula.[5] The influence even extends from one syllable to a preceding one, that is, the assimilation is regressive:

L.	HÁBEO	BÁSIU	LÁC·TE
(VL.	[hájo]	[básjo]	[láxte])
Rom.	HAYO [(h)ájo]	BAYSO [bájso]	LAY·TE [lájte]
Sp.	*he* [e]	*beso*	*leche*
P.	*hei* [éj]	*beijo*	*leite*
C.	*he* [e]	*bes*	*llet*
Pr.	*ai* [aj]	*bais*	*lach*
Fr.	*ai* [e]	*baisier* < BASIÁRIU	*lait* [le]

Note that certain combinations with yod, that is, -*ry* [rj], -*sy* [sj], and the like tended to reverse positions, a process called metathesis, as in BÁSIU > BÁYSO. In addition, a checked *c* [k] before a front consonant in much of Romance territory became a fricative [x] and then was pulled forward to a palatal (yod) position in the mouth, as in LAC·TE > LAY·TE [lak-te > laj-te] (fig. 7).

Note also that the Portuguese forms and orthography represent an intermediate stage in the process, and that the French spelling *ai* [e] (also Provençal) represents an early stage when the vowel combination was [aj]. In Old French this combination was often spelled *e*, showing that the sound

5. Not in Italian, which has *ho, baccio, latte*, and Romanian with *lapte*. Romanian has other forms for HÁBEO (= *am*, by analogy with SUM) and BÁSIU (= *sărut*) of different origin. Cf. also Sard. *bazu* (< BÁSIU).

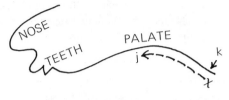

7. Development of [k] to [j]

had already become a single high vowel in most dialects.[6]

The above process was a popular one. A more learned development is often found, side by side in the same language, or a closely related one. At least three types of development are recognized: (1) a learned one, (2) a semilearned, and (3) a popular development. (See sec. 4 for a more extended treatment.)

Examples:

L. ÁERE > *aéro-* (learned combining form, as in Sp. *aeropláno*, Fr. *aéroplan*, etc.)
> Sp. *aire* [ájre] (semilearned)
> Fr. *air*, P. *ar* (popular)
L. ARTÍCULU > C. Fr. *article*, It. Sp. P. *artículo* (learned)
> *artigo(l)o* > P. artigo (semilearned)
> SP. *artejo*, P. *artelho*, Fr. *orteil* (popular)[7]

Further examples of the evolution of stressed /a/ in the principal Romance Languages:

L.	It.	Sp.	P.	Fr.
MÁRE	mare	mar	mar	mer
CÁRU	caro	caro	caro	cher
FÁBA	fava	haba	fava	fève
CÁMPU	campo	campo	campo	champ
PÁSSU	passo	paso	passo	pas
ÁSĬNU	asino	asno	asno	âne

6. French had a special development in the case of an *a* followed by *n* in a free syllable. This combination also generated a yod which had a lifting effect: L. PÁNE > PÁY NE > Fr. *pain* [pɛ̃]. This development was confined almost exclusively to Northern Gaul, although Romanian also has *pâine*.

7. Romanian has *aer*, *artícol*, Catalan *aire*, *artell*, Provençal *air*, and *aire*, *arteil* and *artelh*, etc. Italian *artiglio* is probably borrowed from Pr. *artelh*.

The noun ending -*ariu*, indicating a "doer," had a particularly interesting and divergent development, as attested by the following forms:

L. CABALLÁRIU
It. *cavallaio* (aryo > a[r]yo > ayo) or *cavallaro* (aryo > ar[y]o > aro)[8]
Sard. *caddarzu* (aryo > a[r]zu)
ORm. *călariu* (MRm. *călăras, călăret* is of different origin)
Sp. *caballero* (aryo > ayro > eyro > ero)
P. *cavaleiro* (aryo > ayro > eyro)
C. *cavaller* (aryo > ayro > eyr[o] > er)
Pr. *cavalier* (aryo > yer[o] > yer)[9]
Fr. *chevalier* (aryo > yer[o] > yer)[10]

The -*ariu* (-*aria*) developments then are:

It. -*aio* (-*aia*) or -*aro* (-*ara*)
Sard. *azu* (-*aza*)[11] or -*arzu* (-*arza*)
Rm. -*ariu* (-*aria*)
Sp. -*ero* (-*era*)
P. -*eiro* (-*eira*)
C. -*er* (-*era*)
Pr. *ier* (-*iere*, -*iera*)
Fr. -*ier* (-*ière*)

Note that the Portuguese form (as often) represents an earlier stage of Spanish. Further examples of the evolution of -*ariu* /arju/:

L.	It.	Sp.	P.	Fr.
PRIMÁRIU	*primaio*	*primero*	*primeiro*	*premier*
CALIDÁRIA	*caldaia*	*caldera*	*caldeira*	*chaudière*
OPERÁRIU	*operaio*	*obrero*	*obreiro*	*ouvrier*
MOLINÁRIU	*molinaio*	*molinero*	*moleiro*	*meunier*
USURÁRIU	*usuraio*	*usurero*	*usureiro*	*usurier*

8. The strong yod in Italian absorbed the *r* in *cavallaio*. *Cavallaro* is an alternate dialectal form, while the learned *cava(g)liere* is a French or Provençal borrowing. Portuguese *cavalheiro* is also borrowed (< Sp.?).

9. Perhaps through Germanic influence? Cf. German *Ritter*, English *rider*, etc.

10. See note 9 above.

11. As in *firmazu, firmaza* <PRIMÁRIU, PRIMARIA. Meyer-Lübke, *REW*, lists all such -*z*- with -*dz*- as an indication of sound [dz].

Classical Latin combinations of -DY- and -GY- (spelled -DI- and -GI-) merged with -Y- (spelled -I-) in Vulgar Latin, to remain as a consonant beginning the next syllable, and thus did not affect the preceding *A* — except in French:

L. RÁ·DIU
(VL., Romance RÁ·YO)
It. *raggio* [rá·ĝo]
Sard. *rayu* [rá·ju]
Rm. *raza* (< RÁDIA)
Sp. *rayo* [rá·jo]
P. *raio* [rá·ju]
C. *raig* [ra:ž]
Pr. *rag, rai* [rač, raj]
(but) Fr. *rai* [re] (< [raj] < rá·yo)

The same process holds true for -LY-, which underwent a whole series of transformations; likewise -NY-:[12]

L. ÁLLIU		BÁNEU (< BÁLNEU)	
(VL., Romance	Á·LYO)	(BÁ·NYO)	
It. *aglio*	[áλo]	*bagno*	[báño]
Sard. *azu*	[ázu]	*banzu*	[bánzu]
Sp. *ajo*	[áxo]	*baño*	[báño]
P. *alho*	[áλu]	*banho*	[báñu]
C. *all*	[aλ]	*bany*	[bañ]
Pr. *alh*	[aλ]	*banh*	[bañ]
Fr. *ail*	[a:j]	*bain*	[bɛ̃]

(Note that French also participates here, except for *bain*.)

Tonic /áu/[áw]

This diphthong has survived in certain areas of the old Roman Empire.

In the East and some parts of Italy:

L. ÁURU > Rm. *aur*
L. LÁUDAT > Rm. *laudă*
L. TÁURU > Rm. *taur*, Sicilian *tauru*, Calabrian *táguru* (toe of Italy),

---

12. In both [a] followed by [λ] and [a] followed by [ñ] there is no onglide, hence no lifting in general. But cf. French.

and Apuleian *tovuru* [modified *au* > *ou*] (heel of Italy); cf. Sard. *trau*[13]

In southern Gaul:

L. CÁUSA > Pr. *causa*
L. ÁURU > Pr. *aur*
L. LÁUDAT > Pr. *lauza*
L. TÁURU > Pr. *taur*

Elsewhere it disappeared early by a general process which we already know as assimilation, a compromise in position: áu > ọ́u > ọ́ọ > ọ:

L. ÁURU > It. Sp. *oro*, P. *ouro*,[14] C. Fr. *or*
L. CÁUSA > It. Sp. C. *cosa*, P. *cousa*,[15] Fr. *chose*

The learned Fr. form *cause* represents a traditional spelling, but the sound of /o/ (= [ko:z]) while Sp. *causa* [káwsa] is completely learned. Possibly also Rm. *cauză*. Portuguese as usual shows the intermediate stage of Spanish. Compare other dialects of the Iberian Peninsula. Further examples of the evolution of *au* [aw]:

L.	It.	Sp.	P.	Fr.
AUSÁRE	*osare*	*osar*	*ousar*	*oser*
AUT	*o*	*o*	*ou*	*ou*
PAÚCU	*poco*	*poco*	*pouco*	*peu* (OFr. *pou*)
POSÁRE	*posare*	*posar*	*pousar*	*poser*

Stressed L. /Ĕ/ (VL. /ɛ/ [ɛ̣]) and Stressed L. /ŏ/ (VL. /ɔ/ [ɔ̣])

General Remarks

Generally in free syllables (no coda) /ɛ/ diphthongizes in Italian, Spanish, and French, but not in Portuguese. In a stressed syllable with coda, only Spanish diphthongizes:

---

13. In Sardinian, and in words borrowed into Albanian, *au* regularly > *a:* CÁUSA > OSard. *casa*, LÁURU > Sard. *laru*, Alb. *lar*, AÚRU > Alb. *ar*. Sard. *oro* is borrowed from Italian.

14. The alternate Portuguese forms *oiro* and *coisa* have an entirely different origin. See Williams 92, 7C.

15. See note 14 above.

L.	It.	Sp.	P.	Fr.
PĔDE	*piede*	*pie*	*pe*	*pied*
FĔL	*fiele*	*hiel*	*fel*	*fiel*
MĔL	*miele*	*miel*	*mel*	*miel*
PĔTRA	*pieṭra*	*piedra*	*pedra*	*pierre*

In some places (e.g., France) a nasal following had a lifting effect, converting original /ɛ/ to /e/ [e]:

L. VĔNTU > VẸNT(U) > OFr. *vẹnt* (early) and Pr. *vẹn, vẹnt;* cf. Rm. *timp* < TÉMPU, below

In later development, French-*en* [ēn] > [ã] and identical with the sound of -*an*, as shown by poetic end-rhyme.

In Brazilian Portuguese, -*em*, -*en*- [ē] represents an earlier phase of the language, as contrasted to modern Lisbonese [əj]. Compare the two pronunciations of *bêm* [bē], [bəj] and *vento* [vēntu], [vəjntu].

Italian *benvenuto* probably represents a pretonic development. Compare French "Qu'est-ce que *c'est?*" [sɛ] and *"C'est* moi" [se mwá] where the lack of stress on the first element of the latter phrase serves to raise the vowel *e*.

Examples with nasal: BĔNE > Sp. OFr. *bien* [bjen]. BŎNU > Fr. *bon* [bõ], PŎNTE > Fr. *pont* [põ]. In Italy also, /ɔ/ may become /o/: It. *ponte*, but BŎNU > *buono*. Portuguese has *bom* [bõ].

In Romanian, [ɛn] may > [en], or even [ī] as in *timp* < TĔMPU, and [ɔn] > [un]: PŎNERE > Rm. *punere.* (But not VẸNTU which > *vânt.* See above and below.)

Compare Pr. *ven* (*vent*), *temps, pon,* and so on, and C. *pont, vent, temps* (all with [e] and [o]).

A velar labial [w] (a Latin V or U), on the contrary, had a lowering effect:

L. ŌVU > *ŎVO > It. *uovo* (dialectal *ovo*), Sard. Rm. *ou*, Sp. *huevo* (< *uovo*), P. *ôvo* and (pl.) *ovos* [óvuš], C. *ou*, Pr. *ou, uou,* etc., OFr. *uef* (MFr. *oeuf* is an attempt at a "restored" spelling.)

As stated, in general /ẹ/ > ie [je], while /ọ/ > uọ [wo] > /ue/ [we]. Compare regional treatments below. This is one of the most important phonological changes in Romance, but it was not the same in all countries.

The phonological process proper (called "bimatización" by Menéndez-Pidal) is as follows, in terms of Vulgar Latin notation: /ẹ > ẹ́ẹ > ẹẹ́ > ᵉẹ́ > ⁱẹ́/ (dissimilation) > [je] (assimilation!); /ọ > ọ́ọ > ọọ́ > ᵒọ́ > ᵘọ́/ (Ital. and OSP.) > [wɸ] > uẹ [we] (Sp. and OFr.).

/Ĕ/ and /Ŏ/ Regional Treatments

Central Italy (Italian)

Here stressed VL. /ẹ/ and /ọ/ in free syllables diphthongize, except in proparoxytones, while in checked syllables (syllables with a coda) they do not.

In the free syllables:

FĔLE > It. *fiele*
SĔDET > It. *siede*
PĔTRA > It. *pietra*
FŎRIS > It. *fuori*
NŎVU > It. *nuovo*
MŎRIT > It. *muore*
PŎTET > It. *puo*[16]

In the checked syllables:

FĔSTA > It. *festa* [ɛ]
PĔCTU > It. *petto*
PŎRTA > It. *porta* [ɔ]

And in the proparoxytones: HĔDĔRA It. *edera;* PŎPŬLU > *popolo* (accents retained on first syllables).

Rhetia and the Dalmatian Region

Even in checked syllables, /ie/ and /uo/ (and other diphthongs) regularly developed throughout Friuli, Istria, Dalmatia, but not always in the Engadinian dialect of Rumansch (Rhaeto-Romansch).

16. Cf. Northern Italy: Lombardian *fel*, Piedmontese *pera*, Milanese [nœf] and [mœr]. In Sardinian, there is no diphthongization: *fele, pedra*.

MĔR(U)LU(-A) Istr. *mierlo*, Friul. *mierli*, Vegl. *miarla;* but Engad.
   merl
FĔSTA > Vegl. *fiasta*, Friul. *fieste*, Engad. *feista*
CŎRNU > Istr. *kuorno*, Vegl. *kuarno*, Friul. *kuarn*, Engad. *cüern*
PŎRTA > Istr. *puorta*, Vegl. *puarta*, Friul. *puarta;* but Engad. *porta*

Romania

Diphthongization regularly occurred in both free and checked syllables:

MĔR(U)LA > Rm. *mierlă*
HĔRI > Rm. *ieri*
PĔCTU > Rm. *piept*
FŎRTE > Rm. *foarte;* but FŎRTIA > *forță*[17]
NŎCTE > Rm. *noapte*, FŎLIA > *foa·ie*
MŎRTE > Rm. *moarte;* but MŎRTU > *mort*

Compare, however, PŎRCU > *porc*, NŎVU > *nou*, and TĔMPU > *timp*.
This last may be due to the lifting effect of the nasal. Yet VĔNTU gives
vânt! (Old spelling for *ân*, however = *în*.)

Gaul

Early diphthongization occurred before a palatal, in both North
and South:

PĔCTUS > [pjɛxt(o)s] > *pieyts > Pr. *pieitz*, OFr. *piz* (MFr. *poitrine*
   < PECTORÍNA)
NŎCTE > *nuoyt(e) > Fr. *nuit*, Pr. *nueit*
FŎLIA > [fóλa] > [fwɔλa] > Pr. *fuelha*, OFr. *fueille*, Fr. *feuille*

Later, in the North, diphthongization occurred in any free syllable:

PĔDE > *piede > OFr. *piet* (MFr. *pied* is a restored spelling.)
MŎLA > *muola > OFr. *muele*, Fr. *meule*

In the South, however, these do not diphthongize:[18] PĔDE > Pr.
pede, MŎLA > *mola*.

---

17. For this development, see below and sec. 5.
18. Except before a labial or velar consonant: MÉU(M) > Pr. *mieu*, FÉBRE > *fieure*,
MŎVET > *mueu*, SÉQUO > *siec*, FŎCU > *fuec*.

Iberia

In the West (Portuguese, Galician, and others) and East (Catalan) there is no diphthongizing of these vowels, but in the Center (Castile) even in a checked syllable they diphthongize, that is [ɛ] > [je], and [ɔ] > [wɔ] > [we]:

FĔLE > Sp. *hiel*, P. *fel*, C. *fel*
PĔTRA > Sp. *piedra*, P. *pedra*, C. *pedra*
QUÁERO > *quero* > Sp. *quiero*, P. *quero*
TĔNET > Sp. *tiene*, P. *tem*, C. *té*
TĔRRA > Sp. *tierra*, P. *terra*, C. *terra*
*MŎRIT > Sp. *muere*, P. *morre*, Gal. *more*, C. *mor*
*PŎTET > Sp. *puede*, P. *pode*, C. *pot*
PŎRTA > Sp. *puerta*, P. *porta*, C. *porta*

Menéndez Pidal's theory of "bimatización," referred to above, is that a two-toned conscious effort to keep the open sound produces two impulses with primary stress on the first element and a subsequent shift of stress to the second. (Compare the English emphatic "Why, má-yan!" for "Why, man!") The vowel breaks in the effort to hold it to the end, since the end is the important part of the sound: [ɛ > ɛ́ɛ > eɛ́ > ié > je];[ɔ > ɔ́ɔ > uɔ́ > wɛ > we].

In one sense, we can say that in Spanish *ie* and *ue* are not really diphthongs, but rather consonant ([j], [w]) plus vowel.

In Spanish, a palatal (yod) produced special results, that is, it closed the vowel before it could break[19] (see *a* + yod above):

PĔCTU(S) > Sp. *pecho*[20]; cf. It. *petto*, P. *peito*, C. *pit*, Pr. *pechs*
PŎDIU > Sp. *poyo*;[21] cf. C. *puig* [puːž], Pr. *pog, poi*
FŎLIA > Sp. *hoja*[22]; cf. P. Pr. *folha*, C. *fulla*

---

19. Only in Castile: cf. Aragonese and Leonese *pieito, pueyo*, and *fuella*. Note that Spanish makes no phonemic distinction between [e] and [ɛ]; the pronunciation of /e/ depends on position, and any variation is a minor one. Basque also has the one phoneme in this area.
20. See note 19 above.
21. See note 19 above.
22. See note 19 above.

SPĔCULU > Sp. *espejo;* cf. It. *specchio,* P. *espelho,* C. *espill,* Pr. *espelh,* and even German *Spiegel*
NŎCTE > Sp. *noche;* cf. It. *notte,* P. *noite,* C. *nit,* Pr. *nuech*

The phonological process is: [pę́ktu > péxto > pę́jto (P.) > (Sp.) pę́ĉo]; [spék(u)lu > ispéχlo > espę́ilo > espę́λo (Port.) > espéžo > espéšo > espéχo (Sp.)].

One palatal combination, however, -TY- [tj], from Latin *-ti-* or *-ci-*, early coalesced (throughout the Romance area) into a single consonant sound [ts] and thus had no lifting effect: FŎRTIA > OSp. *fuerça* [fwertsa] > Sp. *fuerza.*[23]

Where *e* > *ię* early and is followed by a yod, there is a double lifting effect, a process not limited to Spanish:[24] TĔPIDU > [tję́beđo] > [tjebjo] > Sp. *tibio.*[25] This development, with retention of the weak syllable in the early stage, is characterized as a semilearned one. A popular one would probably have given *tiedo.* Compare Fr. *tiède.*

Other examples in Spanish are:

CASTĔLLA > OSp. *castiella* [kastję́λa] > Sp. *castilla* [kastíλa]
*SEDĔLLA > *sę́lla > *się́lla > Sp. *silla* [síλa]

In Spanish, it is the effort involved in producing a double *l* (-ll-), with tongue pressed more tightly against the roof of the mouth, that produces the palatal. The same process occurs in Catalan (that is, CASTĔLLU > C. *castell* [kastéλ], but without diphthongization of the vowel).

In hiatus also, Spanish produces a second yod, with the same lifting effect:

DĔUS > [dję́·os] > [dję́·jos] > [djí·os] > Sp. *Dios* (with shift of accent stress to the *o*); cf. It. *Dio* [dío], Sard. P. *Deus,* C. *Deu,* Pr. *Deu* and *Diu,* Rm. *Zeu* (all stressed on the first vowel), and Fr. *Dieu*
MÉU > *mieo* (Leonese) > *m^{i}ę́^{y}o > Sp. *mío;* cf. It. *mio,* Sard. Rm. P. C. Pr. *meu*

---

23. Analogy with adjective *fuerte* may also have helped.
24. This accounts for the French development of SEX > *siéis* > *six* [sis].
25. The vowel lifting did not take place until after the [đ] had been lost and a *yod* created.

An interesting word to trace in Romance is L. ÉGO (= I):

ĔGO > /*ęo > *ⁱęⁱo > ío > ió/ > Sp. *yo;* cf. It. *io* [ío], Sard. *eu,*
eo, deu, eju, Rm. and P. *eu,* C. jo [žo], Fr. *je* (from OFr. *jo* [ĝo]),
and in Vegl. *yu,* Engad. *eu,* Friul. *yo*

An early yod is itself usually absorbed into a preceding palatal, as in:

VL. MULIĔRE > OSp. *mogier* [moĝiér] > Sp. *mujer* [muχér]; cf.
It. *mogliera* (with analogic -a), Sard. *muzere,* Rm. *muiere,* P.
mulher, C. *muller* [muλér], Pr. *molher,* OFr. *moillier*

For the same reason certain verbs in Spanish have no *i* in the third
person preterite plural ending:

OSp. *dixieron* [dišjéron] > Sp. *dijeron* [diχéron]. Also, modern
gruñeron and *bulleron* (from *gruñieron* and *bullieron*); cf. OFr.
vengier [venĝjér], *chief* [čjef]; but MFr. *venger* [vãžé] and
chef [šef]

Castilian *s,* which still today in most of Spain is apico-alveolar,
approaching a palatal quality, also had a lifting effect:

PRĔSSA > OSp. *priessa,* Sp. *prisa*
VĔSPA > Sp. *avispa* (The *a* is apparently by analogy with *abeja,*
assisted probably by apheresis.)

Stressed Ē (VL. /ę/ [e]) and Stressed L. Ō (VL. /ǫ/ [o])

Closed /ę/ and /ǫ/ had several origins. See table of Classic and Vulgar
Latin equivalents (fig. 3).

These vowels in Romance were much more stable under stress than
the open ones. The outstanding exception, however, was in northern France
(French), where -é- and -ó- (in free syllables) were diphthongized.[26] The
general process was as follows: [e > ee > ej > əj > ɔj > wɛ > wa]
spelled *oi* [wa]; [o > oo > ou > u, œ] spelled *ou* [u] and *eu* [œ] respectively.

---

26. The same process occurred in Celtic Italy and in Dalmatia: Geonese and Piedmontese have *teila, beive* (<BĬBIT), Vegl. *kataina* (<CATÉNA), *paira* (< PĬRA), and Bolo-
gnan *flour* (<FLŌRE).

Compare the English process in *they* [ðɛj] and *go* [gɔw] with the French examples:

TĒLA > OFr. *teile* > Fr. *toile*
SĬTI > OFr. *seit* > Fr. *soif*
CRĒDIT > OFr. *creit* > Fr. *croit*
SŎLU > OFr. *soul* > Fr. *seul*
FLŌRE > OFr. *flour* > Fr. *fleur*
GŬLA > OFr. *goule* > Fr. *gueule*
POÉNA > OFr. and Fr. *peine* (before *n* the *ei* remained)
VĒNA > OFr. and French *veine*

In central Italy, Sardinia,[27] Romania,[28] southern France, and Iberia, however, these closed vowels (ẹ and ọ) were usually preserved:

L.		It.	Sard.	Rm.	Sp.	P.	C.	Pr.
TĒLA	>	tela	tela	teară	tela	teia[29] tela	tela	tela
SĬTI(S)	>	sete	sidis	sete	sed	sede	set	set
CRĒDIT	>	crede		crede	cree	crê	creu	cre
VĬDIT	>	vede		vede	ve	ve	veu	ve
SĒTA[30]	>	seta	seda		seda	seda	seda	seda
POÉNA	>	pena	pena		pena	pena[31]	pena	pena
PLĒNU	>	pieno		plin	lleno	cheio[32]	ple	plen
BĬBIT	>	beve		bea	bebe	bebe	beu	beu
FOÉDU	>	fedo	feu		feo	feio[33]		
SŌLU	>	solo	solu		solo	sòˈ	sol	sol
GŬLA	>	gola	bula	gură	gola	gola	gola	gola
VŎTU, -A	>	voto	votu	vot	voto (boda)	voto (boda)	vot (boda)	vot
LŬTU	>	loto	ludu	lut	lodo	lôdo	llot	lot
PŬTEU	>	pozzo	putu	put	pozo	poço	pou	potz

27. But FLÓRE > Rm. *floare*. Note also that Sardinian and Romanian tend to keep the original *i* and *u* of such words as GŬLA, SĬTI(S), LŬTU, PŬTEU, etc.

28. See note 27 above.

29. The *i* of *teia, cheio, feio* was produced by hiatus, from loss of *l* in popular development. The noun *tear* [tjar] (= loom), with stress on *a*, does not have it.

30. Usually SAÉTA in Classical Latin.

31. OP. *pea*. The *n* has been restored in the modern form.

32. See note 29 above.

33. See note 29 above.

Note: Final /e/ [e] of foreign words tend to > -è [ɛ] in Italian: Turkish *kawe* > It. *caffè*. The same is true of Portuguese, even in native forms — in fact, Portuguese uses the acute accent (') to indicate the sound [ɛ], and (ˆ) for [e], contrary to French usage: P. *café* [kɐfɛ́], *rosé* [rozɛ́], and the proper names *José, Nazaré* [žozɛ́], [nɐzɐrɛ́], and so on.

Sp. and P. *cruz* < CRÚCE is a learned development. Compare It. *croce*, Sard. *ruge*, Rm. *cruce*, C. *creu*, Pr. *crotz*, Fr. *croix*.

In southern Italy and Sicily /ẹ > i, ọ > u/: Sicilian *tila* (< TĒLA), *siti* (< SĬTI), *gula* (< GŬLA), *vutu* (< VŌTU). This may be due to Oscan influence: Compare Oscan LĪGĬS, DŪNUM with Latin LĒGIBUS, DŌNUM.[34] But note also Sard. *sidis, ludu*, and others.

As in the case of open vowels, the presence of a palatal (yod), even in an adjacent syllable, often had a lifting effect, particularly in Spain — [e + j] > [i], [o + j] and [j + o] > [u]:

CĒREU > Sard. *chiriu* [kíriu], Sp. *cirio*, P. *círio*, C. Pr. *ciri*, but It. *cero*, Fr. *cierge*[35]

*VĬTRIU (< VĪTREU?) > Sp. *vidrio*, P. *vidro*, C. *vidre*, Fr. *vitre;* but It. *vetro*[36]

LĬMPI(D)U > Sard. *limpiu*, Sp. *limpio*, P. *limpio, limpo;* cf. Sp. P. *límpido, lindo;* Rm. has only *limpede*, C. *limpid*, Fr. *limpide* which are learned

SĒPIA > Sp. *jibia*, P. *siba*, C. *sipia, sepia*, Pr. *sipia, sepia, supia;* but It. *seppia*, Fr. *sèche*

JŬGU > Sard. *yuu*, Rm. *jug*, Sp. *yugo*, P. *jugo*, Fr. *joug* [žug] (of later formation); but C. Pr. *jou*, It. *giogo*

CŌGITO > *CÓYETO > Sp. P. *cuido*, OFr. *cuit*, but C. *cogito*, Pr. cogit

FŬGIO > *FÓYO > It. *fuggio*, Sp. *huyo*, P. *fujo*

Where the yod is intervocalic, it is absorbed or becomes consonantal, and the stressed /e/ persists:

CORRĬGIA > *CORRĒYA > Rm. *cureà*, Sp. *correa*, P. *correia*, C. *corretja*, Pr. *correg, corregei*, Fr. *couroie* (OFr. *coureie);* but Sard. *corria*

34. OSCAN: an Italic Language, an early contemporary and rival of Latin. See figure 5.
35. Cf. Fr. *cire* from CÉRA.
36. From VĬTRU, as are also Sard. *vidru*, Pr. *veire*, Fr. *verre*.

*DĬSSĬDIU (< DĒSĔDIU ?) > *DĒSSĒYO > Sp. *deseo,* P. *desejo;*
but It. *disio,* Sard. *dizizu,* C. *desig*

The same retention of /ę́/ occurs where the yod is a part of the combination -TI- (-CI-) which > a single consonant sound [ts] (cf. note 25 above):

VĬTIU > It. *vezzo,* Sp. P. *vezo,* Pr. *vetz*
TRISTĬTIA > It. *tristezza,* Sp. Pr. *tristeza,* P. C. *tristesa,* Fr. *tristesse*

/ę́/ and /ǫ́/ may also be raised to /i/ and /u̯/ in hiatus. This could
be a case of dissimilation, or more likely the introduction of a transitional
yod, as happens regularly in Portuguese. Compare the transitional yod
in the English pronunciation [bǽjəd] for *bad,* and *hi-yer* [hájər] for *higher.*

[éa] > [ía] (southern France, Italy, Iberia):[37]

MĒA > It. Sard. Sp. Pr. *mia, mía;* but Rm. *mea,* C. *meva*[38]
VĬA > Sard. *bia,* Sp. *via,* It. C. Pr. *via*
SĬAM > It. Pr. *sia;* but Sp. *sea,* P. *seja* < SĔDEAM
HABĒBAM > *HABÉA > Sp. *había,* P. C. Pr. *havia;* but Rm.
     aveam, Fr. *avais* (< *aveis*) and It. has *avevo,* with regularized
     ending

[óa] > [úa] (Italy and Iberia):

TŬA > It. P. *tua,* Sp. *tuya;* but Rm. *ta,* C. *teva* (by analogy with
     meva), Pr. *toa,* OFr. *toie, toe*
DŬAS > OSp. *dues,* P. *duas* (It. *due* < DUAE)

Stressed /e/ followed by unstressed /i/ in the next syllable > [i – i] >
/i/ – /e/: This is a case of (1) regressive assimilation, which is sometimes
called "umlaut" (a German term) or anticipation of a following sound
followed by (2) dissimilation. The process is not complete in all regions
(see secs. 2 and 6).

VĒNI > [wíni, víni] > Sp. *vine* (for final -i > -e, see sec. 4); cf. C.
     vingui, P. *vim,* Pr. *vinc,* Fr. *vins,* but It. *venni,* Rm. *venii*

---

37. The ę remained in the East and in northern France: Rm. *mea, aveam,* OFr. *moie,
voie, soie* (< older *meie, veie, seie*). See above.
38. The Sardinian dialects also have *mea, meja.*

FĒCI > [fitsi] > OSp. *fize* > Sp. *hice;* cf. P. *fiz,* C. *fiu,* Pr. *fi,* Fr. *fis,*
but It. *feci*[39]

In northern Gaul, there was a special process, in which the closed
vowel of [ké] was raised to [í]:

CĒRA > [tjéjra] > Fr. *cire* (OFr. [tsírə], Fr. [si:r]); cf. It. Sp. P. C.
cera, Pr. *cera, ciera, cira,* Sard. *chera,* Rm. *ceară*
MERĊĒDE > Fr. *merci* [mɛrsí] (OFr. [mertsí]); cf. It. C. *mercè,*
Sp. *merced,* P. *mercê,* Pr. *merce, mercei, mercer, merci*[40]

To sum up for the four basic languages studied, the general rule for
development of *E* and *O* is the following:

French: *All* vowels in a *free* syllable break (or diphthongize).
Italian: All *open* vowels in a *free* syllable break.
Spanish: All *open* vowels break.
Portuguese: *No* vowels break, although diphthongization may occur
in hiatus, or as a result of assimilation and metathesis (PRĪMARĬU >
primeiro).

Stressed L. *Ī* and *Ū* (VL. /i/ and /u/)

These high vowels, being of tense articulation, show relatively few
changes. [í] is resistant everywhere:

VENĪRE > It. *venire,* Rm. *veni,* Sp. C. Pr. Fr. *venir,* P. *vir,* Engad.
gnir, Friul. *viñi;* but Vegl. *vener* and Sard. *bénnere* with shift
of accent
FĪLU > It. *filo,* Sard. *filu,* Rm. *fir,* Sp. *hilo,* P. *fio,* C. Pr. Fr. Engad.
Friul. *fil*
AMĪCU > It. *amico,* Sard. *amigu,* Sp. *amigo,* Rm. C. Pr. *amic,* Fr.
Friul. *ami,* Engad. *amih*
FĪCU, -A > It. *figo,* Sard. *figu,* Sp. *higo,* P. *figo,* C. *figa,* Pr. *figa, fia,*
OFr. *fi,* Fr. *figue* (< Pr. *figa*)
FĪLIU > It. *figlio,* Sard. *fizu* (*fillu*), Rm. *fiu,* Sp. *hijo,* P. *filho,* C. *fill,*
Pr. *filh,* Fr. *fils,* Engad. *figl,* Friul. *fi*

39. Rm. *făcui* is a regularized formation.
40. Provençal often exhibits a variety of forms, since its literature represents a long
period when the language was still in a state of flux.

[ú] is generally stable:

CRŪDU > It. Sp. *crudo*, Sard. *cruu*, Rm. Friul. *crud*, P. C. *cru*,
    Pr. *cru, crut*
MŪLA > It. Sard. Sp. P. C. *mula*, Pr. *mula, muola*, Friul. *mule*
LACTŪCA > It. *lattuga*, Rm. *lăptucă*, Sp. *lechuga*, C. *lletuga*,
    Pr. *lachuga*

But the /u/ in French > *ü* [y] in sound (likewise in Engadinian):
Fr. *cru, mule, laitue*, pronounced [kry, myl, letý], and Engad. *crüj, müla*.
Other examples:

MŪTU > It. *muto*, Sard. *mudu*, Rm. C. Pr. *mut*, Sp. P. *mudo*, Fr.
    muet (OFr. *mut*), Engad. *müt*, Friul. *mut*
FŪMU > It. P. *fumo*, Sard. *fumu*, Sp. *humo*, Rm. C. Pr. OFr. *fum*,
    Friul. *fum*, Engad. *füm* (Fr. *fumée* < FUMÁTA)

§4. Atonic or Unstressed Vowels

The history of these vowels varies according to their occurrence in initial, medial, or final syllables. In general, the initial ones are maintained, those medial and final often fall.

In Romance, unstressed /ẹ/ [ɛ] and /ọ/ [ɔ] merged with /ẹ/ [e] and /ọ/ [o], so that there were only five atonic vowels: /a, e, i, o, u/. In final position these were reduced to three: /a, e, o/, the so-called "strong vowels," since unstressed final /i/ early opened (relaxed) to /e/, and unstressed /u/ in final position was almost nonexistent in Vulgar Latin words.

Atonic Vowels in Initial Syllables

Initial attack in a word helped to preserve most of these vowels. Their loss is rare, and then only in certain cases such as a consonant plus vowel plus the letter *r*:

QUIRITĀRE > Q'RITÁRE > It. *gridare*, Sp. P. *gritar*, C. *cridar*,
    Pr. *cridar, criar*, Fr. *crier*, Engad. *crider*, Friul. *kridá*
DIRĒCTU > D'RĒCTU > It. *dritto* (and *diritto*), Rm. *drept*, C.
    dret, Pr. *drech*, Fr. *droit*, Vegl. *drat*, Engad. Friul. *dret;* but
    Sp. *derecho*, P. *direito*, Sard. *derettu* (< DĒRĒCTU?)

Prosthetic (or prothetic)[41] /e/ and /i/

In Vulgar Latin, an initial /s/ followed by another consonant (= /s/ + C), in phrases with a consonant ending the word immediately preceding, developed a vowel between words to create a syllable that would convert what had been initial /s/ (an onset) to a final /s/ (a coda), because apparently in much of Romance territory the cluster /s/ + consonant was not tolerated as the onset of a syllable. This vowel, at first an /i/, later an /e/, occurred to an extent in Vulgar Latin in such combinations as CUM ISPATA and CUM ISCUTU (CL. CUM SPATHA, CUM SCUTU).[42]

This prefixed vowel remained as an *e-* in the West, and an integral part of the word:

SCŪTU > Sp. P. *escudo,* C. Pr. *escut,* OFr. *escu,* Fr. *écu*
SPÁTHA > Sp. P. *espada,* C. *espasa,* Pr. *espaza,* Fr. *épée* (OFr. *espée*)
SCÁLA > Sp. C. Pr. *escala,* P. *escala, escada,* Fr. *échelle*
SPŌ(N)SU > Sp. *esposo,* P. *espôso,* C. *espòs,* Pr. *espos,* Fr. *époux*
SCHŎLA > Sp. *escuela,* P. C. Pr. *escola,* Fr. *école*

This prefix was lost in the East, in Rhetia, and in Italy, but not in Sardinia, where the original *i-* was preserved in some dialects. Compare Ital. *scudo, spada, scala, sposo, scuola;*[43] Rm. *scut, spada, scară, scoală;* Vegl. *sputa;* Engad. *sküt, spada, scuola, spus;* Friul. *skut, spade, skale* — but Sard. *iscudu, ispada, iscala, isposu, iscola.*

Yet literary Italian still says (with prepositions *con, in,* and with *non*) *in istrada, non ispero* (but *le strade, da sperare*).

Apheresis and Accretion (See Section 6)

There were also many cases of apheresis (loss of an initial vowel), usually from confusion with the definite article:

41. Prosthetic means "added," prothetic, "placed before." Modern linguists seem to prefer the latter word.
42. CUM SPATHA, "with (a) sword"; CUM SCUTU, "with (a) shield."
43. Pro(s)thetic *e-* (*i-*) remained long enough in Italy to take with it when it disappeared many initial vowels such as *ae-*/(in *aestimare* > *stimare*), (*e*)*x-*, (*e*)*xtra-*, etc. This left many Italian words beginning with *zd, zg, sc,* etc. Examples: *scorso* < DISCÚRSU, *straordinario* < EXTRAORDINÁRIU. It was the same in the East where Slavic influence probably helped.

ATÁVIA > OFr. *l'ataie* > Fr. *la taie* (pillow case)
ARÉNA > *l'arena* > It. *la rena* (also Sard. *rena*[44]); cf. Fr. *arène*,
Sp. Pr. *arena*, P. *areia*.
HOSPITĀLE > *l'hospedale* > It. *lo spedale;* cf. Rm. *spital*
APOTHĒCA > It. *la bottega*, Sard. *butegga*, Sp. C. *la bodega*, (also
Sp. *botica*), Pr. *la botiga*, Fr. *la boutique*[45]
AEGYPTĀNA > *l'a(e)gitana* > Sp. P. C. *la gitana* (and by analogy a
masculine Sp. *el gitano*, etc.)

The reverse process, accretion, will add a syllable to the basic derivative:

ILLO EPĪSCŎPU > *ello^ebispo* > Sp. *el obispo;* cf. It. *vescovo*,
Sard. *piscamu*, P. *bispo*, C. *bisbe*, but Rm. *episcop*, Pr. *evesque*
and *avesque*, Fr. *évêque*.

In Spanish and Portuguese, failure to recognize the Arabic prefix
al- (*az-*, etc.) as the definite article led to its incorporation into words
borrowed from that language. The other Romance tongues did not follow
this practice. Hence such as the following:

Arab. AS-SUKKAR > Sp. (*el*) *azúcar*, P. (*o*) *açucar;* but It. *zucchero*,
Sard. *tuccaru*, Rm. *zahăr*, C. Pr. Fr. *sucre;* cf. E. *sugar*, Germ.
Zucker
Arab. AL-QUṬUN > Sp. (el) *algodón*, P. (o) *algodão;* but It. *cotone*,
C. *cotó*, Pr. Fr. *coton;* cf. Engl. *cotton*. There are other derivative
forms, such as P. *cotão* and Fr. *hoqueton* (< OFr. *auqueton*),
with specialized meanings.

Other languages also have this type of accretion, as for example
OFr. *l'endemain* (= the tomorrow) > Fr. *le lendemain*. The history of
English shows cases of apheresis and accretion similar to those above,
particularly in borrowed words:

44. The two southern dialects of Sardinian (Cagliaitan and Logudorese) chose ÍPSE,
ÍPSU, ÍPSA for their article. Hence the apheresis indicated is not so obvious as in combinations with ÍLLE, ÍLLO, ÍLLA. But one northern dialect, Sassarese, agrees with Logudorese
in maintaining the prothetic *i-*, while changing the *s* to *l*: e.g., Logudorese *iscriptu, istella*,
Sassarese *ilcritu, iltella*, and Cagliaitan, Tempiese *scrittu, stella*. The last, however, has
istatu (<L. STÁTU). Sardinian is often influenced by Italian. See Posner 142 ff., and
reading selections in Appendix of this text.
45. Portuguese *adega* and OSp. *abdega* show a difference in development.

ME. *a nauger* > E. *an auger* ME. *a nadder* > E. *an adder*
ME. *a napron* (< Fr. *naperon*) > E. *an apron*
Sp. *la riata* > E. *lariat*

Keep in mind that early Romance had, in unstressed position, *no open vowels.*

Individual Vowels

Initial /a/ remained in general.

AMĪCU > It. *amico*, Sard. *amigu*, Rm. C. Pr. *amic*, Sp. P. *amigo*,
Fr. *ami*, Vegl. *amaik*, Engad. *amih*, Friul. *ami*
PARTĪRE > It. Sard. *partire*, Sp. P. C. Pr. Fr. *partir*

The /a/ in an initial /al-/ combination in Portuguese, by the loss of the intermediate /l/, is usually absorbed into the vowel of the following stressed syllable:

CALĔNTE > Sp. *caliente*, C. *calent;* but P. *quente*
PALŬMBA > Sp. C. *paloma*, P. *pomba;* cf. Rm. *porumb* [m.], Pr.
palomba, paloma, Fr. *palombe*[46]
PALĀTIU > P. *paço*, but It. *palazzo*, Sard. *palatu*, Rm. *palat*, C.
palau, Pr. *palatz, palais*, Fr. *palais* (Sp. *palacio* and P. *palácio*
are learned forms.)

Initial /e/ remained in the East, Sardinia, southern Gaul, and Iberia.

NEPŌTE > Sard. *nebode*, Rm. *nepot*, Pr. *nebot* (Sp. *nieto*, P. *neto*,
and C. *nèt* are from NÉPOTE with initial stress.)
SECŪRU > Sard. *seguru*, Sp. P. *seguro*, C. Pr. *segur;* but Rm. *sigur*
MĬNŪTU > Sp. *menudo*, P. *miudo*,[47] C. Pr. *menut*, but Rm. *marunt*,
Sard. *minudu* (Sp. P. *minuto*, C. *minut*, Rm. *minut* are probably
all learned.)
CĪRCĀRE > Rm. *cerca*, Sp. P. C. Pr. *cercar;* but Sard. *chircare*
[*kirkáre*]

---

46. Note: Rm. *corombă*, Fr. *colombe*, It. Pr. *colomba*, Sard. *columba*, C. *coloma* are from an alternate etymon COLUMBA.

47. The *i* in the Portuguese form results from the loss of intervocalic *-n-*, and the consequent production of a diphthong [ju].

In Italy (also Northwest Iberia), there was an old tendency for initial /e/ (if in free syllable) to > /i/; hence It. *nipote, sicuro* (but *cercare*, undoubtedly influenced by other verb forms with stress: *cerco, cerca*, etc.).

In northern Gaul, if free, e- in initial syllable > [ə]: Fr. *neveu* [nəvǿ], OFr. *seur* [səýr] > Fr. *sur* [syr], and *menu* [məný].

Both /a-/ and /e-/, like their tonic counterparts, are affected by a following palatal (yod) or a velar [w].

/a-/ followed by [j] or [w]:

MA(N)SIŌNE > *maisón > Sp. *mesón*, Pr. *maizon*, Fr. *maison* [mezɔ̃][48] It. *mansione*, P. *mansão*, C. *mansió* are learned forms. Old Italian had *magione*.

VARIŎLA > *VAIRǑLA > Sp. *viruela* (< OSp. *veruela*), It. *vaiuolo*, Sard. *arzolu, alzolu*, C. *verola*, Pr. *vairola*, Fr. *vérole;* but P. *variola*

MAXĬLLA > *MAISÉLLA > Sp. *mejilla* (< OSp. *mexilla*, [mešíʎa]), C. *maixella*, Pr. *maisella;* but It. *mascella*, Sard. *massidda*, Rm. *măseà*

JACTĀRE > It. *gettare*, Sard. *bettare*, Sp. *echar*, C. *gitar*, Pr. *gitar*, *getar*, Fr. *jeter* (and P. *deitar*, from JACTÁRE? DE-JACTÁRE? or?); cf. Sp. *jactarse* (= "boast"), P. *jactar* and *jatar*: [kt] > [jt]

AUTŬMNU > It. *autunno*, Sard. *attunzu*, Rm. *toamnă*, Sp. *otoño*, P. *outono*, C. *autumne*,[49] Fr. *automne* [otɔ́n]

SAPUĪMUS > OSp. *sopimos* > Sp. *supimos* (an analogic form, see sec. 6), and P. *soubemos;* but It. *sapemmo*, a regularized form: [sapwi-] > [sawpi-]

ALTĀRIU > *AUTÁIRO > Sp. *otero*, P. *outeiro*, Pr. *autar*, Fr. *autel* [otél]; but It. *altare*, Rm. *altar*

In a few cases, popular development seems to drop the *u* [w]:

AUGŬSTU > It. Sp. P. *agosto*, Sard. *austu*, C. *agost*, Pr. *agost*, *aost, avost*, Fr. *août* [u]; but Rm. *august* (a learned or restored form?)

Sometimes initial atonic /a-/ is changed by assimilation, contamination, crossing, or analogy:

48. Both French and Provençal spellings represent an earlier stage.
49. Like the English "autumn," probably a learned form. The common word is *tardor*.

ABSCÓNDERE > (OSp.) *asconder* > *ex-conder (analogy) > Sp.
P. *esconder*, C. Pr. *escondir;* but It. (*n*)*ascondere*, Rm. *ascunde*
(note shift of stress from *o* to *e* in most languages)
*ANĒTHULU > *anedlo > aneldo (metathesis) > Sp. *eneldo*, P.
endro (analogic *en-*); cf. It. P. *aneto*, C. *anet*, Fr. *aneth*
(< ANĒTHU)

/e-/ followed by [j] or [w] > /i/:

SEMĔNTE > Sp. *simiente*, but P. *semente*, C. *sement*, Pr. *semen* (It.
semenza, Sard. *sementa*, Rm. *semânṭă* are from *SEMĔNTIA.)
PRE(HEN)SIŌNE > *PRESIÓN > It. *prigione*, Sp. *prisión*, P.
prisão, Pr. *preison, prizon*, etc., Fr. *prison;* but Sard. *preyone*,
C. *presó*
SERVIĀMUS > Sp. P. *sirvamos*
SERVIVĒRUNT > Sp. servieron > *sirvieron*
SERVIĔNDO > Sp. *sirviendo*
AEQUĀLE > OSp., P. *egual*, Sp. C. *igual*, OFr. *ivel;* cf. Sard. *galu*,
Rm. *egal*, Pr. *egal, aigal, engal, eagal*, Fr. *égal*, and It. *uguale*
*MĬNUĀRE > OSp. *minguar*, Sp. *menguar*, P. *minguar, mingoar*,
C. *minvar*

(Compare the effect of [w] on a stressed /é/, in LĬNGUA > It. P.
lingua, Rm. *limbă;* but Sp. *lengua*, C. *llengua*, Pr. *lenga*, Fr. *langue*.)

Initial /o-/, in general, tended to remain:

NŌMINĀRE > It. *nominare*, Sp. *nombrar*, P. *nomear*, C. *nomenar*,
Pr. *nominar, nom(n)ar*, Fr. *nommer;* but Sard. *lumenare*,
Rm. *numi*
FŬGĔRE > *FOGÍRE > OSp. *foir;* but It. *fuggire*, Sard. *fuire*,
Rm. *fugi*, Sp. *huir* (from dissimilation), P. C. *fugir*, Pr. *fugir*,
fogir, etc., Fr. *fuir*
*MŌRĪRE, *MŌ(R)RĒRE > It. *morire*, Sard. *morrere*, Sp. C. Pr.
morir, P. *morrer;* but Rm. *muri*, Fr. *mourir* [murír][50]
DŌLŌRE > It. Sard. *dolore*, Sp. C. Pr. *dolor*, P. *dor*, but Rm. *durere*
(ORm. *duroare*), Fr. *douleur* [dulœr][51]

---

50. In French, this [u] is a later development by way of [ow] from [o], as indicated by
the spelling *ou*, and is a regular one.
51. See note 50 above.

CŌRŌNA > It. Sard. Sp. C. Pr. *corona,* P. *corôa;* but Rm. *cunună,*
Fr. *couronne* [kurón][52]
AURĬCŬLA > It. *orecchia,* Sard. *oriya,* Sp. *oreja,* P. *orelha,* C.
orella, Fr. *oreille;* but Rm. *ureche,* Pr. *aurelha*
PORTĀRE > It. Sard. *portare,* Sp. P. C. Pr. *portar,* Fr. *porter;* but
Rm. *purta*

Note: Initial /o-/ in Portuguese (Lisbonese, not most Brazilian) is pronounced [u]: *professor* [prufesór], *o português* [u purtugéš].
Special cases:

Sp. *lugar* < LOCÁLE
Sp. *jugar* < OSp. *jogar*[53] < JOCÁRE (cf. Rm. *juca*)
Sp. *pulgar* < POLLICÁRE (by analogy with *pulga* < *PÚLICA?)
(Cf. Sp. *pulgada* < POLLICÁTA; Portuguese and Catalan
have *pollegada,* Provençal *polgada.*)

/o-/ followed by [j] or [w] lifted to /u/, particularly in Spain:

MŬLĬÉRE > Sard. *muzere,* Rm. *muiere,* Sp. *mujer* (OSp. *mogier*),
P. *mulher,* C. *muller,* but It. *mogliere,* Pr. *molher,* OFr. *moillier*
COGNÁTU > Rm. *cumnat,* Sp. *cuñado,* P. *cunhado,* C. *cunyat,*
Engad. *quinó,* Friul. *kuñat;* but It. *cognato,* Sard. *connadu,*
Pr. *conhat* (ML. lists *cunhat*); Fr. has a euphemistic substitute,
beau-frère[54]

Spanish verb forms illustrate this phenomenon:

DORMI(V)ĔRUNT > Sp. *durmieron;* cf. P. *dormiram*
DORMIĀMUS > Sp. *durmamos*
DORMIÉNDO > Sp. *durmiendo*

Initial /i-/ and /u-/ remained almost everywhere:

HĪBĔRNU > It. P. *inverno,* Sard. *ierru,* Rm. *iarnă,* Sp. *invierno,*
C. *hivern,* Pr. *ivern, invern, uvern, vern,* Fr. *hiver,* Ladin *dinver,*
Engad. *inviern*

52. See note 50 above.
53. The OSp. form explains why this verb is a radical changing one, with present
indicative *juego, juegas,* etc.
54. Regular development would have given *coigné.*

CĪVITĀTE > It. *città,* Sp. *ciudad,* P. *cidade,* C. *ciutat,* Sard. *cittade, cittadi, ziddai,* Pr. *ciutat, ciptat,* Fr. *cité;* but Rm. *cetate*
TĪTIŌNE > It. *tizzone,* Sard. *tittone,* Sp. *tizón,* P. *tição,* C. *tió,* Pr. *tizon,* Fr. *tison;* but Rm. *tăciune*
RĪPĀRIA > It. *riviera,* Sp. C. *ribera,* P. *ribeira,* Pr. *ribiera,* Fr. *rivière*
MŪTĀRE > It. *mutare, mudare,* Sard. *mudare,* Rm. *muta,* Sp. P. C. Pr. *mudar,* Fr. *muer*[55]
*PŪRĬTIA > It. *purezza,* Sp. C. Pr. *pureza,* P. *purêza;* cf. It. *purità,* Rm. *puritate,* OSp. *poredad* OP. *puredad,* Fr. *pureté,*[56] Pr. *purdat, puretat,* etc. < PŪRITÁTE

Initial /au-/ [aw] in Italy and Rhetia often tended to > *u-*:

AUDĪRE > It. *udire,* Engad. *udir*
*AUCĔLLU > It. *uccello,* Engad. *utschè,* Friul. *uĉiel*

Elsewhere, the development was the same as for the tonic /au/.[57]

AUDĪRE > Rm. *auzi,* Sp. C. *oír,* P. *ouvir,* Pr. *ouzir,* Fr. *ouir*
*AUCĔLLU > C. *ocell,* Pr. *auzel, aucel,* Fr. *oiseau*

Special Treatments[58]

VERVÁCTU > Sard. *barvattu,* Sp. *barbecho,* P. *barbeito,* C. *guaret,* Pr. *garach* (perhaps through the obscuring or lowering effect of an *r.* Cf. English *Clark* < *clerk,* and *sergeant,* pronounced [sar·ĝṇt].) Fr. *guéret*
SILVÁTICU > Rm. *sălbatic,* Sp. *salvaje* (but *selva* < SĬLVA), C. Pr. *salvatge,* Fr. *sauvage* (OFr. *salvage*), Engad. *sulvedi,* Friul. *salvadi;* but It. *selvatico,* P. *selvagem.* (This is a case of assimilation: *i-a* > *a-á.*)
FORMÓSU > Rm. *frumos,* Sp. *hermoso;* cf. It. P. *formoso,* C. *formos.* (This is a case of dissimilation, or obscuring by *r.*)

55. But note that French /u/ = *ü* or [y]: *muer* [mųé], *juger* [žyže] (< JŪDĪCÁRE). Also in N. Italy and W. Rhetia.
56. See note 55 above.
57. See /a/ followed by [w] above and also sec. 3.
58. For general discussion, see sec. 6.

ROTŬNDU > *RODÓNDO > Sp. P. *redondo*, Pr. *redon*, OFr. *reond*, Fr. *rond*. This dissimilation could be a case of analogy with the prefix *re-;* cf. It. *tondo, rotondo*, Sard. *tundu*, Rm. *rotund*, C. *rodó*, Engad. *raduond*. Friul. *turont* shows a case of metathesis. (The Italian nouns *ronda, ronde* may be borrowed from French.)

HOROLŎGIU > It. *orologio*, Fr. *horloge*, but Sp. *reloj*, P. *relogio*, C. *rellotge*, Pr. *relotge*

SORORE > OSp. OFr. Pr. *seror*, Vegl. *seraur* (cf. It. *sorella* < SORÓR + ĬLLA); It. *suora*, Sard. *sorre*, Rm. *soră*, Sp. C. Pr. *sor*, Engad. *sour*. Friul. *sur*, Fr. *soeur* are from an alternate nominative form (SÓROR) with initial stress.

Assimilations to /a/ (cf. SILVÁTICU above):

AERĀMEN > VL. *ARÁME > Rm. *aramă*, Sp. *alambre, arambre*, P. *arame*, C. Pr. Engad. *aram*, OFr. *arain*, Fr. *airain* (It. *rame*, Sard. *ramine* are victims of apheresis [sec. 6].)

BILĀNCIA > Sp. *balanza*, P. C. *balança*, Pr. *balansa*, Fr. *balance;* but It. *bilancia*

An analogous type of assimilation, which German calls "umlaut," is that of *i* + *e* (or *e* + *í*) > *i* + *i*. This is the kind of change by "anticipation," discussed in sections 3 and 6.[59] Example:

VĪGĬNTI > *VĪYĒNTE > *VI-INTE > Sard. *vinti*, P. *vinte*, C. Pr. *vint*, Fr. *vingt*, Friul. *vinky;* but It. *venti*, Sp. *veinte*, Engad. *vainch*, Vegl. *venč* (Rm. *douăzecĭ* is a different formation.) Cf. FĒCĬ (with initial stress) > *FĪCĬ > Sp. *hice*, P. *fiz*, C. *fiu*, Pr. Fr. *fis;* but It. *feci* and Rm. *făcui* (a regularized form)

Atonic Vowels in Medial Position

As has already been seen, in the discussion on proparoxytones (sec. 2), these weaker pretonic and posttonic vowels tended to drop, although Italian retains many of them (NŌBILE > *nobile*).

---

59. The Germanic languages, as well as Turkish, Hungarian, Finnish (and others) have this "umlauting": cf. Germ. *Buch, Bücher, Stadt, Städte,* OEngl. *fōt, fōtī* > *foot, feet.* Other examples in English are *tooth, teeth, goose, geese.*

CŌLĂPHU > It. *colpo*, Sard. *colpu*, Sp. P. *golpe*, C. *cop*, *colp*, OFr. *colp*, Fr. *coup*, Engad. *cuolp*

FŎLLĬCĀRE > Sp. *holgar*, P. C. *folgar;* but It. *follegiare*, Rm. *infulica*[60]

Popular vs. Semilearned Development

If the loss of the medial weak vowel is delayed, a semilearned development takes place: SÁECŬLU > *sécolo* (It.), **ségolo* > **séglo* > **siéglo* > Sp. *siglo*. The cognate forms in other languages are Rm. *secol*, Sard. *seyu*, C. Pr. *segle*, Fr. *siècle*, Engad. *secul*. P. *século* is a learned form.

If this development had been completely popular, the process would have been: (Pop.) SAÉCULU > **séklo* > **séλo* > Sp. **sejo*, P. **selho*, Fr. **sieil*, It. **seglio*, and so on.

Quite often one finds both popular and semilearned developments, as well as learned forms of the same word: LĬMPIDU > Sp. *lindo* (pop.), *limpio* (semipop.), *límpido* (learned). (See the discussion which follows.)

Doublets

All languages have "doublets," that is, two or more forms of the same word which have come down to the modern period by various channels, or represent different stages in the evolution of the term. In English, for example, the Greek δίσκος has five or more derivatives: *discus*, *disk* (*disc*), *desk*, *dish*, *dais*, while the word *housewife* occurs also in the forms *hussy* and *huswife* with specialized meanings and pronunciations.

The terms "learned," "semilearned," and "popular" are used to classify derivatives as to their origin and development. Learned forms are generally borrowed either directly from the original language or are heavily influenced by church usage, scholastic writings, and the like. Semilearned forms generally show a delayed development before being subjected to the regular changes occurring in the vernacular. Popular words exhibit the characteristic developments that basically distinguish one language from another.

Proper names are apt to be more conservative, and represent an earlier form, for example, the French *François* as opposed to *français*, both from FRANCĬSCUS.

---

60. Note semantic shift from FOLLICÁRE ("to have a foolish good time") to Sp. *holgar* ("to be idle"). The Sp. noun form *huelga* means a "labor strike," while the Andalusian *juerga* is a "wild party." Italian *follegiare* retains the original idea of "to play the fool." One of the meanings of the Romanian verb is "to swallow."

In some instances, a nominative case form and an accusative one give differing results. A good example of this is the Italian *drago, dragone* < L. DRÁCO (nom.), DRACÕNEM (acc.). The first might be considered a learned form.

One of the characteristics of a semilearned development is the tendency to resist the loss of weak syllables. This can be well illustrated by the Spanish triplets cited in section 2: *límpido* (learned [poetic]), *limpio* (semilearned), and *lindo* (popular), all from the Latin LÍMPIDU.

In the case of FÁBRÍCA, we have the learned forms *fabbrica* (It.), *fábrica* (Sp., P.), and *fabrique* (Fr.), as well as the popular French form *forge* and It. *forgia*, Sp. *forja*, both borrowed from the French. The Spanish form *fragua*, however, is completely popular, with multiple metathesis. The Portuguese *forja*, and *frágua*, are undoubtedly borrowings.

Other examples of doublets are:

ARÃTRU > Sp. *arado, aladro*
(Germanic) FÁLDA (= single fold) > Sp. *falda, halda*
PE(N)SÃRE > It. *pensare, pesare*, Sard. *pesare*, Rm. *păsa*, Sp. P. C.
      Pr. *pensar, pesar*, Fr. *penser, peser*, Engad. *penser, passar*,
      s'impissar, Friul. *pensá*
ÁQUILA > C. *águila* and *áliga* (metathesis)
FÓEDU > Sp. *feo, hedo*

Final Unstressed Vowels

In general, the so-called "strong" vowels (/a/, /e/, /o/) tended to remain, the "weak" ones (/i/, /u/) to drop or change. This varied, however, with regions.

Individual Vowels

-/a/ remained in most places:

AMÍCA > It. *amica*, Sard. Sp. P. C. Pr. *amiga*
PŎRTA > It. Sard. P. C. Pr. *porta*, Sp. *puerta*
ÍNTRAT > It. Sp. P. C. *entra*, Pr. *intra*
ÁMAT > It. Sp. P. C. Pr. *ama*

By the end of the eighth century, however, this -/a/ had weakened to [ə] in northern Gaul, and likewise between 800 and 1000 in Romania (spelled -*e* in French, and -*ă* in Romanian): Fr. *amie, porte, entre, aime;* Rm. *amică, poartă, intră.*

(Note that an unstressed /a/ in Portuguese, whether final or not, has a neutral sound listed phonetically as [ɐ] and similar to the slurred /a/ sounds in unstressed English syllables, as in Anna, Canada, etc.)

In Rhetia, the preservation of final -/a/ depended on the particular dialect involved: Engad. *amia, porta;* Friul. *amiye, puarte.*

-/u/ > -/o/ in Italy and Spain, and -/o/ remained:[61]

VĪNU > It. Sp. *vino*, P. *vinho*[62]*;* but C. *vi*
ÁMŌ > It. Sp. P. C. *amo*[63]
AMĪCU > It. *amico*, Sp. P. *amigo;* but C. *amic*

Any losses are analogic or proclitic, as in *UNO > It. Sp. *un*, P. *um*, and *BONO > It. *buon*, Sp. *buen*, P. *bom;* i.e., *uno bueno hombre* > Sp. *un buen hombre*, etc.

-/u/ did remain sporadically in Romanian, although normally dropping. In Sardinian, however, it has persisted regularly as a final vowel (or been restored):

ŎCULŬ > Rm. *ochiu*, Sard. *oju, ogu*
VĔTULU > Rm. *vechiu*, Sard. *vettsu, vriku, egru*
DIRĒCTU > Rm. *drept*, Sard. *derettu*
CÓRPUS > Rm. *corp*, Sard. *corpus*
SCŪTU > Rm. *scut*, Sard. *iscudu*
PŎRCU > Rm. *porc*, Sard. *porcu*
PÁSSU > Rm. *pas*, Sard. *passu*
UMBĬLĬCU > Rm. *buric*, Sard. *imbiligu*

-/u/ generally dropped in Rhetia:

61. Catalan regularly dropped the -/o/. In first person singular indicative verb endings, however, it has been restored.
62. In modern Portugal the final unstressed -*o* is pronounced [u], just as in other atonic positions in the Lisbonese dialect. This is also the case in Brazil, except in the far South and in a few inland areas.
63. See note 61 above.

ŎCŬLU > Engad. *ögl*, Surmiran *îgl*, Sursilvan *egl*, Sutsilvan *il*
PĬLU > Engad. *pail*, Surm. Surs. *peil*, Suts. *pel*
VĔTULU > Engad. *vegl*
DIRĒCTU > Engad. *dret*
CÓRPUS > Engad. *corps*
PŎRCU > Engad. *porch, püerch*
PÁSSU > Engad. *pass*

-/e/ and -/i/ remained in Italy, Sardinia, and the East:

VÁLLE > It. *valle*, Rm. *vale*, Sard. *badde*
SŌLE > It. *sole*, Sard. *sole*, Rm. *soare*
CANTĀRE > It. Sard. *cantare;* but Rm. *cânta* with loss of inf. *-re*
FĒCI > It. *feci* (Rm. has regularized *făcui*)
HĔRĬ > It. *ieri*, Rm. *ierĭ;* cf. Sicilian *ayeri*

In Iberia, -/i/ > -/e/, which regularly dropped after /d/, /l/, /n/, /r/, /s/, in Spanish and in Portuguese (although the latter does tend to retain /e/ after /d/). Note that Catalan tolerates practically all final consonants — even some consonant groups (including -*ll* [λ]) — except /n/; Portuguese regularly nasalizes all final /n/ combinations: -*an(e)*, -*an(o)*, -*en(e)*, etc., (> -*ão*, -*am*, -*em*, and so on), including -*ana* (GERMÁNA > *irmã*):

CANTĀRE > Sp. P. C. *cantar*
SŌLE > Sp. P. C. *sol*
PÁNE > Sp. *pan*, P. *pão*, C. *pa*

But:

CLÁVE > Sp. *llave*, P. *chave* (C. *clau*)
ÁXE > Sp. *eje*, P. *eixe* (C. *eix*)
TŌRRE > Sp. P. C. *torre*
PÁTRE > Sp. P. *padre*, C. *pare*
PŎNTE > Sp. *puente*, P. *ponte* (C. *pont*)[64]
VÁLLE > Sp. *valle*, P. *vale* (C. *vall* [vaλ])

---

64. But OSp. had *puent* (CID), and Aragonese *muert* (for *muerte*), and OSp. *diz, faz* (for *dice, face* [modern *hace*]). Cf. modern Portuguese verb forms *diz, fiz* (Sp. *dice, hice*), etc. Italian, on the other hand, not only retains final vowels but even adds them where they did not previously exist: SŬM and SŬNT > It. *sono*.

In some other cases, Portuguese has retained final -e where lost in Spanish and Catalan:

CIVITĀTE > Sp. *ciudad*, C. *ciutat*, P. *cidade*
VERITĀTE > Sp. *verdad*, C. *veritat*, P. *verdade*

And in numerous cases of hiatus, an original derived -/e/ has become -/i/ by dissimilation (= diphthong):

CÁDĬT > CÁ(D)E > Sp. OP. *cae* > P. *cai*
*ANIMĀ(L)ES > P. *animáis;* but Sp. *animales*
AMĀTIS > OSp. OP. *ama(d)es* > Sp. P. *amáis*
RĒGE > *ree > Sp. *rey*, P. C. *rei*

In Gaul and Rhetia all final vowels except -/a/ tend to fall:[65]

PŎNTE > Fr. *pont*, Pr. *pon*, Engad. *punt*, Friul. *puint*
VÁLLE > Fr. Pr. Engad. Friul. *val*
CABÁLLU > Fr. *cheval*, Pr. *caval*, Engad. *chavagl*, Friul. *k'aval*
HĔRĬ > Fr. *hier*, Pr. *er, ier*, Engad. *her*
LŪNA > Fr. Friul. *lune*, Pr. *luna*, Engad. *glüna*
VĪNU > Fr. Pr. Engad. Friul. *vin*
AMĪCU > Fr. Friul. *ami*, Pr. *amic*, Engad. *amih;* cf. C. *pont, vall, cavall, ahir, vi, amic*[66]

In French and Catalan vowels not directly final also fell:[67]

MŪROS > Fr. C. *murs* (pl.); but Sp. *muros* (sg. *muro*)
PÁNES > Fr. *pains*, C. *pans* (pl.); but Sp. *panes* (sg. *pan*)
FLŌRES > Fr. *fleurs*, C. *flors* (pl.); but Sp. *flores* (sg. *flor*)
CŬRRIT > Fr. *court;* but Sp. C. *corre* (retained because of *-rr-*)

Such Modern French forms as *je chante* (< CÁNTO, ind., and CÁNTEM, sbj.) are analogic or restored forms. Old French had for both *jo chant.*

---

65. Was this due to a specifically intense tonic stress? It is also found in northern Italy and Dalmatian. Cf. Old Milanese *grand, molt, amig* (< GRÁNDE, MŪLTU, AMĪCU) and Vegl. *amaik, ven* (AMĪCU, VĪNU). A Celtic influence?

66. Catalan and Provençal are often very close, being considered by some authorities as dialects of the same language.

67. Except -/a/ > -/e/ in French, and also (in plurals) in Catalan: PÓRTA > Fr. *porte*, C. *porta*, PÓRTAS > Fr. *portes*, C. *portes*.

§5. A Description of Consonants

As stated in section 2, consonant sounds have been classified in different groups according to their (1) manner of production (explosives or stops, fricatives, nasals, and so on), (2) place of articulation or production (bilabial, labiodental, interdental, alveolar, palatal, velar, uvular, guttural), and (3) whether the sound has voice (vibration of the vocal cords) or none. See also figure 2.

At the risk of repetition, some kind of restatement or description of consonant classifications may be in order. See also section 2 and Definitions.

MANNER OF ARTICULATION

Occlusives, or *Explosives:* consonant sounds characterized by closure of lips, or by the tongue against various parts of the roof of the mouth, or the teeth followed by an explosion (of sound) as air is released. There are two basic types: (1) simple stops, or occlusives, and (2) affricates which contain an element of friction following the explosion.

Fricatives (also known as spirants, or continuants): consonant sounds with considerable friction, but produced without complete closure of articulation, so that the sound may be prolonged in certain cases. Sometimes the term "liquids" is used to designate varieties of *l* sounds (laterals) and different types of *r* (vibrants), both of which are often fricatives.

Nasals are a special kind of consonant sound involving closure of the oral passage but with the air stream passing out through the nose to produce friction and nasal resonance.

POINT OF ARTICULATION

Bilabials: consonant sounds produced mainly by closing or partially closing the lips.
Labiodentals: consonant sounds produced by upper teeth and lower lip.
Interdentals: consonant sounds produced with tongue tip between teeth.
Dentals: consonant sounds produced by tongue against or near the teeth. (Note that in some languages *t*, *d*, and nasal *n* have dental articulation, in others they are alveolar.)
Alveolars (or *Gingivals*): consonant sounds produced with tip of tongue against the gum ridge.
Palatals: produced by tongue against the roof of the mouth or palate.
Velars: produced with rear of tongue near or touching the velum (soft palate).
Uvulars: produced by uvula flapping or vibrating against the rear of the tongue.
Glottals: sounds produced in the larynx.

VOICE

Vibration of the vocal cords. It is present in all vowels, and its presence or absence in consonants marks the distinction of such pairs as /p/-/b/, /t/-/d/, /k/-/g/.

(There are many other types of consonant sounds, with adjectives such as *cacuminal*, *coronal*, *pharyngeal*, but they have no importance for our study of Romance languages.)

The evolution of consonants in Romance depends (as with vowels) on position. If initial, they usually remained; when medial, the voiceless consonants voiced or eventually disappeared; where final, they tended to fall. There are exceptions, of course, according to individual languages and regions.

Evolution of Initial Consonants

Most remained,[68] as is the case with the simple occlusives /p/, /b/, /t/, /d/, /k/, /g/:

PÁNE > It. Sard. *pane*, Rm. *pâine*, Sp. Pr. Friul. Engad. *pan*, P. *pão*, C. *pa*, Fr. *pain*, Vegl. *pun*

BÍBĔRE > It. *bere*, Sard. *biere*, Rm. *bea*, Sp. P. *beber*, C. Pr. *beure*, Fr. *boire*, Vegl. *bar*, Engad. *baiver*, Friul. *beri*

TĔCTU > It. *tetto*, Sp. *techo*, P. *teito*, Pr. *tech*, Fr. *toit*, Engad. *tet*

TĒLA > It. Sard. Sp. P. C. Pr. *tela*, P. *teia*, Rm. *teară*, Fr. *toile*, Engad. *taila*, Fruil. *tele*

DĔNTE > It. Sard. P. *dente*, Rm. *dinte*, Sp. *diente*, C. Fr. *dent*, Pr. *den*, Vegl. *diant*, Engad. *daint*, Friul. *dint*

CŌLŌRE > It. Sard. *colore*, Rm. *culoare*, Sp. C. Pr. *color*, Fr. *couleur*, Engad. *culur*, Friul. *kolor*

GŬLA > It. Sp. C. Pr. *gola*, Rm. *gură* (= "mouth"), P. *goela*, Fr. *gueule*, Vegl. *gaula*, Engad. *gula*, Friul. *gole;* but Sard. *bula*

These same consonants + /r/ are also regularly preserved:

PROBĀRE > It. *provare*, Sard. *proare*, Rm. *proba*, Sp. *probar*, P. C. *provar*, Pr. *proar*, Fr. *prouver*, Engad. *provar*, Friul. *provà*

BRŪNU > It. Sp. *bruno*, Rm. Pr. Fr. *brun*, C. *bru*, Engad. *brün*

TRACTĀRE > It. *trattare*, Rm. *trata*, Sp. P. *tratar*, Sp. *trechar*, C. *tractar*, Pr. *trachar, traitar*, Fr. *traiter*, Engad. *trattar*

DRACŌNE > It. *drago, dragone*,[69] Rm. *drac*, Sp. *dragón*, P. *dragão* C. *drac, dragó*,[70] Pr. *drac, dragon*,[71] Fr. *dragon*

CRĒSCĔRE > It. *crescere*, Rm. *creşte*, Sard. *kreskere*, Sp. *crecer*,[72] P. *crescer*, C. *creixer*, Pr. *creser*, Fr. *croître*, Vegl. *kraskro*, Engad. *creschantar*, Friul. *kresi*

GRÁNU > It. Sp. *grano*, Rm. *grâu*, P. *grão*, C. *gra*, Pr. *gran*, Fr. *grain*, Vegl. *grun*, Engad. Friul. *gran*

68. For special treatment of dentals and sibilants in Romanian, see below. Note that some Greek words when taken into Latin voiced: κυβερνᾶν > L. GUBERNÁRE.

69. These doublets in Italian, Catalan, Provençal are from different Latin case forms, i.e., DRÁCO (nom.) and DRÁCONEM (acc.).

70. See note 69 above.

71. See note 69 above.

72. Note shift of stress in infinitive from first syllable to second in Sp., C., Pr., etc.

(Note that initial BR- was not a Classical Latin combination. BRŪNU, for instance, is of Germanic origin, borrowed into Latin.)

In a few cases the [k] of initial *ca-, cu, cr-* voiced and > [g]:

CÁTTU > It. *gatto,* Sp. P. *gato,* C. *gat,* Pr. *cat, gat;* but Sard. *batu* and Fr. *chat*[73]

CRĒTA > Sp. P. C. Pr. *greda,* but It. *creta,* Rm. *creta,* Fr. *craie;* cf. C. *gleda*

CRÝPTA > It. *grotta,* Sard. *grutta,* Sp. P. C. *gruta,* Fr. *grotte;* but note also Pr. *crota,* Fr. *crypte* (a learned form)

CO-, CU-, GO-, GU- generally remained /k/ and /g/ everywhere.

CŎRPUS > It. P. *corpo,* Rm. *corp,* Sp. *cuerpo,* C. *cos, corpora,*[74] Pr. *cors, corpora,*[75] Fr. *corps,* Engad. *corps*
GŬRDU > Sp. P. *gordo,* C. Pr. *gort,* Fr. *gourd*

CA- (VL. /ka/) remained except in northern Gaul, where it regularly fronted to palatal [č] to > Modern French (about 1300) [š],[76] and in Rhetia, where fronting also took place. The process was probably [ka > kia > ča > ša]:

CABÁLLU > It. *cavallo,* Rm. *cal,* Sard. *caḍḍu,* Sp. *caballo,* P. *cavalo,* C. *cavall,* Pr. *caval;* but Fr. *cheval,* and Engad. *chavagl,* Friul. *k'aval*

(For the evolution of GA-, see below.)

CE- [ke], CI- [ki] > *k'* (palatalized, or fronted) from the Empire on (VL. /č/), except in Sardinia and Dalmatia, and continued its evolution in

---

73. For *ca-* in French, see below.

74. The form *corpora* is from the Latin neuter plural of CÓRPUS, taken into Catalan and Provençal as a feminine singular.

75. See note 74 above.

76. This shift, which is peculiar to French and Rhetian, is thought by some to be due to Celtic habits of speech (the Substratum theory). But it is not found in the Norman and Picard dialects.

The sound in Rhetian, however, is the affricate [č], spelled *ch-* in Engadinian, *tg-* in Surmiran, Sutsilvan. In Sursilvan it remained *ca-* [ka]: Engad. *chavra (chevra),* Sursil. *caura,* Surm. Suts. *tgora* (< CÁPRA).

two main lines. The physiological changes involved in the tongue shifts for the two chief evolutions ([k > kj > č] and [k > kj > tj > ts > s > θ]) can be illustrated by the diagram of a buccal section in figure 8 (*t′* =

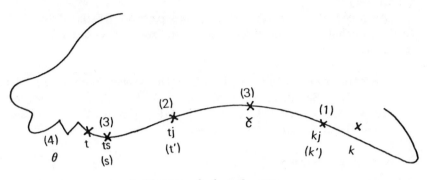

8. *Diagram of a buccal section*

palatalized *t*, or [tj]; *k′* = palatalized *k*, or [kj]; both these positions are hard to hold).[77] The two main lines of evolution are these:

1. [kj] > [tj] > [č] (= [tš]) in the East (Italy, Romania, and parts of Rhetia):

CĔRVU > It. *cervo* [čérvo], Rm. *cerb* [čɛrb], Engad. *tschierv*
CĪLĬU > It. *ciglio* [číʎo], Engad. *tschail;* cf. Sic. *ĝiggya*

2. In the West, [kj] > [tj] > [ts] > [s] (> [θ] in Castilian):

CĔRVU > Sp. *ciervo* [sjérƀo, θjerƀo], P. *cervo* [sérvu], C. *cervo* [sérvo], Pr. Fr. *cerf* [sɛrf], Friul. *sierf*
CĪLĬU(A) > Sp. *ceja*, [séχa], P. *cílio, celhas* [sílju, séʎas], C. *cell, cella* [sɛʎ, sɛʎa], Pr. *celh* [seʎ], Fr. *cil* [sil], Friul. *seye*

The affricate [ts] represents the stage of development in OSp., OP., OPr., and OFr.; the fricative [s] that of French, North Italian, some Rhetian dialects, and by the 1400s, Peninsular Spanish, the Spanish of Hispanic America, and Portuguese, Catalan, etc. The Spanish of most of Spain, however, shows a further shift to an interdental position, which took place apparently during the seventeenth century.

77. Note that these shifts are an attempt at "compromise" between a back consonant (velar [k]) and a front vowel [e], [i], that is the vowel pulls the consonant forward into one of several positions. This is one type of assimilation.

Dalmatia and Sardinia stand apart from the other Romance areas in showing a regression to (or preservation of) [k]: cf. Sard. *cerbu* (< CĔRVU), *celu* (< CAÉLU), [kidzu] (< CĬLĬU), and Vegl. *kaina* (< CĒNA).[78]

As noted above, northern Gaul (and parts of Rhetia) differed still further, in that CA- (and GA-) also palatalized.[79] CA- > k′a > [kja] > [tja] > [ča] > [ša]:

CÁRNE > OFr. *char* [čar], Fr. *chair* [šɛr], Engad. Friul. *charn;* cf. It. Rm. Sp. P. *carne,* Sard. *carre,* C. *carn,* Pr. *carn, cart, cher*
CABÁLLU > OFr. *cheval* [čəvál], MFr. [šəvál], Engad. *chavagl,* Friul. *k′aval*

GA- > g′a > [gja] > [dja] > [ĝa] > [ža]:

CÁMBA (< Grk. καμβα) > GÁMBA > Fr. *jambe* (OFr. [ĝãmbə], later [žã:b],[80] Engad. *chamma,* Friul. *g′ambe;* cf. It. Sp. *gamba,* Rm. *gambă,* Sard. *camba,* OSp. *cama,* C. *cama, gamba,* Pr. *camba* (and *gambaut* = Fr. "enjambée")
GÁLBĬNU > OFr. *jalne* [ĝalnə] > Fr. *jaune* (cf. Rm. *galbăn*); It. *giallo,* P. *jalde, jardo, jalne,* Sp. *jalde* are all borrowed from Old French (possibly also Vegl. *dzuolo*); cf. Engad. *gelg*

In Vulgar Latin, GE- and GI- combined with Classical Latin J- [j] as the consonantal *y* [j]:[81] GĔNĔRU > *yenero* [jénero] (cf. *yaket* < JÁCET).

The phone [j] (often spelled *y*) persisted to a certain extent, in central Iberia, the northern Pyrenees, Sicily, and parts of Italy:

---

78. The Sardinian dialects use various spellings for this [k] sound, chiefly *c* and *ch;* where known, they are used in this text rather than the phonetic representation. See selections in Appendix.

79. Not in southern France, nor along the English Channel, or in Normandy and Picardy. Cf. the English *cat, cavalier* (< Norman). Present day American English shows a similar palatalization of CA- in certain regional treatments (viz. Virginian): Cf. [kja] for *car* as opposed to "standard" Southern pronunciation [ka].

80. Cf. the explosive *j* in English *John* (< OFr. *Jehan*) with the fricative [ž] of modern French *Jean* [žã].

81. Cf. the change that has taken place in Greek; Mod. Grk. *γύνη* = "yee-nee" [jíni], and the dialectal *γιατρός* for *ἰατρός* Also *γιά* for *διά*.

Sp. *yero* (< ÉR(V)U), *yace* (< JÁCET), but Pr. *ers*, C. *erp;* Sp. *yema*, Béarnais *yeme* (< GÉMMA); Sicil. *yinokyu* (< GENÚC'LU), but Sard. *benuju*

Elsewhere it gathered force and > [dj] > [ǧ] or [dz], as in

DĬÚRNU > It. *giorno*, [ǧórno], OFr. [ǧɔrn], but Fr. *jour* [žur], C. *jorn* [žɔrn], etc., without occlusive element

JÁCET > Rm. *zace;* cf. Fr. *ci-gît*, formerly *gist* [ǧist]

Spanish shows a triple, or "three-pronged" development for these consonantal J- combinations (including JA-): (1) J remains [j] (popular), (2) J > [x] (learned, or semilearned), and (3) J- drops completely (popular).

(1) ĬAM (JAM) > Sp. *ya;* cf. It. già [ǧa], Sard. *ya*, Rm. *deja*, P. *já*, [ža], C. Pr. *ja*, Fr. *jà* [ža]

(2) GÉNTE > Sp. *gente* [xénte]; but It. *gente* [ǧénte], Sard. *gente*, P. *gente* [žénti], C. *gent* [žent], Pr. *gen*, Fr. *gens* [žã]

(3) GERMÁNU > *yermano > Sp. *hermano* (> Sard. *ermanu?*); but It. *germano* [ǧermáno], P. *irmão*, C. *germà* [žermá], Pr. germán [žermán]

Other samples of this type are:

GÉLU > Sp. *hielo* (OSp. *yelo*);[82] but It. P. *gelo*, Rm. *ger*, Pr. Fr. *gel*

JANUĀRĬU > Sp. *enero;* cf. It. *gennaio*, Sard. *bennarzu*, Rm. *ianuarie* (and *ghenar* by way of Mod. Grk.?), P. *janeiro*, C. *gener*, Fr. *janvier*, and Pr. *genier, genvier, genovier, ginovier, janovier. gembei, gervier, gier*[83]

The shift from [j] to OSp. [ž] to modern [x] (spelled *j-*) usually occurred before [a], [o], [u].[84]

---

82. Note that modern Spanish *y-*, or *hi-* + vowel (= [ŷ]), has affricate articulation in initial (phrase) position and after [n] and [l]: *yegua, hierba (yerba), cónyuge, el yugo*, etc.

83. See note 40 above.

84. Since the front vowels [e] and [i] have tongue positions closest to the yod element [j] in these *ge-, gi-* combinations, they tend to inhibit any drastic change in position of this palatal element, that is they are more likely to assimilate in sound (cf. P. *irmão* < *yermano). On the other hand, the middle-back vowels [a], [o], [u] tend to pull the yod [j] strongly toward *their* positions, thus causing a more extreme difference or change in sound by an assimilation in position, i.e., [j] is a front semiconsonant, while [x] is a back consonant.

JAM MÁGIS > Sp. *jamás* (It. *già mai*, Fr. *jamais*, C. *jamai*, Pr. *ja . . . mais*)

DĬURNĀTA > Sp. *jornada* (It. *giornata*, P. C. Pr. *jornada*, Fr. *journée*)

JŎVIS > Sp. *jueves* (It. *giovedì*, Rm. *joi*, C. *dijous*, Pr. *jous*, Fr. *jeudi*) (< JÓVIS DÍE = "Jove's Day")

JŎCU > Sp. *juego* (It. *giuoco*, Sard. [ĝogu], Rm. C. Pr. *joc*, P. *jôgo*, Fr. *jeu*)

JŬVENE > Sp. *joven* (It. *giovane*, Rm. *june*, P. *jovem*, C. *jove*, Pr. *joven*, Fr. *jeune*)

JŪSTU > Sp. *justo* (It. *giusto*, Sard. [justu], Rm. C. Pr. *just* P. *justo*, Fr. *juste*)

Note in the above examples that Spanish has a jota [χ], Italian [ĝ], Sardinian [ĝ] or [j], the others cited [ž]. Also, forms quoted as Sardinian generally refer to Logudorese, and are usually spelled phonetically as listed by Meyer-Lübke (e.g., [fidzu] for *fizu*) since the four dialectal spellings often vary considerably.

Further samples of k' > [č], [ts], [s], and [θ], (the last only in Castilian via OSp. [ts] and [s]):[85]

CĒRA > It. *cera* [čera], Rm. *ceară* [čjárə], Sard. [kera], OSp. *çera*, Sp. P. C. Pr. *cera*, Fr. *cire*

CĔNTU > It. *cento*, Sard. [kentu], OSp. *çiento*, Sp. *cien(to)* P. *cem*, *cento*, C. Fr. *cent*, Pr. *cen*

CÁELU > It. *cielo* [čelo], Rm. *cer*, Sard. *celu* [kelu], OSp. *çielo*, Sp. *cielo*, P. *ceu*, C. Pr. *cel*, Fr. *ciel*

CÓENA > It. C. Pr. *cena*, Sard. [kena], Rm. *cina*, OSp. *çena*, Sp. *cena*, P. *ceia*, Fr. *cène*

CIVITĀTE > It. *città*, Rm. *cetate*, OSp. *çibdad*, Sp. *ciudad*, P. *cidade*, C. *ciutat*, Pr. *ciutat*, *ciptat*, Fr. *cité*

85. This sound in Old Spanish was regularly spelled *ç* before *e* or *i* as in *çera*, *çiento* *çibdad*. This *c cedilla* was in origin a Gothic character, a *z* with a large hook on top.

The loss of the occlusive element produced the [s] in most Romance tongues (but see Italian, Sardinian, Romanian); there is no good phonological explanation for the Castilian [θ], except that it is more forceful and represents a reinforcement of [s]. Some have suggested that it was a court mannerism (?). It is a shift still farther forward in position of articulation, just as the change of OSp. *x* [š] in *dexa* to modern *deja* [χ] is a shift backward. In both cases the sound is still a fricative. The OSp. palatal sound of *x* [š] is clearly indicated by such spellings as Fr. *Don Quichotte*, It. *Don Chisciotte* — transcriptions for *Quixote* (now *Quijote* in modern Spanish).

QU- [kw] followed by [a] mostly remains (when accented):

QUÁNDO > It. P. *quando*, Sp. *cuando*, C. *quan;* but Sard. *candu*, Rm.
  cand, Pr. *can*, Fr. *quand* [kã][86]
*QUÁTTŎRO > It. P. *quatro*, Sp. *cuatro*, C. *quatre;* but Pr. *catre*,
  Fr. *quatre* [katr],[87] and Sard. *battoro*, Rm. *patru*
QUĀLE > It. *quale*, Sp. *cual*, P. C. *qual;* but Sard. *cali*, Rm. *care*,
  Pr. *cal*, Fr. *quel* [kɛl][88]

Note that Sardinian, Romanian, Provençal, and French have lost the
[u] sound, although the last keeps it in spelling, while Sardinian often
dissimilates the initial consonant. Also, Spanish has adopted the spelling *cu*
for all [kw] sounds, and Italian uses *qu*, regardless of which vowel follows,
for [kw].

Unstressed [kwa], however, regularly > [ka]:

QUATTUÓRDĔCIM > Sp. *catorce*, P. *catorze* (and Braz. *quatorze*),
  C. Pr. *catorze*, Fr. *quatorze* [katórz]; but It. *quatordici*
  [kwatórdiči] and Sard. *battordige*

QUI-, QUE-, QUO- uniformly lost the [w]:[89]

QUI > It. Engad. *chi*, OSard. [ki], OSp. *qui* [ki], C. Pr. Fr. *qui* [ki]
QUEM > It. *che*, OSard. [kin], Rm. *cine*, Sp. *quien*, P. *quem*, Engad.
  cha, C. Pr. *que*, Fr. *que* [ke][90]
QUĪNDECIM > It. *quindici* [kwíndiči], Sard. *bindigi*, Sp. *quince* [k],
  P. C. Pr. *quinze* [k], Fr. *quinze* [kɛ̃z]
QUÁERO > *kwero > It. *chiedo*, Sp. *quiero*, P. *quero*, Pr. *quier*,
  OFr. *quer* (= [k-])

86. *Qu* represents in modern French /k/. OFr. spelled these forms *kant, qand, catre,
qatre* (cf. Rm., Sard., and Pr. spellings).
87. See note 86 above.
88. See note 86 above.
89. For [ke], [ki], Italian and some forms in Sardinian, have chosen to use the diagraph
ch: che, chi. Even here Rhetian shows palatalization: Engad. *ch* is always [č] (=Surm.,
Surs., Suts. *tg*).
90. It. *che*, Sard. *chi* [ki], Rm. *ce*, Sp. *que*, C. *que*, etc., may have come exclusively from
L. QUID, although a crossing is possible here with QUEM.

QUĪNQUE > VL. CÍNQUE [kínkwe] > It. *cinque*, Sard. [kimbe],
Rm. *cincĭ*, Sp. P. *cinco*, C. Pr. *cinc*, Fr. *cinq*[91]
*QUŌM(OD)O > It. *come*, OSard. *co*, Rm. *cum*, Sp. P. *como*, C.
com, Pr. *com*, *coma*, *con*, Fr. *comme*

Germanic W- in words like *wárdon*, *wērra*, *wìsa* and the like had in
Germanic a bilabial voiced *w* which the Romans could not pronounce
without an accompanying *g*: hence the Latin derivatives GUARDÁRE
[gwardáre], GUÉRRA [gwér̄a], GUĪSA [gwísa].

GWA- kept the [w] except in French and Sardinian:

GUARDĀRE > It. *guardare* [gw-], Sp. P. C. Pr. *guardar* [gw-]; but
Fr. *garder*, Sard. *bardare*, *baldare*

GWE- and GWI- preserved the [w] only in Italian, although most
languages retained the *u* as a spelling device:

GUÉRRA > It. *guerra* [gw-], Sard. *gerra*, Sp. P. C. Pr. *guerra* [g-],
Fr. *guerre* [g-]
GUĪSA > It. *guisa* [gw-], Sp. P. C. *guisa*, Pr. *guiza*, Fr. *guise* [g-]

These words of Germanic origin did not get over into Romanian.
This change was extended also to some Latin words:[92]

VÁDU > It. *guado*, C. *gual*, Pr. *gua*, Fr. *gué;* but Rm. *vad*, Sp. *vado*,
P. *vau;* cf. verb forms VÁDO > It. *vo*, Sp. *voy*, P. *vou*, Fr. *vais*,
etc., also Eng. *wade*
VASTĀRE > It. *guastare*, Sp. P. C. Pr. *gastar*, Fr. *gâter*, but It.
devastare, Rm. *devasta*, Sp. P. C. *devastar*, Fr. *devaster*
VĚSPA > Fr. *guêpe*,[93] but It. P. C. Pr. *vespa*, Sard. *espe*, Engad.

91. Note that pre-Latin PÍNKWE had > QUÍNQUE by a process of assimilation,
whereas QUÍNQUE to KÍNKWE is an example of dissimilation. Cf. Grk. *pente*, German
fünf, Hindu *pancha*, Russ. *piata*, all cognates of English *five*, L. QUÍNQUE.
92. Northern and eastern Gaul kept the *w*- sound: *ouarder* (sixteenth-century grammar
in Picardy). Today Walloon has [wɛsp], Picard and Lorain [wɛp] for French *guêpe* [gɛp].
In southern Gaul -*w*- > -*gw*- in perfect tenses: HABUI > *abgwi* > *aguí*, VOLUI
> *volguí*. Catalan has similar forms: *haguí*, *volguí*. For development of *w* element in differ-
ent regions, see Bourciez, secs. 269b, 336 ff, 404c, 464b, 516a, and others.
93. The French form is probably a hybrid, from the Frankish *wabisa* + L. VESPA >
*wespa. It occurs as *wapces* in the Glosses of Reichenau (Rohlfs 32). Germanic words may
also have influenced others of the Latin etyma cited above.

vespra, Rm. *viespe*, Sp. *avispa* (*a-* by analogy with *abeja*?); cf. Eng. *wasp*, Germ. *Wespe*

In Old Spanish, initial [v] (often written *u-*) had already become identical with [b], and was lost as a phoneme, and /b/ is now [b] at the beginning of a breath group and after a nasal, but a fricative [ƀ] in all other situations. The letter *b* tended to be used, however, at the beginning of a word, a *v* in interior position: *bever* (mod. *beber*) < *BĬBĒRE, and *bivir* (mod. *vivir*) *VIVĪRE. Modifications of spelling were made by the Spanish Academy in the nineteenth century.

Initial L-, R-, M-, N-, S-,[94] V- are generally preserved, with the exceptions for V- noted above:

LĚCTU > It. *letto*, Sard. *lettu*, Sp. *lecho*, P. *leito*, C. *llit*[95] Pr. *lech*, Fr. *lit*, Engad. *let*
RŎTA > It. *ruota*, Sard. *roda*, Rm. *roată*, Sp. *rueda*, P. C. Pr. *roda*, Fr. *roue*, Engad. *rouda*
MŬLTU > It. *molto*, Rm. *mult*, Sp. *mucho*, P. *muito*, C. OFr. *molt*, Pr. *molt*, *mon*, *mot*
NŎVU > It. *nuovo*, Sard. Rm. C. *nou*, Sp. *nuevo*, P. *nôvo*, Pr. *nou*, *nau*, Fr. *neuf*, Engad. *nouv*
SĒTA > It. *seta*, Sard. Sp. P. C. Pr. *seda*, Fr. *soie*, Engad. *saida*
VÁNO > It. Sp. *vano*, Sard. *vanu*, Rm. C. *va*, P. *vão*, Pr. *vam*, Fr. *vain*

Initial /r̄/ in Romance was generally written *r* but strongly trilled, and sometimes written in Old Spanish as *rr-* or R-; this was also true of an interior *-nr-*: OSp. "dixo el rrey (Rey)," and the spelling *onrra* for *honra*. Compare It. Sard. *re*, Rm. *rege*, P. C. Pr. *rei*, Fr. *roi*, Engad. *rai*

In Spanish, Moorish pronunciation of [ś] as [š] may have influenced the sporadic evolution of Latin S- to [š] which subsequently became [χ]; however, the articulatory proximity of Spanish (Iberian) /ś/ (apicoalveolar) to the palatal [š] (Spanish and Semitic) might lead to these changes:

SAPŌNE > OSp. *xabón* [šaƀon] > Sp. *jabón;*[96] cf. It. *sapone*, Sard.

---

94. Every original Latin word beginning with a checked *s* (/s/-) prefixed a pro(s)thetic *i* or *e:* STÁTU > ISTÁTO, ESTÁTO and SCRIBO > ISCRÍBO, ESCRÍBO. For more extended discussion, see sec. 4.
95. Initial *l-* tended to palatalize in Catalan: *llit* [ʎit], *lluna* (< LÚNA) [ʎúna].
96. Why "SOAP"? Were the Moors cleaner than the Medieval Spaniards?

sabone, Rm. *săpun,* P. *sabão,* C. *sabó,* Pr. *sabon,* Fr. *savon,* Engad. *savun*

SALŌNE > OSp. *Xalón* > Sp. *Jalón*

Initial H- of Latin was lost in Vulgar Latin, and in Romance generally not written. By hypercorrection in spelling, it sometimes was prefixed to words which had no *h* originally. In later forms, the lost *h* was often restored in spelling, except in Italian, Sardinian, and Romanian, and usually not in Rhetian.

HABĒRE > It. *avere,* Sard. *aere,* Rm. *avea,* OSp. Pr. *aver,* P. C. *haver,* OFr. *aveir,* Fr. *avoir,* Sp. *haber*

HONŌRE > It. *onore,* Rm. *onoare,* Sp. P. C. *honor,* Pr. *onor, aunor,* OFr. *onour,* Fr. *honneur,* Engad. *onur*

The only exceptions in Italian are the verb forms of the present indicative of *avere: ho, hai, ha, abbiamo, avete, hanno.* This silent written *h* helps to distinguish the four forms (all the singular and the third person plural) from other homophones.

On the other hand, French words with an [h], of Germanic origin, lost this element but still do not allow elision or liaison, for example, *la halle* [la al] — the so-called "aspirate h." The Latin word ÁLTU for some obscure reason (perhaps influence of Germanic *hoch?*) was attracted into this category: OFr. *halt* > Fr. *haut.* One says *le haut* [ləo].

Note that Spanish uses an *h-* as a spelling device, prefixed to words otherwise beginning with *ue-: huelo, hueles, huele, huelen,* but *olemos, oléis* from the verb *oler,* and *huebra* < ŌPERA, *hueso* < ŌSU, and so on. This probably resulted from a desire to differentiate between spellings of *uelo* (= *velo*), *uelo* (= *huelo*), and the like, since *u* and *v* were used interchangeably in old manuscripts. Note that this same *h-* must be used nowadays before *ie-,* as in *hielo* (< GĔLU). Some forms, however, change the *i* to *y,* thus obviating the need for *h-,* for example, the present indicative (and subjunctive) forms of *errar: yerro, yerras. Hierba* and *hiedra* have not only the etymological *h-,* but are also spelled *yerba* and *yedra. Yegua* (< ĔQUA), on the other hand, has only the *y-* spelling.

Romanian does have some initial *h*'s deriving from Greek *chi* (X, χ) or other non-Latin sources:

Grk. CHÁOS > Rm. *haos*
Grk. CHÁRTA > Rm. *hartă*
Grk. CHRÍSTOS > Rm. *Hristos*
Turkish HARĪM > Rm. *harem*

Initial *F-* remained in most Romance tongues, but a popularized bilabial version [φ] > [h] in Spanish (later silent), resulting in many Spanish words beginning with *h-*, from original Latin *F-*. The original [f], however, was retained in many other Spanish words (see *F* in any Spanish dictionary), especially before the diphthong *ue*,[97] and before *r*. Two forms of the same word are not uncommon: *hondo, fondo* (< FŬNDU). Examples of *F-* > Sp. *h-* are:

FABULĀRE (*FABELLÁRE) > OSp. *fablar* [φablár], Sp. *hablar*, It. *favellare*, P. *fallar*, Pr. *faular*, OFr. *fabler* (but MFr. *hâbler* < Spanish?); cf. Rm. *fabulă*, C. *faula* < the noun FÁBULA

FĪCATU > OSp. *figado*, Sp. *hígado*, It. *fegato*, Sard. *figadu*, Rm. *ficat*, P. *fígado*, C. Pr. *fetge*, Fr. *foie*[98]

FĔLE > OSp. *fiel*, Sp. *hiel*, It. *fiele*, Sard. *fele*, Rm. *fiere*, P. C. Pr. *fel*, Fr. *fiel*

FĪLIU > OSp. fijo,[99] Sp. *hijo*, It. *figlio*, Sard. *fizu, fillu*, Rm. *fiu*, P. *filho*, C. *fill*, Pr. *filh*, Fr. *fils*, Engad. *figl*

FŎLIA > OSp. *foja* [φoχa], Sp. *hoja*, It. *foglia*, Sard. [fodza], Rm. *foaie*, P. *folha*, C. *fulla*, Pr. *folha*, Fr. *feuille*, Engad. *fögl*

FUGĪRE > OSp. *foir*, Sp. *huir*, It. *fuggire*, Sard. *fuire*, Rm. *fugi*, P. C. *fugir*, Pr. *fugir, fogir, fuir*, Fr. *fuir*, Engad. *fügir*

That the spelling *f-* in older Spanish is only traditional for an aspirate [h] or [φ] is attested by the use of *f-* for words borrowed from Germanic through French:

OSp. *fonta* (Cid) < Fr. '*honte;* cf. It. *onta*, Pr. *anta, onta*, etc.
OSp. *fardido* (Cid) < Fr. '*hardi;* cf. It. *ardito*, Pr. *ardit*, mod. Sp. P. *ardido*

Examples of Spanish retention of *f-* before the diphthong *ue* [we] and *r*, are:

FŎRTE > Sp. *fuerte*, It. Sard. P. *forte*, Rm. *foarte*, C. Pr. Fr. *fort*
FŎCU > Sp. *fuego*, It. *fuoco*, Sard. *fogu*, Rm. C. *foc*, Pr. *foc, fuc*, Fr. *feu*, Engad. *fö*
FRÓNTE > OSp. *fruente*, Sp. *frente*, It. Sard. P. *fronte*, Rm. *frunte*, Pr. *fron*, C. Fr. *front*, Engad. *frunt*

---

97. Even here *h-* occurs: *huesa* < FŎSSA, *huelga* < the verb form *FOLLICAT.
98. For various etyma forms and shift in stress, see Meyer-Lübke, *REW*, 8494.
99. Cervantes still uses this initial *f-*, as in *fidalgo*, etc.

(But even today in Mexico and elsewhere in the Hispanic World, one hears [hwérte], [hwego] for *fuerte, fuego*. This is actually [φwerte], [φwego] and may go back to the Basque substratum. For examples of this "rustic" pronunciation, see spellings of peasant speech in Lope de Vega's *Fuenteovejuna*.)

In the East, the dental-alveolars T-, D-, S- before *i* and *ie* (< Ĕ) > [ts], [z], and [š] respectively.[100]

TĔRRA > Rm. *țară* [tsárə]
DĪCIT > Rm. *zice* [zíče]
SĔPTE(M) > Rm. *șapte* [šápte]

The combinations, CL-, GL-, PL-, BL-, FL-, TL-, and so on, changed anciently throughout most Romance territory (except Dalmatia, Gaul, Catalonia, and Rhetia), usually palatalizing the *l*.[101]

In Italy all groups palatalized, the *l* changing to yod [j]:

PLĒNU > It. *pieno*, BLÁNCU > It. *bianco*, FLÁMMA > It. *fiamma*, CLÁVE > It. *chiave*, *GLÁCCIU > It. *ghiaccio;* cf. FÁBULA > *flaba (metathesis) > It. *fiaba*

Sardinian has a variety of changes, some of them influenced by Italian:
PL- > *pr-* or *pi-:* PLÁNU > Sard. *pranu*, PLÁNGERE > *piangere*.
FL- generally remains: FLÁMMA > *flamma*, FLÓRE > *flore;* but FLŎCCU > *fioccu*.
CL- > [ǧ]: CLÁVE > Sard. [ǧae] CLÁVU > [ǧau].
GL- lost the *g:* *GLÁNDE > Sard. *lande*, GLĒBA > *lea*.
BL- > *bi*, or dissimilated even more extremely: BLŬNDU > *biondo*, *BLASTIMÁRE > *frastimare*.

---

100. Also with interior dentals: PETĪRE > Rm. *peți* [petsí], TŌTĪ > Rm. *toț* [tots], AUDĪRE > Rm. *auzi* [awzí], MISĔLLU > Rm. *mișel* [mišél], FORMŌSI > Rm. *frumoși* [frumóši].
    This change occurred regularly after *e* > *ie*, but before the adoption of Slavic words in the eighth century, in which it did not occur. Also, it does not ordinarily occur where *e* > *i* before nasals: TĒMPU(S) > Rm. *timp*, DĒNTE > Rm. *dinte*, but SENTĪRE > Rm. *simți* [simtsí], and elsewhere throughout this verb.
    101. Palatal *l* has a variety of symbols: [ɫ], [l̬], [l'], or [λ]. In Spanish and Catalan this sound is spelled *ll*, in Portuguese and Provençal *lh*, in Italian *gl*, in Old French by a vowel + *il* or *ille* (occasionally *-il* alone, as in OFr. *fils* [fiλs], now [fis]).

In Romania, [kl] and [gl] changed, the others did not:

CLÁVE > Rm. *cheie*, *GLÁNDE > *ghinda*, but PLĒNU > *plin*,
and *BLASTIMÁRE > *blestima*, FLŌRE > *floare*

In French, Provençal, Catalan, Dalmatian, and the Rhetian dialects of the Engadine and Friuli, the original groups were maintained:

PLĒNU > Fr. *plein*, Pr. and C. *ple*, Vegl. Engad. *plain*, Friul. *plen*
*BLASTIMĀRE > Fr. *blâmer*, Pr. C. *blasmar*, Vegl. *blasmur*, Engad. *blastmar*, Friul. *blestemá*
*GLÁCIU, -IA > Fr. *glace*, Pr. *glasa*, C. *glaç*, Vegl. *glas*, Engad. *glatsch*, Friul. *glase*
FLÁMMA > Fr. *flamme*, Pr. C. *flama*, Engad. *flamma*, Friul. *flame*
CLÁVE > Fr. *clef*, Pr. C. *clau*, Vegl. *kluf*, Engad. *clav*, Friul. *klaf*

In Iberia, [bl-] and [gl-] sometimes lost the initial explosive element:

*GLÁNDĪNE, GLÁNDE > Sp. *landre*, P. *lande*
*BLASTIMĀRE > Sp. P. *lastimar*, but Fr. *blâmer*, Pr. *blasmar*, C. *blasmar*, *blastomar*, and *blasfemar*

In Spain, PL-, FL-, CL- regularly > [λ], and in Portugal [š], but in Catalonia (as stated above) remained unchanged. In early Spanish, scribes often wrote single *l* for the *ll* sound:

PLÁNU > Sp. *llano*, P. *chão* (C. *pla*)
PLORĀRE > Sp. *llorar*, P. *chorar* (C. *plorar*)
PLĒNU > Sp. *lleno*, P. *cheio* (C. *ple*)
FLÁMMA > Sp. *llama*, P. *chama* (C. *flama*)
CLAMĀRE > Sp. *llamar*, P. *chamar* (C. *clamar*)
CLÁVE > Sp. *llave*, P. *chave* (C. *clau*); but Sp. *clavo* < CLÁVU

Sometimes the palatalization did not develop; this may be a case of learned development or late borrowing:

PLÁNTA > Sp. P. *planta;* but cf. Sp. *llanta*, "tire" — popular development
PLÁCĬTU > Sp. *plazo*
FLÁCCU > Sp. *flaco*
FLŌRE > Sp. P. *flor*
CLÁRU > Sp. P. *claro*

And in Spanish FL- sometimes lost the *f*:

FLÁCCĬDU > Sp. *lacio* (P. *flácido*)
FLÁMMŬLA > Sp. (Doña) *Lambra* (a character in medieval Spanish literature)

In Portuguese, FL-, BL-, PL-, CL- often had an alternate development of *l* > *r:*

PLÁNCTU > P. *pranto* (OP. *chanto*); cf. Sp. *llanto,* Sard. *prantu*
PLÁCĬTU > P. *prazo* (Sp. *plazo*)
CLÁVU > P. *cravo* (Sp. *clavo*); cf. Sard. [ĝau]
FLÁCCU > P. *fraco* (Sp. *flaco*)
BLÁNCU > P. *branco* (Sp. *blanco*)

The wide variety of change in these combinations with *l* can be seen by the following example of [kl-] in the Latin word CLAMÁRE, "to call":

It. *chiamare* [kl- > kj-] [kjamáre]
Rm. *chema* [kl- > k-] [kemá]
Sard. *jamare* [kl- > ĝ] [ĝamáre]
Galician *chamar* [kl- > č-] [čamár]
Port. *chamar* [kl- > š-] [šamár]
In traditional Spanish and in some Andean regions *llamar* [kl- > λ-] [λamár]
Andalusian-American Spanish generally *llamar* [kl- > j-] [jamár][102] or [ŷamar]
C. Engad. Pr. *clamar* [kl- > kl-] [klamár]
Fr. *clamer* [kl- > kl-] [klamé(r)]
Vegl. *klamuar* [kl- > kl-] [klamwár]
Friul. *klamá* [kl- > kl-] [klamá]

Similiar differences are to be found for other combinations:

L. PLANU > It. *piano,* Sard. *pranu,* Rm. Pr. Fr. Engad. Friul. *plan,* Sp. *llano,* P. *chão,* C. *pla*

A number of Galician examples have been adopted into standard Spanish, such as

102. Initially and after /n/ and /l/ this becomes [ŷ] ([ŷamár]) and is [ž] ([žamár]) in some regions.

*PLÁTTU > *chato*
PÓP(U)LU > *PLÓPPU (metathesis) > *chopo* (cf. C. *xop* [šop])
PLUS > [chuš]: "ni chus ni mus" (neither more nor less)

Initial X- and Z- existed in Latin only in words borrowed from Greek. Hence, there are few popular derivatives. Portuguese, however, has adopted the letter *x* for the sound [š] in prevocalic position (in addition to *ch*), and has many words borrowed from Indian tongues, African terms, learned forms from Greek, loan words from other languages, and the like:

P. *xelim* [šélī] (< Eng. *shilling*)
P. *xênia* [šénja] (< Grk. = the flower of same name)
P. *xadrez* [šadréš] (< Arab. = chess; cf. Sp. *ajedrez*)
P. *xícara* [šíkara] (< Carib = cup) Sp. *jícara*
P. *xoxo* [šóšo] (Brazilian = loud kiss, smack), etc.

Catalan, like Portuguese, uses *x* for its spelling of the sound [š], some of the words corresponding to Spanish ones with *j-*, some to those with *ch-*, and so on. Examples:

C. *xapa* [šápa] (= Sp. *chapa*)
C. *xarop* [šaróp] (= Sp. *jarabe*)
C. *xicot* [šikót] (= Sp. *chico*)

Spanish too has some native Indian words with initial *x-*. They were originally pronounced [š], but have been reduced today in sound to [s] or [χ]: *Xochimilco* [sočimílko], *xochitl* [sóčitl], *Xalapa* or *Jalapa* [χalápa]. Other words are learned forms from Greek, with the sound of [ŝ]: *xenia* [šénja], *xilófono* [šilófono], *xilol* [šilól] (Eng. *xylol*, chem.)

For these learned borrowings from Greek, French has preserved the original [ks] sound: Fr. *xénophobe* [ksenɔfɔb]; Fr. *xylophone* [ksilɔfɔn].

Z- however is a standard initial spelling device in modern languages, although derived from various sources. In French, Catalan, Provençal, Portuguese, Romanian it is a voiced [z], in Spanish [s] or [θ], in Italian [ts] or [dz]:

L. Grk. ZŌNA > Fr. *zone* [zo:n], P. C. *zona* [zóna], Rm. *zonă* [zónə], Sp. *zona* [sóna, θóna], It. *zona* [dzóna], etc.
L. DĔCEM > Rm. *zece* [zéče]
Arab. ZAĠÁL > Sp. P. *zagal;* but C. *sagal*

Medial or Intervocalic Consonants

The oldest and most widespread change is a tendency for mute or unvoiced occlusives to > voiced occlusives to > fricatives, and then to fall. This is a general process, to be found in most languages, and one which works sometimes in cycles. For a list of voiced and unvoiced consonants, see figure 2.

Why should these unvoiced (mute, or surd) consonants voice? Because they take on voice from preceding and following vowels. Why do they become fricatives? Because the fricatives generally represent a measure of relaxation.

Early traces documented in Latin times are forms such as PAGÁTUS (= PACÁTUS), MĒGUM (= MĒCUM), AMÁDUS (= AMÁTUS), and so forth. The process generalized about the fifth century, the East differing from the West.

-P-T-K-

In Romania, Dalmatia, Southern Italy -P-, -T-, -K- were generally preserved:

LACTŪCA > Rm. *lăptucă*, Sicil. *lattuca*
PACĀRE > Rm. *împăca*, Vegl. *pakur*
SĬTIM > Rm. *sete*
MUTĀRE > Rm. *muta*
RĪPA > Rm. *rîpă*, Vegl. *raipa*, Sicil. *ripa*
STRÁTA > Vegl. *struota*, Sicil. *strata;* but Rm. *stradă*

In the West, there was a uniform weakening:[103]

LACTŪCA > Sp. *lechuga*, Pr. *lachuga*, C. *lletuga*
PACĀRE > Sard. *pagare*, Sp. P. C. Pr. *pagar*, Engad. *pajar*, Friul. *payá*
SECŪRU > Sard. *seguru*, Sp. P. *seguro*, C. Pr. *segur*, Engad. *sgür*, Friul. *siyur*
*SĒTA > Sard. Sp. P. C. Pr. *seda*, Engad. *saida*, Friul. *sede*
MUTĀRE > Sard. *mudare*, Sp. P. C. Pr. *mudar*, Friul. *mudá*
RĪPA > Sard. Sp. C. Pr. *riba*, P. *riba(-mar)*, Engad. *riva*, Friul. *rive*

---

103. Including northern Italy: Lombard *paga, amiga, roeda* (< RÓTA). Some exceptions are found in dialects of the Pyrenees, near the Basque provinces: Béarnais [apéλa] (< APĬCŬLA), Aragonese [nokera] (< NUCÁRIA).

STRÁTA > Sard. *istrada,* Sp. P. C. Pr. *estrada,* Engad. *strada,* Friul. *strade*

In northern Gaul, the process was the same, but a later development carried it still further: Fr. *laitue, payer, sûr* (< *sëur*), *soie, muer, rive,* OFr. *estrée* (cf. Eng. *street*). The modern form *estrade* is semilearned, or borrowed. (Cf. -b-, -v-, -d-, -g-, below.)

In central Italy, the process varied: It. *lattuga, pagare, riva, strada,* but *securo, sicuro,* and *seta, mutare.* The full range of this change is well illustrated by medial -P- in the following word:

PAPILIŌNE > It. *padiglione* (dissimilation), Rm. *pavilion,* Sp. *pabellón,* P. *pavilão,* C. *pavelló,* Pr. *pavilhon, parpathon, pabalhon,* Fr. *pavillon* and *papillon,* Ladin *pavel,* Friul. *paveye* and *paveyon,* Venez. *paveĝa,* Lomb. *babeya* (etc. in other dialects)

(Note that the Spanish consonants *b* (*v*), *d,* and *g* [in medial position] are normally fricatives rather than explosives: [ƀ], [đ], [ǥ]. See below.)

The complete process from Latin to modern Romance is as follows:

1. [p] > [b] > [ƀ] or [v]
2. [t] > [d] > [đ] and falls [ø]
3. [k] > [g] > [ǥ] or [j] and falls [ø]

This process of change is a general one, found in most languages. Compare Hawaiian, in which most intermediate consonants have disappeared, or unvoiced, or been displaced, so that the language now has only twelve phonemes, five of them vowels! For instance, the English phrase "Merry Christmas" appears in Hawaiian as *Meli Kalikimaka.* And the well-known *aloha* is said to be cognate with the Polynesian *ia orana.*

-B (V)-, -D-, -G-

Original Latin *B* and *V* early became confused in many localities and often had a parallel development. As a rule, however, all three (four?) sounds persisted, with some exceptions and special traits:

In the East, intervocalic *G* and *D* remained, *B* (*V*) fell (= ø):

LIGĀRE > Rm. *lega*
CRŪDA > Rm. *crudă*
SUDŌRE > Rm. *sudoare*

But:

VĪVA > Rm. *vie*
SCRĪBO > Rm. *scriu*
CABÁLLU > *caal > Rm. *cal*[104]

In central Italy they persisted:

LIGĀRE > It. *legare*
NŪDA > It. *nuda*
VĪVA > It. *viva*
CABÁLLU > It. *cavallo*
PLÁGA > It. *piaga*
SUDŌRE > It. *sudore*
SCRĪBO > It. *scrivo*

But not in Sardinia:

LIGĀRE > Sard. *liare*
VĪVA > Sard. *bia*
CRŪDU > Sard. *cruu*
CABÁLLU > Sard. *caddu*

Iberia and southern Gaul: in posttonic position /g/ remained (although becoming a fricative [ǥ] in Spanish): PLÁGA > Sp. *llaga* [λáǥa], P. *praga*, *chaga*, C. Pr. *plaga*.

But it often fell before the accent (pretonic):

LIGĀRE > Sp. P. Pr. *liar* (P. also *ligar*), but C. *lligar*
REGĀLE > Sp. P. C. *real*, Pr. *reial, real*

-D- > [đ] or fell (Iberia), later > [z] in southern Gaul:

FEUDĀLE > Sp. P. C. *feudal*,[105] Pr. *feuzal*
GUIDĀRE > Sp. P. C. *guiar*, Pr. *guizar*

104. These losses occurred before the eighth century. Note Slavic borrowings: Slav. *ljubiti* > Rm. *iubi*, *byvolu* > *bivol*.

105. Portuguese regional pronunciation of *d* may be fricative or explosive, and *de-, di-* even affricate [ĝ] (very light), e.g., *cidade* [sidádı], [siđáđı] [sidáĝı]; *diante* [djántı] or [ĝančı]. The affricate sound is very common to some Brazilian areas, which maintain a hard *d*, however, in *da-, do-, du-*. Note also the affricate *te-* and *ti-*, symbolized here as [č].

Intervocalic B (V) became fricative at first, later diverged, being strengthened in some cases, in others disappearing or vocalizing:

NŎVU > Sp. *nuevo* [nwéƀo], P. *nôvo* [nóvu], Pr. C. *nou*
CABÁLLU > Sp. *caballo* [kaƀáλo], P. *cavalo* [kaválu], Pr. *caval* [kavál], C. *cavall* [kaváλ]; cf. OGasc. *cabat*
BĬBĔRE, *BIBÉRE > Sp. *beber* [beƀér], P. *beber* [bebér], C. Pr. *beure* [béwre]

In northern Gaul very early, perhaps by the sixth century, the unvoiced intervocalic P-T-K's > voiced and along with the originally voiced B (V)-D-G's were affected alike.[106]

-G- and -D- > the fricatives [j] and [d] respectively, by relaxation. The latter has completely disappeared, the former has been absorbed where it was part of a diphthongal combination:

PACĀRE > *PAGĀRE > Fr. *payer* [pɛjé]; but *je paie* [pɛ]
PLÁGA > Fr. *plaie* [plɛ]
*SĒTA > *SEDA > [sejđə] > Fr. *soie* [swa]
NŪDA > [nyđə] > Fr. *nue* [ny]
SUDĀRE > [syđér] > Fr. *suer* [sɥe]
MUTĀRE > [myđér] > Fr. *muer* [mɥe]

-B- (-P-) > -*v*- and was preserved along with Latin -V-:

NŎVA > Fr. *neuve*
CABÁLLU > Fr. *cheval*
RĪPA > Fr. *rive*
CREPĀRE > Fr. *crever*

(Compare It. *cavallo*, Rm. *cal*, Sard. *caddu*, P. *cavalo*, Pr. *caval;* but It. *crepare*, Sard. *crebare*, Rm. *crepa*, P. *quebrar*, Pr. *crebar* with preservation of the bilabial occlusives. Spanish has [ƀ]: *caballo, quebrar.*)

In Rhetian (Engadinian), intervocalic B (*V*) and D are regularly preserved, even when they > final, while G varies in its development:

---

106. French carried this process to its greatest extent, dropping many of the consonants:
    LOCÁRE > OFr. *loer* > Fr. *louer*
    LAUDÁRE > OFr. *loder* [lođér] > Fr. *louer*
    RÚGA > Fr. *rue* (cf. Sp. *rúa*, P. C. *rua*)
    SECÚRU > OFr. *sëur* > Fr. *sûr*

NÓVU > Engad. *nouv,* CABÁLLU > *chavagl,* *BIBĒRE > *baiver,*
SCRĪBO > *scriv,* NŪDU > *nüd,* *SÉTA > *saida,* LAUDÁRE
> *lodar;* but LIGĀRE > *liar,* PACĀRE > *pajar,* SECŪRU >
sgür

Intervocalic *K'* and *G'*

-CE-, -CI- and -GE-, -GI- suffered many of the changes undergone
also in initial position. For examples, note the following:

MERCĒDE > It. *mercede* [č], Sp. *merced* [θ] [s], P. *mercede* [s], Pr.
merce(i) [s], C. *mercè* [s], Fr. *merci* [s]

DŬLCE > It. *dolce,* Sard. *dulce,*[107] Rm. *dulce* [č], Sp. *dulce,* P. *doce,*
C. *dolç,* Pr. *dous,* Fr. *douce,* Vegl. *dolk,* Engad. *dutsch,* Friul.
dolts

VICĪNU > It. *vicino,* Sard. *biginu,* Rm. *vecin,* Sp. *vecino,* P. *vizinho,*
C. *veí,* Pr. *vezin,* Fr. *voisin* [z], Vegl. *vičain,* Engad. *vaschin,*
Friul. *vizin*

PÁCE > It. *pace,* Sard. *page,* Rm. *pace,* Sp. *paz,* P. *paz* C. *pau,* Pr.
patz, Fr. *paix* [pε], Engad. *pasch,* Friul. *pas*

DĔCEM > It. *dieci,* Sard. *dege,* Sp. *diez,* P. *dez,* C. *deu,* Pr. *detz,*
Fr. *dix* [s], Vegl. *dik,* Engad. *desch,* Friul. *dis*

LĒGE > It. *legge,* [ĝ], Rm. *lege* [ĝ], Sp. *ley,* P. Pr. *lei,* C. *llei,* Fr. *loi,*
Engad. *ledscha*

RĒGE > It. Sard. *re,* Rm. *rege,* Sp. *rey,* P. C. Pr. *rei,* Fr. *roi,* Vegl. *ra,*
Engad. *rai*

REGĪNA > It. Engad. *regina,* OIt. Sard. Sp. *reina,* Rm. *regină* [ĝ],
P. *rainha,* C. *reina, regina* [ž], Pr. *reina, regina,* Fr. *reine*

VAGĪNA > It. Pr. *guaina,* Sard. *baina,* Sp. *vaina,* C. *beina,* Fr.
gaîne, Friul. *vazine,* Venez. *vazina,* Pied. *vena*

As stated above, intervocalic P, T, K regularly voiced if single:[108]

SÁPĔRE > *SAPĒRE > Sp. P. C. Pr. *saber,* Fr. *savoir,* Engad.
savair, Friul. *savé;* but It. *sapere,* Sard. *sapir*

---

107. Note that Sardinian is almost unique in preserving in many words the original
velar quality [k] of C unvoiced, even before *e* and *i*. There are exceptions, however, as in
PÁCE > *page,* DĔCEM > *dege,* LÚCE > *luge,* etc.

108. But, as just mentioned, subject to regular fronting and changes in k' combinations
(CE, CI). In French -CA- (-GA-) > -y (+ vowel) [-j-]. PACÁRE > Fr. *payer* [pεjé],
PAGÁNU > Fr. *païen* [paj$\bar{ε}$'].

VĪTA > Sp. P. C. Sard. *vida*, Pr. *vida*, *via*, Fr. *vie*, but It. *vita*, Rm. *vită*, *viaţa* (Engad. *vita*, Friul. *vite* < It. ?)

PACĀRE > It. Sard. *pagare*, Sp. P. C. Pr. *pagar*, Fr. *payer*, Engad. *pajar*, Friul. *payá;* but ORm. *paca*, Vegl. *pakur*

If double or supported, however, these remained unvoiced, but usually simplified (see Doubling, sec. 7):

CÁTTU > Sp. P. gato, C. *cat*, Pr. *cat*, *gat*, Fr. *chat* Engad. *giat*, Friul. *gat;* but It. *gatto*, Sard. *batto*[109]

VÁCCA > Rm. *vacă*, Sp. P. C. Pr. *vaca*, Fr. *vache* [vaš], Vegl. *baka*, Friul. *rak'e;* but It. *vacca*, Sard. *bacca*

Intervocalic P, T, K followed by R also voiced:

CÁPRA > Sard. *craba* (met.), Sp. P. C. Pr. *cabra*, Pr. *craba* (met.) and *chevra*, Fr. *chèvre*, Engad. *chavra*, Friul. *k'avra;* but It. *capra*, Rm. *capră*

MÁTRE > It. Sp. P. *madre*, C. *mare*, Pr. *maire*, Fr. *mère;* but Rm. *mitră*, from Grk. METRA ["matrix" ?]

SACRĀTU > Sp. P. *sagrado*, C. Pr. *sagrat;* but Fr. *sacré*, It. *sacrato*

Intervocalic KWA > [gwa]:

ÁQUA > Sp. P. *agua*, C. *aigua*, Pr. *aiga*, *agua*, *augoe*, Fr. *eau;*[110] but It. *acqua*, Sard. *abba*, Rm. *apă*, Engad. *aua*, *ova*, Friul. *age*

AEQUĀLE > It. *uguale*, Sp. P. C. *igual*, Engad. *egual;* but Sard. *galu*, Pr. *egal*, *esgal*, *aigal*, Fr. *égal*

Other -KW- combinations also voiced, but lost the W element:

ALIQUOT > Sp. P. C. *algo;* but Pr. *alque*, *alques*, OFr. *alques*, Engad. *alc* (possibly from ÁLIQUID?)

ALIQUEM > Sp. *alguien*, P. *alguem*

SEQUI > *SEQUIRE, *SEQUERE > Sard. *segire*, Sp. P. C. Engad. *seguir*, Pr. *segre*, *seguir;* but It. *seguire* [segwíre]

---

109. Italian has always been fond of double consonants and has even doubled many single ones, e.g., LÉGE > It. *legge*, ÁGUA > It. *acqua*. A double consonant in Italian has double length, i.e., *gat-to*, *vac-ca*. See Double Consonants and Clusters below.

110. Old French has a variety of forms for this word: *ague*, *aigue*, *aighe*, *aige*, *aive*, *aiue*, *awe*, *iave*, *eve*, *ewe*, *yaue*, and *eaue*. Also the plural ÁQUAS > *Aix* (as in *Aix-la-Chapelle*).

In medial position, GW had a wide variety of developments, preserving the labial-velar element in some cases, in others dropping or dissimilating it. Two good examples are the following:

LÍN*GUA* > It. P. *lingua* [gw], Sard. *limba*, Rm. *limbă*, Sp. *lengua*, C. *llengua* [gw], Pr. *lenga*, Fr. *langue* [g], Vegl. *langa*, Engad. *lengua*, Friul. *lenge*

ÍN*GUÍ*NE (IN*GU*EN) > It. *inguine* [gw], Sard. *imbena*, Sp. *ingle*, C. *engonal* (< INGUINÁLE), Pr. *engue*, Fr. *aine*, Friul. *lenzit*

The Liquids -L-, -R-, and the Nasal -N-

These persisted primitively. Later changes occurred, such as the loss of *l* and *n* in many Portuguese words:

GŬLA > It. Sp. P. C. Pr. *gola*, Sard. *bula*, Rm. *gură*, Fr. *gueule*, Vegl. *gaula*, Engad. *gula*, Friul. *gole*

COLŌRE > It. Sard. *colore*, Rm. *culoare*, Sp. C. Pr. *color*, Fr. *couleur*, Engad. *culur*, Friul. *kolor;* but P. *côr*

PĬRA > It. Sp. P. C. Pr. *pera*, Sard. *pira*, Rm. *pară*, Fr. *poire* (OFr. *peire*), Vegl. *paira*, Engad. *pair*, Friul. *per*

AMĀRE > It. Sard. *amare*, Sp. P. C. Pr. Engad. *amar*, Fr. *aimer*, [ɛmé],[111] Engad. *amer*, Friul. *amá*

LŪNA > It. Sard. Sp. Pr. *luna*, C. *lluna*, Rm. *lună*, Fr. Friul. *lune*, Vegl. *loina*, Engad. *glüna;* but P. *lua*

When intervocalic N became final through loss of a following consonant, this *n* was dropped in Catalan, and in French spelling it is used as an indication of a nasal vowel; in Portuguese its loss resulted in a nasal diphthong:[112]

PÁNE > It. Sard. *pane*, Rm. *pâine*, Sp. Pr. Friul. Engad. *pan*, Vegl. *pun*, but P. *pão* [pãw], C. *pa*, Fr. *pain* [pɛ̃]

MÁNU > It. Sp. *mano*, Sard. *manu*, Rm. *mână*, Pr. Engad. Friul. *man*, Vegl. *mun*, but P. *mão* [mãw], C. *ma*, Fr. *main* [mɛ̃]

---

111. In this -er conjugation in French, the *r* has become silent in the infinitive, except sometimes in liaison and of course in other verb forms, e.g., the future *aimerai* [ɛm(e)ré], etc.

112. This Portuguese nasal diphthong [ãw] is usually spelled *am* when unstressed: *cantam* [kántãw]. One of the rare exceptions is *Cristóvão*.

(For double -NN-, see below.)

There are many early cases of regressive dissimilation, especially of the R:

PEREGRĪNU > *PELEGRĪNU > It. *pellegrino*, Fr. *pèlerin* (cf. Eng. *pilgrim*), Pr. *pelegrin, pelerin, peregrin;* but Sp. P. *peregrino*
PRURĪRE > *PRUDĪRE, *PRÚDERE > It. *prudere*, Sard. *prudire*, Pr. *pruzir;* cf. P. *pruir, prurir*, C. *pruir*
QUAÉRĔRE > *Q(U)EDERE > It. *chiedere*, but Sard. [kerrere], Rm. *cere*, Sp. P. Pr. *querer*, Pr. OFr. *querre*, (Fr. *quérir*), Friul. *čerí*

R and L are also frequently subject to metathesis,[113] for example:

CREPÁRE > Sp. P. Pr. *quebrar*, but It. *crepare*, Sard. *crebare*, Rm. *crepa*, Pr. *crebar*, Fr. *crever*
CŎRVU > Sard. *crobu* (and *corvu*)
FÁBRĬCA > Sp. *fragua*, P. *frágua;* cf. It. *forgia* < Fr. *forge*, C. Pr. *farga*
PÓP(U)LU > *PLÓPO > It. *pioppo*, Rm. *plop*, Gal. Sp. *chopo*, P. *choupo*, C. *xop, clop* (and *poll*)
FÁB(U)LA > *FLÁBA > It. *fiaba* (Cf. nonmetathesized developments, It. *fola, favola*, Rm. *fabulă*, Sp. *habla*, P. *fala*, Engad. *fabla*, C. *faula*, Pr. *faula, fabla*, Fr. *fable*. From a diminutive FABULÍLLA, Provençal has doublets *flabel* and *fablel*.)

Exchange of L for R (rhotacism) and vice versa was quite widespread in Iberia and elsewhere:

PŎPŬLU > Rm. *popor*
VĔTŬLU > *VEC'LU > *vecru > Sard. *vricu*[114]
AERÁMINE > *ARAM'NE > *alam're > Sp. *alambre*
ÁMPLU > Sard. *ampru*
ÁRBŎRE > It. *albero*, Sp. *árbol*, Vegl. *yuarbol*, Engad. *alber*, but Sard. *arbure*, Rm. *arbore*, P. *arvore*, C. Pr. Fr. *arbre* (and Pr. *albre*). In a word of this type, with two *r*'s, the exchange of one or the other for an *l* is a clear case of dissimilation. Cf. Sassarese Sard. *altilta* < ARTÍSTA

---

113. For discussion, see below.
114. This word exhibits not only *l-r* exchange but also metatheses.

-M-

In most cases, an M in medial position remained except where it became final in French and was written -*n* or -*m* to represent a nasal vowel sound:

FÁME (FÁMĬNE) > It. *fame*, Sard. *famine*, Rm. *foame*, Sp. *hambre*,[115] P. *fome*, C. Pr. *fam*, Fr. *faim* [fɛ̃], Vegl. *fum*, Engad. Friul. *fam*

HÓMO (HÓMĬNE) > It. *uomo*, Sard. *omine*, Rm. Friul. *om*, Sp. *hombre*, P. *homem*, C. Pr. *home*, Fr. *on, homme* [õ, ɔm], Vegl. *yomno*, Engad. *hom*

CAMĪSIA > It. *camicia*, Rm. *cămaṣă*, Sp. P. C. *camisa*, Pr. *camiza*, Fr. *chemise*, Vegl. *kamaisa*, Engad. *chamischa*, Friul. *k'ameze*

FŪMU > It. P. *fumo*, Sard. *fumu*, Rm. C. Pr. *fum*, Sp. *humo*, Fr. *fumée* (< FUMÁTA), Engad. *füm*

PULMŌNE > It. *polmone*, Sard. *prumone*, Rm. *plamân*, Sp. *pulmón*, P. *pulmão*, C. *pulmó*, Pr. *polmon*, Fr. *poumon* [pumõ'], Engad. *pulmun*, Friul. *palmon*

-F-

Medial F was not common in standard Latin. Such words as RÚFUS, GLÍFA for example were dialectal forms corresponding to Latin RÚBEUS (RÚSSUS, RÚSSEUS) and GLÉBA. Words borrowed from Greek with PH (= *p*', with breathing) > VL. F or P and these were maintained as unvoiced consonants in some cases, voiced in others:

RŪFU > C. *ruf*

RÁPHĂNU > It. *rafano*, Sp. *rábano*, P. *rabão*, C. Fr. *rave*, Pr. *rafe, rave*, Engad. *rava*

CÓLĂPHU > It. *colpo*, Sard. *colpu*, Sp. P. *golpe*, C. *colp*, Pr. *colp, colbe*, Fr. *coup*, Engad. *cuolp*

STÉPHĂNU > It. *Stefano*, Rm. Ṣ*tefan*, Sp. *Esteban*, P. *Estévão*, C. Pr. *Esteve*, Fr. *Etienne*

Latin compounds with initial F in the second element either maintained the F, occasionally voiced it when singular, or (in Spanish) treated it as an initial:

115. For discussion of *mbr* in Spanish, see below.

DEFĒNSA > It. *difesa*, Sp. *defensa, dehesa, devesa*, P. *defésa, devesa*,
C. *devesa*, Pr. *deveza*, Fr. *défois, defense*, Engad. *defaisa*

SUFFOCĀRE > It. *soffocare*, Sp. C. *sofocar*, P. *sufocar*, Pr. *sofocar*,
sofogar, Fr. *suffoquer*

*AFFOCĀRE > It. Sard. *affogare*, Sp. *ahogar*, P. C. Pr. *afogar*

*SUFFUMĀRE > Sp. *sahumar*

SUFFLĀRE > It. *soffiare*, Rm. *sufla*, Sp. *sollar, soplar*, P. *soprar*,
Engad. *sofflar*, Pr. *soflar, soprar*, Fr. *souffler*[116]

TRIFŎLĬU > It. *trifoglio*, Sard. *trovozu*, Rm. *trifoiu*, Sp. *trébol*, P.
trevo, Pr. *trefolh, trefuelh*, Fr. *trèfle*, Engad. *trafögl*

PROFĔCTU > It. *profitto*, Sp. *provecho*, P. *proveito*, C. *profit*, Pr.
profech, Fr. *profit*

Since H had become silent in Vulgar Latin, it regularly disappeared
in medial position, except as a spelling device in modern languages to
separate syllables (Spanish) or in combination with other letters to represent
new sounds.[117]

COHÓRTE > It. Sp. C. *corte*, OSard. *corte*, Rm. *curte*, C. Pr. *cort*,
Fr. *cour*

PREHÉNDERE > It. Sard. *prendere*, Rm. *prinde*, Sp. P. *prender*, C.
prendre, Pr. *penre*, Fr. *prendre*

DEFÉNSA > Sp. *dehesa* [de·ésa]

HAC HÓRA > OSp. P. *agora*, Sp. *ahora* [aóra]

Spelling devices with *h*:

CH = It. Rm. Sard. [k], Sp. [č], P. Fr. [š]
GH = It. Rm. Sard. [g]
LH = P. Pr. [λ]
NH = P. Pr. [ñ]

In Sardinian, *ch* alternates with *c* and *qu* in the various dialects to
designate the [k] sound, as in *chi, qui; chervu, cerbu; quircadu, circau*. In
Engadinian the sound [č] is sometimes spelled *ch*, sometimes *tsch*, while the
combination *sch* (as in German) = [š] and *s-ch* (with dash) is [šč].

---

116. For standard -FL- development, see above.
117. For initial H, see above (see also, -F- above).

Medial S (SS)

In medial position, a single intervocalic *S* usually voiced [z], although continuing to be spelled *s* in most cases.[118] A double S (SS) remained unvoiced [s], unless through contraction of the word it came into contact with a voiced consonant, or lost its intervocalic position to become final and later fall. Support from a voiceless consonant, however, tended to preserve the unvoiced *s*. Old Spanish had both single *s* [ż] and double *ss* [ś], but in the sixteenth century all intervocalic [z] unvoiced and in spelling were reduced by the Spanish Academy to a single *s* in the nineteenth century.

AUSĀRE > It. *osare* [z], Sp. *osar* [osár], P. *ousar* [z], C. *gosar* [z], Pr. *ausar, auzar* [z], Fr. *oser* [ozé]

RŌSA > It. *rosa* [z], Sard. *rosa*, Rm. *roză*, Sp. *rosa* [s], P. C. Pr. *rosa* [z], Fr. *rose* [z]

CAÚSA > It. C. *cosa* [z], Sp. *cosa* [s], P. *cousa, coisa* [z], Pr. *cauza*, Fr. *chose* [šo:z]

PÁSSU > It. P. *passo* [s], Sard. *passu* [s], Rm. C. Pr. *pas* [s], P. *passo* [s], Fr. *pas* [pa]

ÁS(I)NU > It. *asino* [s], Sard. *ainu*, ORm. *asin*, Sp. P. *asno* [z], C. *asse*, Pr. *aze, aine*, Fr. *âne* (OFr. *asne* [z])

HÓSP(I)TE > It. *ospite* [s], Rm. *ospete* [s], Sp. *huesped* [s], P. *hospede* [s], C. Pr. *oste*, Fr. *hôte* (OFr. *oste* [s])

FĔSTA > It. Sard. P. C. Pr. *festa* [s], Sp. *fiesta* [s], Fr. *fête* (< *feste*)[119]

Double Consonants and Clusters

In general, double consonants persisted in Romance spelling, but were actually simplified except in Italian (and Sardinian), where they still have double value. Other languages reduced the articulation generally. In French, for example, the double spelling is a learned restoration, to represent a distinction in pronunciation. The RR, however, has persisted in nearly all languages as [r̄] and even intensified in the case of Spanish. In French the

---

118. Italian continues to waver between voiced and unvoiced -/s/-, dialectal and regional variants. That is, *casa* [káza] or [kása], *caso* is regularly [kázo]. Grandgent says that " the stage usage has (voiced) ṣ in all words. Outside of Tuscany, we find ṣ [z] in all cases in the North, *s* [s] in all the Marches, Rome, and the South." He thinks the Tuscan *s* may once have been voiced and is in the process of transition to unvoiced *s* (Grandgent 105).

119. For combinations of -SC-, -PS-, etc., see sec. 4. Cf. also S in final position and initial S + consonant (sec. 4).

[ř] and [r] were leveled and are now generally [R]. In Spanish and Catalan the LL took on palatal value [λ] (-ll-). NN palatalized to [ñ] because of increased pressure to preserve the double value.[120]

FLÁMMA > It. *fiamma* [fjám·ma], Rm. *flamă*, Sp. *llama*, P. *chama*, C. Pr. Fr. *flamme*

BĚLLA > It. Sard. *bella* [bέl·la] (and Sard. *bedda*), Sp. *bella* [béλa], P. *bela* [l], C. *bella* [bέλa], Pr. *belha, bella, bela* [λ], Fr. *belle* [bεl]

ÁNNU > It. *anno*, Sard. *annu*, Rm. *an*, Sp. *año*, P. *ano*, C. *any* [añ], Pr. *an*, Fr. *an* [ã]

PÁSSU > It. *passo*, Sard. *passu*, Rm. C. *pas*, Sp. *paso*, P. *passo*, Pr. *paso*, Fr. *pas* [pɑ]

TĚRRA > It. Sard. P. C. Pr. *terra* [ř], Sp. *tierra* [tjeřa], Fr. *terre* [tε:r][121]

CATTU > It. *gatto* [gat·to], Sard. *battu* [t·t], Sp. P. *gato*, C. Pr. *gat*, Fr. *chat* [ša]

Note: Italian is so fond of double consonants that it has doubled many single ones (see below and sec. 7).

FĚBRE > It. *febbre*
TŌTU > It. *tutto*
CÁTHĚDRA > It. *cattedra*
Germ. LAÚBJA > It. *lubbione, loggia* (< Fr. *loge*)

-NS-, -RS-

With some exceptions, the first element in these combinations was absorbed and disappeared. The N preceding an S had already been dropped in Vulgar Latin speech in most words. Retention of the first consonant can be considered a learned development.

Í(N)SŬLA > It. *isola*, Neap. *Ischia* (?), Sard. *isa*, Sp. Engad. *isla*, P. *ilha*, C. *illa*, Pr. *ila, ilha, isla, iscla, isola*, Fr. *île;* but Rm. *insulă*

---

120. This tilde *n* (ñ) was a scribal abbreviation in Spanish for -*nn*- and was adopted for all palatal *n*'s, regardless of origin. In Catalan, the spelling -*ny*- is used for this sound.

121. Fr. /r/ (*r* or *rr*), is now generally uvular [R] or even pharyngeal. Only in parts of the South does one hear the flapped *r*.

PE(N)SĀRE ("to weigh, grieve") > It. *pesare*, Sard. *pesare*, Engad. *pasar*, Rm. *pasa*, Sp. P. C. *pesar*, Pr. *pezar*, Fr. *peser;* but the more "intellectual" form (= "to think") > It. *pensare*, Sp. P. C. Pr. *pensar*, Fr. *penser*, Engad. *pensar*

VERSŪRA > Sp. *basura*, P. *vassoura*

(DE +) SŪRSU > It. *su*, Rm. *sus*, OSp. *suso*, P. *sus*, Fr. *dessus*, and as a combined form in MSp. *suso(dicho)*, C. *sus(dit)*

Note that so-called "double" consonants have the same occlusion as "singles," consisting of implosion, plosion, and explosion, except that the "holding" or plosion, that is the time and tension of the articulation, is prolonged. This can be illustrated by the Latin word BŬCCA and its Italian derivative *bocca*, with Spanish *boca* for comparison (fig. 9).

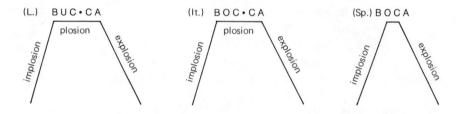

9. *Contrasts in consonantal articulation: double/*single

Italian has many of these "double" or prolonged consonants: *ecco, fatto, fiamma, febbre*, etc.; Sardinian also: *abba* (< ÁQUA), *caddu* (< CABÁLLU). Compare German *Mann* vs. *man*, and English *this city* vs. *the city*. The other Romance languages have not preserved the double consonants except as a spelling device: Fr. *belle* [bɛl], *passe* [pas], *flamme* [flam], P. *essa* [ɛsa], *passa* [pása]. The one exception is the double RR which has persisted as a separate phoneme.

-ATĬCU

This particular suffix was originally an adjectival ending, but became a very popular noun formation, especially in Provençal and Old French. From them it spread to other Romance tongues. The standard formations are: Fr. *-age*, C. Pr. *-atge*, It. *-aggio*, Rm. *-aj* or *-atic*, Sp. *-aje*,[122] P. *-agem*.

---

122. The native popular development in Spanish was -ÁTĬCU > *-azgo*, as in PORT-ÁTĬCU > *portazgo*, with standard masculine *-o* ending, as contrasted to *portaje*.

The nouns in Portuguese are always feminine, in the other languages masculine:

VIÁTĬCU > Fr. *voyage*, C. Pr. *viatge*, It. *viaggio*, Sp. *viaje*, P. *viagem;* cf. Engad. *viadi*

SILVÁTĬCU > Fr. *sauvage*, C. Pr. *salvatge*, It. *selvaggio*, Rm. *sălbatic*, Sp. *salvaje*, P. *selvagem* (It. *selvatico, salvatico* are learned.)

VL. ABÁNTE + ÁTICU > Fr. *avantage*, C. Pr. *avantatge*, It. *vantaggio*, Sp. *ventaja*, P. *vantagem*,[123] Rm. *avantaj* (borrowed?)

-C'L- (-T'L- > -CL-)

This combination differed somewhat in development from that in initial position, with Italian having two end products.

-C'L- regularly > Sp. [x],[124] P. C. Pr. OFr. [λ], Sard. various, Fr. [j] (with loss of *l* element), and It. [kj] or [λ], Rm. [kj], Rh. [l], or [λ] (spelled *gl*):

ÓC(U)LU > Sp. *ojo*, P. *olho*, C. *ull*, Pr. *olh*, Fr. *oeil* [œ:j], It. *occhio*, Rm. *ochiu*, Engad. *ögl*, Surm. *igl*, Surs. *egl*, Suts. *il;* cf. Sard. *ogu, oju, occhiu*

APĬC(U)LA > Sp. *abeja*, P. Pr. *abelha*, C. *abella*, Fr. *abeille* [abέ:j], It. *pecchia* (apheresis); but Engad. *aviöl*

VERMĬC(U)LU > It. *vermiglio* [vɛrmíλo], Sp. *bermejo*, P. *vermelho* C. *vermell*, Pr. *vermelh*, Fr. *vermeil* [vɛrmέ:j]

TRABÁC(U)LU[125] > It. *travaglio* [traváλo], Sp. *trabajo*, P. *trabalho*, C. *treball*, Pr. *trebalh, tribalh, trabalh*, Fr. *travail*

VĔT(U)LU > *VEC'LU > It. *vecchio*, Sp. *viejo*, Rm. *vechiu*, P. *velho*, C. *vell*, Pr. *velh*, Fr. *vieil* [vjέ:j], and Sard. *egru, vriku, vettsu* (this last form from Italian?)

The complete process, with various steps in the regular developments of -C'L-, are as follows:

---

123. The Italian, Spanish, and Portuguese forms show a good example of apheresis, with *l'avantaggio, l'aventaje, l'avantagem* > *la vantaggio, ventaje*, (mod. *ventaja*), *vantagem* respectively.

124. The development of Spanish *ojo* from ÓC(U)LU was along the lines: [óklo] > [ójlo] > [óljo] > [óλo] > [óĝo] > [óžo] > [óšo] > [óxo].

125. This etymon, first proposed by Diez (Grandgent 325) has been rejected by many modern philologists in favor of TRIPÁLĬU, because of the *b* in Provençal and Old Spanish forms; however er, see -LY- below.

(1) KL > k'λ > [kj] (Ital. and Rm.)
(2) KL > k'λ > [λ] (Ital. P. C. Pr. Rh. OFr.) > [ǵ] > [ž] > [š] >
   [χ] (Sp.)
(3) KL > k'λ > [λ] > [j] (MFr.)

In Spanish, a double velar + L (-KKL-) produced an unvoiced
affricate [č] instead of [χ]. Compare:

FÁCŬLA > Sp. *faja* (single velar C'L)
FÁCCULA > Sp. *hacha*[126] (double velar CC'L)
COCHLEĀRE > *COCCLJÁRE > Sp. *cuchara;* cf. It. *cucchiaio,*
   Sard. *cogarzu,* P. *colher,* C. *culler, culleara,* Pr. *cullier, culliera,*
   Fr. *cuillièr(e)* [kɥijέr]

The development of intermediate GL was similar to that of -CL-:

TĒG(U)LA > It. *tegghia* [tέg·gja], *teglia* [tέλa] (*tegola* is semilearned),
   Sard. C. Pr. *teula,* Sp. *teja,* P. *telha,* Fr. *tuile.*

-LY-, -LLY-

This combination, spelled LI or LE in Latin, and followed by a
vowel, regularly palatalized with divergent end products: in Romanian
the palatal [λ] disappeared, leaving [j], in French it also eventually lost
the *l* element, in Italian, Catalan, Rhetian, and Provençal it has persisted
to this day, while Spanish carried the development through to [χ] and
Sardinian regularly produced [z] or [dz]. Compare the development of
-CL- above.

ÁLLĬU > Ital. *aglio,* Sard. *azu,* Rm. *aiu,* Sp. *ajo,* P. *alho,* C. *all,*
   Pr. *alh,* Fr. *ail* [a:j]
TRIPĀLĬU > It. *travaglio,* etc. (See TRABÁCULU above and
   fn. 125.)
CŌLEU, CÓLEA > OIt. *coglia,* Rm. *coiu, coaie,* Sard. *coza,* Pr.
   colh, colha, Fr. *couille;* cf. It. *coglione,* Sp. *cojón,* C. *colló* <
   COLEÓNE
FĪLĬU > It. *figlio,* Sard. *fizu,* Rm. *fiu,* Sp. *hijo,* P. *filho,* C. *fill,* Pr.
   filh, Fr. *fils,*[127] Engad. *figl*

126. Likewise possibly a postulated *MUCCULÁCCULU > Sp. *muchacho* (a dirty-
nosed little boy?). Cf. It. *moccione* and Sard. *mucconozu, muccozu.*
127. From nominative sg. FĪLĬUS or plural oblique FĪLIOS. In OFr. = [fiλs], spelled
fiz or *filz,* in Mod. French the *l* is silent [fis]. The English Fitz of Fitz-Hugh (etc.) is from the
OFr. form.

FŎLĬU, FŎLIA > It. *foglio, foglia*, Sard. *foza, folu*,[128] Rm. *foaie*, Sp. *hoja*, P. *folho, folha*, Pr. *folh, folha*, C. *full, fulla*, Fr. *feuille* [fœ:j], Engad. *fögl*
MÁLLEU > It. *maglio*, Sard. *mazu*, Rm. *maiu*, Sp. *mallo*, P. *malho*, C. *mall*, Pr. *malh*, Fr. *mail*

-CT- [kt]

This group regularly palatalized the velar, raising the preceding vowel in Spanish, Catalan, and French (unless already a high one), but in Italian and Sardinian it > *-tt-*, in Romanian *-pt-*, and in Engadinian simplified to *t*:

NŎCTE > Sp. *noche*,[129] P. *noite*, C. *nit*, Pr. *noch, nuch, nech, neit*, Fr. *nuit* (via *nueit); but It. Sard. *notte*, Rm. *noapte*, Engad. *not*
LÁCTE > Sp. *leche*, P. *leite*, C. *llet*, Pr. *lach*, Fr. *lait* [le]; but It. Sard. *latte*, Rm. *lapte*, Engad. *lat*
DIRĒCTU > Sp. *derecho*, P. *direito*, C. *directe* (learned), Pr. *drech, dret*, Fr. *droit;* but It. *dritto, diritto*, Sard. *derettu*, Rm. *drept*, Engad. *dret*

-MN-, -MB-, -MC-, -MPS-, -ML-, -MT-

These consonant combinations suffered varying changes, following regional lines. In most cases assimilation (or dissimilation) played an active role. (See sec. 6.)
In French, -MN- regularly gave *-mm-* [m] and in final position *-m* as a nasal sign only. Spanish regularly dissimilated to *-mr-* and then *-mbr-* with a transitional explosive sound [b]. Portuguese and Romanian lost the *n* element. Italian tended to be more conservative. Other languages varied (see -NY- below):

FĒMĬNA > Fr. *femme* [fam], Sp. *hembra*, P. *fémea*, C. *fembra* (< Sp.), Pr. *femna, fenna, frema*, It. *femmina* (note doubling), Sard. *femina*, Rm. *femeie*

Note- Sp. *hambre* and Sard. *famine* are derived regularly, as per above, from FÁMĬNE, whereas the other language forms are from a

128. Sard. *folu* may be borrowed (< Italian?).
129. The Spanish development was [kt] > [jt] > [tj] > [č]. Portuguese thus exemplifies an earlier stage. Such Spanish words as *delito* (< DELĪCTU), *tratado* (< TRACTĀTU), *fruto* (< FRŪCTU) show semilearned development, while *acto, contacto, exacto*, and the like are straight borrowings from Latin.

generalized nominative FÁME(S): It. *fame*, P. *fome*, C. *fame*, Pr. *fam*, *fame*, *fami*, Fr. *faim* (< FÁMINE?), Rm. *foame*, Engad. *fam*. There are many other such double etyma, like LÚMEN, LÚMINE; NÓMEN, NÓMINE, and so on.

-MB- remained in most languages, the *b* eventually becoming silent (when final) in French, and disappearing in Spanish, Catalan, Rhetian, and occasionally in Provençal:

PALŬMBA > It. *palomba*, Rm. *porumb* (m.), Sp. C. *paloma*, P. *pomba*, Pr. *palomba*, *paloma*, Fr. *palombe*
PLŬMBU > It. *piombo*, Sard. *piumu*, Rm. *plumb*, Sp. *plomo*, P. *chumbo*, C. Pr. *plom*, Fr. *plomb* [plõ], Engad. *plom*

-MC- > -*nc*- in French: PŬMĬCE > Fr. *ponce;* but It. *pomice*, Sard. (*pedra*) *fumiga*, Rm. *pumice*, Sp. *pómez*, P. *pomes*.[130]

-MPS- > -*ns*-: CAMPSĀRE > It. Sard. *cansare*, Sp. P. C. *cansar*.

-M'L- will regularly generate a transitional *b*:

TREMULĀRE > Sp. *temblar*, Pr. *tremblar*, *tramblar*, *temblar*, Fr. *trembler;* but It. *tremolare*, Sard. *tremulare*, Rm. *tremura*, C. *tremolar*, Engad. *tremblar*

-MT- readily assimilated to -*nt*- or -*nd*-, although French (among others) sometimes has retained (or restored) a conservative spelling:

CŎM(I)TE > It. Rm. *conte*, Sp. P. *conde* (OSp. also *cuende*), C. Pr. Fr. *comte*
CŎMP(U)TU > *CÓM(P)TU > It. P. *conto*, Sp. *cuento*, C. Fr. *conte*, *compte*, Pr. *comte*, *comde*, *conde*

-*NY*-, -*GN*- (-*MN*-, -*MNY*-)

These combinations, like the double *n* [ñ] in Spanish, regularly developed palatal consonants. The -MN-, however — when it didn't become -*mbr*- (see -MM- above) — palatalized only in Spanish (and in Catalan sporadically). Spellings for the palatal *n* differ for each language:[131]

130. The Spanish and Portuguese forms may be from the Latin nominative PÚMEX.

PŪGNU > It. *pugno* [púño], Sard. *punzu*, Rm. *pumn*, Sp. *puño*, P. *punho*, C. *puny*, Pr. *ponh, punh*, Engad. *puogn*, Fr. *poing* [pwɛ]¹³²

CASTÁNEA > It. *castagna*, Sard. *castanza*, Rm. *castană, gastîñe* (= ?) (listed in Meyer-Lübke, *REW*, 1472), Sp. *castaña*, P. Pr. *castanha*, C. *castanya*, Fr. *chataigne* [šatɛñ], Engad. *chastagna*

SŎMNU > It. *sonno*, Sard. *sonnu*, Rm. *somn*, Sp. *sueño*, P. *sono*, C. *son*, Pr. *som*, Fr. *somme*

SŎMNĬU > It. *sogno*, Sp. *sueño*, P. *sonho*, C. *somni*, Pr. *som, somi, somnhe, somni*, Fr. *songe* [sõ:ž], and Sard. *sognu, sonnu, sonniu*

-PT-, -BT-

-PT- and -BT- regularly assimilated to *-tt-* (as in Italian and Sardinian today), then simplified to *-t-*. Modern French, however, has sometimes restored the original spelling (PT) while Romania retained the original sound:

CAPTĀRE > It. *cattare*, Sp. P. C. *catar;* but Rm. *capta, cata*, Pr. *captar*, Fr. *capter* [kapté]

SĔPTEM > It. Sard. *sette*, Sp. *siete*, P. *sete*, C. Pr. Engad. *set*, Fr. *sept* [sɛt]; but Rm. *şapte* [šapte]

RŬPTA > It. *rotta*, Sp. P. C. *rota*, Fr. *route* (< RŬPTA VÍA); but Rm. *rupută* (regularized p.p.) and (*între*) *ruptă*

SUBTĪLE > It. *sottile*, Sard. *suttile*, Sp. C. Pr. *sotil*, Sp. *sutil*, P. Friul. *sutil*, OFr. *sotil*, but Fr. *subtil*, Rm. *subţire*

Occasionally the P of -PT- vocalizes (through [b] > [b̵]) to *u*; the same is true of -B- and -V-:

CAPTĪVU > Sp. *cautivo*, Pr. *cautiu, caitiu, captiu;* but It. *cattivo*, Rm. *captiv*, Sard. *battia* (f.), P. *cativo*, C. *captiu*, Fr. *chétif* (and *captif*)

CÚBĬTU > Sp. *codo*, Rm. *cot*, Sard. *cuidu*, P. *côvado*, Pr. *cobde, coide, covede*, Fr. *coude;* but It. *gomito* (< OIt. *gombito*), C. *colze*

131. Latin NY, GN regularly gave [ñ], spelled *gn* in Italian and Rhetian, *ñ* in Spanish, *nh* in Portuguese and Provençal, *ny* in Catalan, and *gn* or *ign* in French. When the sound became final in French, however, it reduced to [ɛ], spelled *ing* (as in *poing* and *coing*), but kept the *gn* order and palatal sound in related forms such as *poignée* and *poignet* where the palatal was not final. The same combinations in Romanian normally gave *mn* or merely *n*. Sardinian again shows various treatments. Check the above examples.

132. See note 131 above.

-PS-

-PS- often > -SS-:

ĬPSU, ĬPSE > It. *esso*, Sard. *su, is-, issu*, OSp. *esso, esse*, Sp. *eso, ese*, P. *isso* [ísu] *êsse*, C. *eix*, Pr. *eis*
GȲPSU > It. *gesso* [ǧés·so], Sp. *yeso*, P. *gesso*, C. *guix, ges*, Pr. *geis, gis;* but Fr. *gypse*, Rm. *ghips, ipsos*

-BS-

-BS- tended to lose the *B*, particularly if followed by another consonant:

SUBSTĀRE > It. *sostare*, P. *sustar*, Pr. *sostar*
SUBSCRĬPTU > It. *soscritto*, Sp. *suscrito, subscrito*, P. *subscrito*, Fr. *souscrit*

-PY-, -RY-, -SY- (-BY-, -MY-, -VY-)

In these combinations the *yod* [j] regularly transposed (metathesisized) into the preceding syllable ([pj] > [jp], [rj] > [jr], [sj] > [js]), or merged with the consonant (*b, m, v*), in French especially. Italian tended to double the consonants *p* and *b*. (The [rj] change has already been treated in -ÁRIU, sec. 2.) Other variations can be seen in the examples below:

SÁPĬAM > It. *sappia*, Sp. *sepa*,[133] P. *saiba*, C. *sàpiga*, Pr. Engad. *sapcha*, Fr. *sache*
ÁREA > It. *aia*, Rm. *arie*, Sp. C. *era*, P. *eira*, Pr. *aira, iera*, etc., Fr. *aire* [ɛr]
BASIĀRE > It. *baciare*, Sard. *bazare*, Sp. C. *besar*, P. *beijar*, Pr. *baizar*, Fr. *baiser* [bɛzé]
RŬBEU > It. *roggio*, Sard. *ruyu*, Rm. *roib* (= "fox," or "horse"), Sp. *rubio, rojo*, P. *ruivo*, C. *roig* [rož], Pr. *roi*, Fr. *rouge* [ru:ž]
SÍMĬA > It. *scimmia*, Sp. *simia, jimia*, P. C. Pr. *simia*, Fr. *singe* [sɛ̃:ž], Engad. *simgia*
CÁVEA > It. *gabbia, gaggia*, Sp. *gavia*, P. *gávea*, C. *gàbia*, Fr. *cage* [ka:ž], Engad. *chabgia*

133. SÁPIA > *saipa* > *seipa* > *sepa*, the semiconsonant [j] supporting the *p* and preventing it from voicing. Not so in Portuguese. See Boyd-Bowman 107, rule 1.

-KY-, -TY-

Vulgar Latin [kj] and [tj] regularly combined into one sound which then differentiated into the palatal [č] or the alveolar [ts] > [s] (cf. Consonants, sec. 1):[134]

BRÁCHĬU > It. *braccio* [č], Rm. *braţ* [ts], Sp. *brazo*, P. *braço*, C. *braç*, Pr. *bratz*, OFr. *braz* [brats], Fr. *bras* [bra], Engad. *bratsch*, Friul. *bras;* but Sard. *rattu*

PŬTEU > It. *pozzo* [pót·tso], Rm. *puţ*, OSp. *poço* [pótso], Sp. *pozo*, P. *poço*, C. *pou*, Pr. *potz*, Fr. *puits* [pɥi], Engad. *puoz*, Friul. *potse;* but Sard. *putu*

FŎRTIA > It. *forza* [fórtsa], Rm. *forţa*, Sp. *fuerza*, P. *fôrça*, C. *força*, Pr. *forsa*, Fr. *force*, Engad. *forza*, Friul. *fuartse*

-TTY- had the same development as single -TY-:

*MŬTTĬU > OSp. *moço* [mótso], Sp. *mozo*

MATTIĀNA > OSp. *maçana* [matsána] > C. *maçana* [masána], P. *maçã*, and Sp. *manzana*, Fr. *mancienne* (both with anticipated nasals; cf. Portuguese nasal diphthong in *muito* [mwi̊tu])

-RCL-, -SCL-

Most of these "impossible" combinations compromised by squeezing out one of their members or combined into more pronounceable groups. In Spanish, both of these > *ch* [č]. In other languages they developed along characteristic patterns:

MÁRC(U)LU (MÁRTULU?) > Sp. *macho* ("mallet"); cf. MÁLLEU above

MÁSC(U)LU > It. *maschio*, Sard. [mášu], Rm. *mascur*, Sp. *macho* (and *maslo*), P. *macho*, C. Pr. *mascle*, Fr. *mâle* (OFr. *masle*)

Other combinations of the sort and their development can be seen in these examples (with special reference to Spanish and Portuguese):

---

134. There are always exceptions, of course, like STÁTIO, STATIÓNE. Here Old Italian gave *stazzo, stazzone*, Sard. *istattu, istattsu*, but modern Italian through [č] to voiced [ĝ]: *stagione*. Spanish has *estación*, Portuguese *estação*, Catalan *estació* (semilearned?).

-NKTL- > *nch*, etc.: SÁNCTULU (= "little saint") > Sp. *Sancho;*
cf. It. *Santocchio* (< SANCTÚCULU)

-MPL- > *nch*, etc.: ÁMPLU > Sp. P. *ancho;* but It. *ampio,* Sard.
ampru, C. Pr. Fr. *ample*

-FFL- > *ll*, etc.: ADFLÁRE > Sp. *hallar* (< *FAFFLÁRE), P.
achar; but Rm. *afla*

-NFL- > *nch*, etc.: INFLÁRE > Sp. P. *hinchar;* but It. *enfiare,* Sard.
unflare, Rm. *umfla,* C. P. *inflar,* Pr. *enflar, esflar, uflar,* Fr. *enfler*

-NGL- > *ñ*, etc.: ÚNGULA > Sp. *uña,* P. *unha,* It. *ugna;* but It.
unghia, Sard. [únĝa], Rm. *unghie,* C. *ungla,* Engad. *ungla,*
Pr. *ongla, oncla,* Fr. *ongle*

-X-

The evidence indicates that this Latin letter represented [ks]. The
development of the sound in Vulgar Latin and in the Romance languages
varied from region to region, with more changes occurring in Spanish
than in any other case.

In Castilian territory the [ks] > [js] > [sj] > [š]. This last phone
leveled with [ž] from Latin J and G (e, i) in the fifteenth and sixteenth
centuries, and the resulting[š]gradually became [x] by 1650. In the nineteenth
century the Spanish Royal Academy did away with the spelling *x*, except
in Latinisms such as *examen, sexta*, and words such as *dixe* are now
spelled with *j* (*dije*). In Mexico, especially, the *x* has been retained in words
of Indian origin to represent a primitive [š] (*México, Xalapa, Oaxaca*),
now [x], and in Yucatán one still hears the [š] (*Uxmal*) among the Maya-
speaking inhabitants or among foreigners who may have [š] in their own
phonological inventory. It is to be noted that the evolution of X to an
ultimate [x] did not take place when it was supported by a consonant as in
FRÁX(I)NU > *fresno*, SÉXTA > *siesta*, and where X has been retained
before a consonant, generally represents [s] (*extraño* [estráño], *experiencia*
[esperjénsja]).[135]

In the other Romance languages the -X- [ks] usually became a sibilant
or retained its original Latin value.

In Catalan and Portuguese the descendents are [š] (*x*) and [s] (*ss*) and
the letter X has been extended to represent [š] of other origins than Latin X:

---

135. In the latter type [s] (= *x* preceding consonant), hypercorrection often produces
[ks] or [gs] through pedantic school teaching, i.e., *sexta* [séksta] and *extraño* [ekstráño]. This
is *not* the popular pronunciation, however.

Arabic [š] (P. *xadrez* C. *aixedres*), Latin -PS- (P. C. *caixa*). In Catalan the [č] is represented normally by *tx*.[136]

The -X- in Italy generally became [s] (*ss*), as it did in France, and the popular French orthographic *x* (*paix*, and the plurals *chateaux, cheveux*) simply represent a former final -*s* or -*z* written with a peculiar flourish so as to resemble somewhat an *x*.[137]

The prefix EX- in Italian and Romanian, by apheresis or loss of *e*- (along with prosthetic *e*-) was generally reduced to [s] or [z], depending on whether it was followed by a mute or voiced consonant:

EXPÓNĔRE > Rm. *spune* [spúne], but It. *esporre* [espóře]

EXCUTULĀRE > It. *scotolare* [sk-], Rm. *scutara* [sk-]

EXVENTĀRE > It. *sventare* [zventáre], Rm. zvinta [zv-]; cf. Sard. *izventare*, C. Pr. *esventar* [-ez-], and Fr. *éventer* < OFr. *esventer*[138]

Before the front vowels *e* and *i*, however, Italian generally palatalized the [ks], spelled *sce, sci* [še, ši].

Examples of standard treatments of -X-, showing the variety of treatments, are:

EXÉMPLU > It. *scempio* [š-], *esempio* [ez-], Sp. *ejemplo* [eχ-], P. *exemplo* [ez-], C. *exemple* [egs-], Fr. *exemple* [egz-]

EXPECTĀRE > It. *aspettare* [as-], Sard. *istettare*, Rm. *aştepta* [aš-], P. *expectar* [iš-, eš-]

EXÁMEN, EXÁMĬNE > It. *sciame* [š-], Sp. *enjambre*, P. *enxame* [enš-] (*en-* by analogy with prefix IN-), C. *eixam* [eš-], Pr. *eisam* [ejz-]

---

136. The letter *x* in Catalan has the sound of [š] at the beginning of a word or after a consonant: *xic* [šik], *llanxa* [ʎánša]. In words beginning with *ex-* followed by a vowel or *h*, it has the sound of [gz]: *exacte* [egzákte]. Followed by [s] it equals [k]: *excessiu* [eksésju]. It combines with *t* to produce [č]: *fletxa* [fléča]. And following *i* it also has the sound [š]: *això* [ašó], *moix* [moš], *ixen* [íšen]. (See Gili 18.)

Further examples of *x* origins other than Latin X: P. *oxalá* (Sp. *ojalá*) < Arab. WAŠA' ALLAH, "Allah grant . . . "; P. *peixe*, C. *peix* (Sp. *pez*) < L. PÍSCE [píske]. The L. etymon for P.C. *caixa* is CÁPSEA.

137. Some words (e.g., *bals*) have the original *s*.

138. For a more complete treatment, see note 43 above and sec. 6.

FIXĀRE > It. *fissare*, Rm. *fixa* [-ks-], Sp. *fijar*, C. P. *fixar* [-ks-], Fr. *fixer* [-ks-]

DĪXĬT > It. P. *disse* [-s-], Sp. *dijo*, Fr. *dit* (< *dist*); C. *digué* is a different formation

*VEXĪCA > It. *vescica* [-š-], Sard. [bušika] [-š-], Rm. *başica* [-š-], Sp. *vejiga* [-x-], P. *bexiga* [-š], C. *veixiga* [-š-], Pr. *veziga* [-z-], Fr. *vessie* [-s-]

SEXÁGĬNTA > It. Sard. *sessanta* [-s-], Sp. *sesenta* [-s-], P. *sesenta* [-z-], C. *seixanta* [-š-], Pr. *seissanta* [-s-], Fr. *soixante* [-s-] (< *seissante*)

FRÁXĬNU > It. *frassine* [-s-], Sard. *frassu* [-s-], Rm. *frasin* [-s-], Sp. *fresno* [-z-], P. *freixo* [-š-], C. *freixe* [-š-], Pr. *fraise* [-z-], Fr. *frêne* (< *fresne*)

TRÁXI > It. *trassi*, Sp. *traje*, P. *trouxe* [trósi], C. *traguí*

-Z-

The statements made about initial Z- apply equally well to medial -Z-; that is this letter represented a sound foreign to Latin and was found mainly in Greek borrowings, like BAPTIZĀRE. Originally [dz], the sound > [ts], [s], [z], [ž], [ĝ], [θ], among others, with a wide variation in different tongues. In Old Spanish, the letter first represented the voiced dental affricate [dz], later [z], as distinguished from the unvoiced [ts], later [s], which was spelled with a Gothic letter in the form of a z surmounted by a large hook. This latter character was reduced in manuscript printing to a c cedilla (= ç).[139] [z] and [s] leveled to [s] in the fifteenth and sixteenth centuries, the sound that is still heard in Andalucía and Spanish America. In most of Spain it became [θ] about 1700. In Modern French, Portuguese, Provençal, Catalan, et al., [z] regularly survives, spelled z [z], or s [z] (in intervocalic position: *rose, rosa*, etc.). See above.

The distinction between such words as *casar* and *cazar, cocer* and *coser* has been lost in Andalusian and American Spanish. As a rule of Academy spelling, c and z alternate (similarly to g and j) before front and back vowels, namely, *ce, ci*, but *za, zo, zu*, with final z changing to c in the plural of nouns. Note the alternation in these samples:

Sp. *voz* (sg.), *voces* (pl.)
vencer (= "to conquer")

---

139. Still used today in French, Catalan, Portuguese, but merely as a spelling device for [s] before *a, o, u*, or when final.

venzo (= "I conquer")
vences (= "you conquer"), etc.
¡*venza*! (subj. command form: "Conquer!")
(Compare Portuguese *voz, vozes,* and *venço, vences, vença,* etc.)

In Italian *z* (*zz*) usually represents an unvoiced explosive [ts], otherwise [dz]. A few examples of -Z- derivations should suffice:

BAPTIZĀRE (Grk.) > It. *battezzare* [dz] (formerly *battegiare* [ĝ]),
Rm. *boteza* [z], Sp. *bautizar* [θ, s], P. *batizar* [z], C. Pr. *batejar*
[ž], Fr. *baptiser* [z] (OFr. *batoyer* [j]); but Engad. *battiar*
(AL +) ÇÚCCAR (Arab.) > It. *zucchero,* [ts], Sard. *tuccaru,* Rm.
zahăr, Sp. *azúcar* [θ, s], P. *açucar* [s], C. Pr. Fr. *sucre* (note that
the Spanish and Portuguese forms have retained the Arabic
article, the others not)

Final Consonants

-M

In spoken Latin, with rare exceptions, final -M early ceased to be pronounced: PÓRTA(M), MÚRU(M), TÚRRE(M). This is attested to for instance by poetic elisions, by grammarians' statements, and by inscriptions at Pompeii.

-M remained only in monosyllables, and > -*n,* for example:

REM > OSp. Pr. *ren,* OP. *rem,* Fr. *rien*[140]
QUEM > Rm. *cine,* Sard. (Cagl.) *chini,* Sp. *quien,* P. *quem*
*MUM, *TUM, SŬUM > Fr. *mon, ton, son*

(Note that Portuguese final -*m* is a spelling device to indicate a nasal vowel, and in Spanish a loan word or a learned word ending in -*m* pronounces the -*m* as -*n*: Sp. *álbum* = [álbun]. In fact, Spanish speakers regularly pronounce -*m* in foreign words as -*n,* saying "then" for "them.")

CŬM > Sp. It. *con,* P. Pr. *com,* Sard. Engad. *cun,* Rm. *cu;* but in Sp.
P. compounds *co(n)migo, contigo, consigo,* etc. (< CUM +
MÉCUM, CUM + TÉCUM, etc.), the -*m* of the second
(i.e., final) CUM is lost.

---

140. Catalan *res* comes from the nom. form of the noun, as also probably Sard. *reze.*

Latin SŬM should have > *son* but an early loss of *-m*, or desire to avoid conflict with *son* from SŬNT, gave a basic *SO (except in Italian, Engad., and Romanian):

> SUM > OSp. *so*, Sp. *soy*,[141] P. *sou*, Pr. *soi*, *sô*, *son*, OFr. *sui*, Fr. *suis*,[142] C. *sóc;* but It. *sono*, Rm. *sunt*, *sânt*, Engad. *sun;* cf. Sard. *seu*, *soccu*, *soggu*

-N

-N usually fell in words like the following:

> NÓMEN > It. P. *nome*, C. Fr. *nom*, Rm. *nume*, Pr. *nom*, *nome*, *nomi;*
> but Sard. *lúmene*, Sp. *nombre* (< NÓMINE)
> *ARÁMEN > It. *rame*, Rm. *aramă*, P. *arame*, C. *aram*, Pr. *aram*,
> *eram*, Fr. *airain;* but Sard. *ramine*, Sp. *alambre* (< ARÁMINE)
> EXÁMEN > It. *esame*, P. *exame;* but Rm. Sp. C. Fr. *examen*

In monosyllables, final -N is preserved in a few words, but often only as a sign of vowel nasality:

> IN > Fr. *en* [ã], P. *em* [ē]; but It. Sard. Rm. *in* [in], Sp. C. Pr. *en* [en]
> NŌN > Fr. *ne* [nə], *non* [nõ], Sp. C. *no*, P. *não*, Pr. *no*, *non*, Rm. *nu*,
> *n'*, and It. Sard. *non* [non][143]

-S

Final -S was already lost before consonants in rustic and archaic Latin speech.[144] They never quite succeeded in restoring it in Italy (Italian tolerates no final *-s*). In the West, however, yes — thanks to schools and (perhaps) native habits. Also in Sardinian: *crabas*, *muros*, *canes*, etc. In

---

141. The *y* on *soy* (and *voy*, *doy*, *estoy*) is thought to come from a postfixed *yo*, i.e., *so yo*, etc. This is the generally accepted theory.

142. The *-s* of *suis* is an analogic one, as also in the first person *vends*, for example, which was *vent* in OFr. The analogic model was the *-ir* declension verbs in *-is*, *-is*, *-it*. Other verb forms such as *vois*, *viens*, etc., follow the same analogy.

143. This *-n* first began to disappear in such enclitic combinations as Sp. *non me*, *non lo*, etc.

144. Cf. Cicero's remarks to the effect that failure to pronounce the -S was a mark of rusticity: "... jam subrusticum videtur, olim autem politus" (*Orat.* 48. 161).

Old French, there was a final [s] or [z], but in Modern French the manifestation is usually [∅] (i.e., silent), with rare exceptions. The Old French ending -*als*, -*els*, which developed into -*aus*, -*eus*, and so on, is now spelled -*aux*, -*eux*, through a confusion in writing of a final -*s* or *z* as -*x*: OFr. *bels* > *beaus* > Fr. *beaux;* *chevels* > *cheveus* > *cheveux;* cf. OFr. *voiz* > MFr. *voix*. This spurious -*x*, like the -*s*, represents a former sound in French, but is silent, with a few exceptions such as: *six* [sis], *dix* [dis], but *six francs* [si frã].

Modern -*s* in Romance (often from the accusative plural of Latin) is usually a sign of plurals, and a second person verb ending:

CÁUSAS > Sp. *cosas*, P. *cousas*, C. *coses*, Fr. *choses*, Engad. *chosas*, but It. *cose*[145]

ÁMAS > Sp. P. Pr. *amas*, C. *ames*, Fr. *aimes* [εm]; but It. *amai* (cf. Rm. *ai* < HÁBEAS); note the -*t* in Engad. *amast*

MĬNŬS > Rm. Sard. *minus*, Sp. P. *menos*, C. *menys*, Pr. *mens*, *menhs*, Fr. *moins* [mwε̃]; but It. *meno*, Engad. *main*

MÁG(I)S > Sp. *más*, P. *mas*, *mais*, C. *mes*, Pr. *mais*, *mai*, *mas*, *mar*, *mei*, *mes*, *mos*, *mor*, Fr. *mais* [mε], It. Rm. *mai*, Engad. *mo*, *ma*

SĔX > Sard. *seze*, Rm. *șase*, Sp. P. *seis*, C. *sis*, Pr. *seis*, *sei*, Fr. *six* [sis], Engad. *ses*, and It. *sei*[146]

-X

As stated elsewhere, Latin X was merely a single letter for the double sounds of KS, GS, and occasionally other combinations. Words with this sound combination in final position in Latin were rare, except as nominative forms, hence did not occur in the basic Vulgar Latin parallels. The final -*x* in such French words as *six* [sis] and *voix*, *poix* [vwa, pwa] represents the sound of [s] or is a restored spelling. See above for discussion of -*s* and -*x* confusion.

145. This is because, while most noun forms regularly developed from the oblique case in VL., Italian and Romanian chose the nominative case for their plurals. Cf. CÁSA, CÁSAE > It. *casa*, *case*, Rm. *casă*, *case*. See sec. 6 for discussion.

146. As already stated, French final [s] has been lost, except in some cases of elision, where it persists as [z], e.g., *les hommes* [lezóm], *ils ont* [ilzó̃], and in certain words such as *hélas* [elás] and some proper names: *Laurens* [lɔrá̃:s].

Italian (like Japanese) does not tolerate a final consonant, Catalan and Provençal almost any. Spanish is intermediate, at one time tolerating forms like *noch*, *nuef* (CID), and *relox* [r̄eloš]. Today the syllable final consonants that are permitted by Spanish oral behavior are /d, l, n, r, s, θ/.

A "legitimate" form such as SEX ("six") gives a variety of derivatives, with the [ks] reduced in most cases to [s] (spelled -*x* in French). Note that Italian drops the final consonant(s), whereas Romanian and Sardinian add a syllable:

SĔX[147] > It. *sei*, Sard. *seze*, Rm. *şase*, Sp. P. *seis*, C. *sis*, Pr. *sieis*, Fr. *six*, Vegl. *si*, Engad. *ses*, Friul. *sis*

Examples of other words (nouns) in both nominative and basic Vulgar Latin forms, with their derivatives are:

LĔX—LÉGE > It. *legge*, Rm. *lege*, Sp. *ley*, P. *lei*, C. *llei*, Pr. *lei, leg*, Fr. *loi* (OFr. nom. = *lois*), Engad. *ledscha*

RĔX—RÉGE > It. Sard. *re*, Rm. *rege*, Sp. *rey*, P. C. Pr. *rei*, Fr. *roi* (OFr. *rois, reis* in nom.), Vegl. *ra*, Engad. *rai*

NĬX—NĬVE > It. P. *neve*, Sard. *nie*, Rm. *nea*, Sp. *nieve*, C. Pr. *neu*, OFr. *noif*,[148] Vegl. *nai*, Engad. *naiv*, Friul. *nef*

VOX—VŌCE > It. *voce* [vóče], Sard. *boge*, Rm. *boace*, Sp. P. *voz* (formerly *voçe* [vótse]), C. *veu*, Pr. *votz*, Fr. *voix* [vwa] (< OFr. *voiz* [vɔjts]), Vegl. *baud*, Engad. *vusch*, Friul. *vos*

Since the basic Vulgar Latin form for most of such derivatives has two syllables, the development of the nonfinal consonant in each case follows the patterns already illustrated above under Medial or Intervocalic Consonants.

-Z

The letter Z did not occur as a final letter in Latin, but the orthographic form is found in some of the modern languages, where it has the value of [θ] or [s] (Spanish) as in *voz, feliz*, and the numerous family names *Álvarez, Gómez*, and so forth, or of [š] (Portuguese), as in *xadrez, voz, feliz*, the verb forms *faz, diz*, and the like.

In Old French final -*z* was quite common in noun and verb endings. It regularly stood for -*ts* or -*ds*, and other combinations such as -*sts*, -*ks*, -(*r*)*ns*, -*ls* (palatal *l*).[149] For instance, *venz* was the nominative singular and

---

147. Also listed above under final -*s*.

148. The Modern French form *neige* is presumed to be a back-formation derived from the verb *neiger* (< NIVIĀRE or NIVICĀRE).

149. See Paton 22–24.

oblique plural of *vent* ("wind") and also the second singular present in-dicative form of the verb *vendre* ("to sell"). The modern forms are *vent(s)* and *vends* respectively, with silent *s*, *d*, and *t*. The indeclinable Old French noun *voiz* (< VOX, VŌCES) is an example of the reduction of *ks* to *z* [ts]. In the French second plural verb ending *-ez* (< -ÁTIS, -ĒTIS, ĪTIS, etc.) the *-z* is a vestige of a former [*ts*] except in cases of liaison such as "Vous avez un beau livre," where the *z* (like the *s*) is voiced: [vuzavezœ̃ . . .]. The same is true of such rare examples as the preposition *chez* (< a locative CÁSAE?): *chez elle* [šezɛ́l] but *chez lui* [šelɥí].

Other Final Consonants

Final -T in third singular and plural verb forms tended to fall toward the end of the empire (due to dialect influences?):

CÁNTAT > It. Sp. P. C. Pr. *canta*, Rm. *cîntă*, *cântă*, Engad. *chanta*
VĒNDĬT > It. Sp. P. *vende*, C. Pr. *ven*, Rm. *vinde*, Engad. *venda*
CÁNTANT > It. *cantano* (with added -o), Rm. *cîntă*, Sp. Pr. *cantan*,
   P. *cantam*, C. *canten*, Engad. *chantan*
VÉNDŬNT, *VÉNDENT > It. *vendono*, Rm. *vind*, Sp. C. *venden*,
   P. *vendem*, Pr. *vendon*, Engad. *vendan*

The -*t* remained for some time in northern Gaul (cf. ROLAND *chantet*, *chantent*, and modern French *chante-t-il?* and plural *chantent-ils?* [šãtətíl]), but fell later except in plural spelling and liaison in question word order. It has also been kept in Sardinian: *cantat, vendet*.
   Other examples of loss of -T:

CANTÁVIT > CANTÁUT > P. *cantou* > It. *cantó*, Sp. *cantó;* cf.
   Rm. *cantă*, C. *cantá*, Pr. *cantét*, Fr. *chanta*, Engad. *chantet*
AUT > It. *o, od*, Sard. *a*, Rm. *au*, Sp. C. Engad. *o*, P. Fr. *ou*, Pr. *o*,
   oz, vo

-ST > -*s* or fell completely:

EST > Sard. *est, è* Sp. Pr. *es*, C. *és*, It. *è*, P. *é*, Engad. *ais*, Fr. *est* [ɛ]
   (but -*t* pronounced in liaison: *Il est à Paris* [ilɛtaparí])
POST > It. Rm. *poi*, OSard. *pus*, Sp. *pues*, P. Pr. *pois*, C. *puix* [puš],
   Fr. *puis* [pɥi]

Final -R fell initially (cf. forms MATE, FRATE = MATER, FRATER found in inscriptions), but was restored in most regions. It is questionable that Vulgar Latin had many final -R's: *POR for PRO is a notable exception. Even L. QUÁTTUOR and SĔMPER > VL. *QUÁTTORO and *SĔMPĔRE.

Final -L generally disappeared: INSÍMUL > It. *insieme*, OSp. *ensiemo*, C. Pr. *ensems*, but Fr. *ensemble*, and Engad. *insembel*.

Final -D was lost, except in Italian, where it survives as a literary or euphonic device:

> AD > It. Sard. Rm. Sp. P. C. Pr. Engad. *a*, Fr. *à*; but It. *addio* < AD DÉO, also Sard. *ad*
>
> QUID > It. *che*, Rm. *ce*, Sard. *chi*, Sp. P. C. Pr. Fr. *que*, Engad. *che*, *cha*, Friul. *tse*
>
> ÁLID > *ALE > OSp. OP. *al*, Pr. *al*, *als*, OFr. *el*

Final -C fell:

> DĪC > It. Sp. Pr. Engad. *di*, Fr. *dis* (< *di*); but P. *dize* (< *DICE, a regularized form)
>
> FAC > It. *fa'*, Rm. Engad. *fa*, Pr. *fai*, OFr. *fai* > Fr. *fais;* but Sp. *haz* and P. *faze* < *FACE, a regularized form
>
> HĪC > OSp. *i*, *y* ("there"), Sp. *(ha)y*, Fr. *y* (*il y a*), C. *hi*, Pr. *i* (Is there a crossing with ĪBI?)[150]
>
> NĔC > *NE > It. *nè*, Sard. *nen*, P. *nem* (with nasal vowel), Sp. C. Fr. *ni*, Pr. *ni*, *né*, Vegl. *ne*, Engad. *ne*, Friul. *ni;* but Rm. *nici*
>
> VL. ÁCCU + HĪC > It. *qui*, Rm. *aici*, *aci*, Sp. P. C. *aquí;* cf. OFr. *ez vos*, *as vos*

§6. Special Cases (Sporadic Changes)

Various special developments have been mentioned in connection with the phonological evolution of vowels and consonants in the main body of this work, such as apheresis, dissimilation, metathesis, and so on. Some of these phenomena, often referred to as sporadic changes, need further

---

150. In the older stage of these languages (e.g., Old French), the adverbial form often seems to translate better as "there" than as "here," hence the probability that we have a merging of HIC and IBI into a single unit, a theory not unacceptable to Meyer-Lübke (among others): "*i* kann auch IBI 4252 sein" (*REW*, 4129).

discussion, which is hereby added in the pages that follow, along with other items not covered above. Latin indications of short and long vowels are not respected in this section except where they are relevant.

Excellent examples of several of these phenomena (apheresis, doubling, dissimilation, contamination, etc.), occurring in a single word, are found in the development of Latin UMBĬLĪCU:

UMBĬLĪCU (*IMBÍLICU) > It. *bellico,* Sard. *imbiligu,*[151] Rm. *buric,* Sp. *ombligo,* P. *embigo, umbigo,* C. *llombrigol, meliu,* Pr. *ombelic,* Fr. *nombril,* Engad. *unglih,* Friul. *(l)umbrison,* etc.

Apheresis and Accretion

Apheresis, which is the omission or loss of an unstressed syllable (or sound) at the beginning of a word, often results from wrong division of the word in combination with an article or other part of speech. Sometimes the word will gain a sound or syllable (= accretion). Examples of both are numerous in all languages. In English, for example, *an auger* was originally *a nauger, an apron, a napron.*

Italian is especially rich in these formations, since the loss of prosthetic *i-* (*e-*) led to a wholesale discard also of many prefixes and other initial syllables, for example:

EX-: It. *scusa* (EXCÚSA), *sciame* (EXÁMEN = "swarm"), *squisito* (EXQUISÍTU), etc.

EXTRA-: It. *strabello* (EXTRABÉLLU), *straordinario* (EXTRA-ORDINÁRIU)

(H)IS-: It. *Spagna* (HISPÁNIA), *storia* (HISTÓRIA), *scuola* < *iscuola* (SCHÓLA), etc.

DIS-: It. *sfavore* (DISFAVÓRE), *sgradevole* (DISGRADÁBILE), *sleale* (DISLEGÁLE), etc.

Other representative examples of these processes in various languages are illustrated by the following:[152]

---

151. Logudorese; the other dialects have *biddiu, biddicu, umbìligu.* The Latin etymon is a diminutive formation from ÚMBO, knob or boss. The earlier form *UMBALUS is cognate with Grk. 'ομφαλός (navel).

152. Both processes occurred also in words borrowed from Latin by languages not in the Romance family, e.g.: (*apheresis*) HOSPÍTIU > M. Grk, *spiti,* Alb. *spitu* (= "home," "house"); (accretion) ÁURU > Alb. *lauru.*

EPÍSCOPU > It. *vescovo*, Sp. *obispo* (< *elo* ⸢*bispo*), P. *bispo*, C. *bisbe;* but Fr. *évèque*

ERÍCIU > It. *riccio;* cf. P. *ouriço*

ACÚCULA > Pr. *gulha* (and *agulha*)

APOTHÉCA > LAA/POTECA > It. *bottega*, Sp. *bodega* and *botica*, C. *botiga*, Pr. *botiga*, *botica*, Fr. *boutique;* but P. *adega* (< *a*(*bo*)*dega*)

OCCASIÓNE > It. *cagione*

HÉDERA > OFr. *l'hierre* > Fr. *lierre*

IN-DE-MÁNE > OFr. *l'endemain* > Fr. *le lendemain*

ÍNGUINE > Pr. *lengue*, Friul. *lenzit*

ECCLÉSIA > It. *chiesa*, Pr. *gleiza*

GEMELLÍC(I)U > *emellizo* > Sp. *mellizo*

AUTÚMNU > Rm. *toamnă*

ÓSTREA > Pr. *lustra*

EXERCISES

(Use dictionaries if necessary)

(1) What do the following give in Italian?

EXTRACÁRU, EXTRAVAGÁNTE, EXTRÁNEU
DISBARCÁRE, *DISCOPÉRTU, DISDIGNÓSU, DISMONTÁRE,
DISNUDÁRE, EXPLICÁRE, EXPÉ(N)SA, EXTÉNDERE

(2) Using the same process, what do the following become? (Check in dictionary.)

ELEEMÓSYNA (= "alms") > It. (?), Sp. (?)
EPIPHANÍA (Epiphany) > It. (?)
AEGYPTÁNA > Sp. P. C. (?), Fr. (?)
*ARÁME (= "brass") > It. (?)
HOSPITÁLE > It. (?)

(3) Can you trace back?

It. *sviluppo, staccato, sprezzo*

Extra Apheresis and Accretion

UMBÍLICU (See above and decide what happened in each case.)

SULFÚRE > Sp. *azufre* (with Arab. article *al-*), P. *enxofre* (contamination or mixing?)

INSÚLSU (= "unsalted") > Sp. *soso* ("tasteless"); cf. P. *ensosso*

ÁMITA > *ANTA > OFr. *ante* > Fr. *tante* (See Meyer-Lübke, *REW*, 424.)

ARÉNA > It. *rena*

ELISIPÓNE > P. *Lisboa*

ARÁNEU > It. *ragno*

AEQUÁLÉ > Sard. *galu*

ÚVA PÁSSA > Sard. *pabassa*

Assimilation and Dissimilation

Assimilation is the general tendency to make two or more sounds more alike in articulation. The assimilation can be complete, as in SÉPTE > It. *sette*, or partial: CÓM(I)TE > It. *conte*. The sounds involved may be adjacent or in separate syllables. The assimilation may be one of position (PT > TT), or in manner of articulation (explosive, fricative, etc.), or the addition or deletion of voice (voicing-unvoicing). The process covers a wide range of changes which go by special names (anticipation, umlaut, nasalization, etc.). Unless one of the sounds is more dominant than the other, the assimilation is likely to be a reciprocal one, that is, each sound affects the other. For instance, CÓM(I)TE > Sp. *conde*, the *t* assimilates the nasal *m* to its own dental position [n], while the *n* voices the *t* to *d*.

Examples of various types of assimilation follow:[153]

MATTIÁNA > Sp. *manzana* (anticipation of last *n*, helped also by nasality of initial *m*)

MÚLTU > P. *muito* [mũítu] and dialectal Spanish *muncho* (nasalization of *ui*, *u* vowels by *m*)

AUGÚRIU > Pr. *argurio* (*u* > *r*)

MIRABÍLIA > Sp. *maravilla*, P. *maravilha* (*i* > *a*); cf. It. *meraviglia*, Fr. *merveille*

SALMÚRIA > Rm. *sarmaură* (l > r)

BÚRSA > C. *bossa* (r > s)

ÚRSU > Sp. *oso*, C. *os* (r > s); but It. *orso*, Sard. *ursu*, P. *urso*, Fr. *ours*, etc.

PÉCTU > It. *petto* (*k* > *t*)

BÁSIU > *BÁISO > *béiso > *béeso > *beso (*ai* > *ei* > *e*); P. *beijo* represents the intermediate stage

FĒCĪ > *FÍCI > Sp. *hize* (with anticipation, followed by relaxing of final -*i* to -*e*) (ẹ > i̭); cf. P. *fiz*, Fr. *fis*, but It. *feci*

Perhaps assimilation accounts also for the unique change of VĬCES > OFr. *veiz*, Fr. *fois*, that is, by unvoicing of the *v* from preceding mute consonants in combinations like *dous veiz, treis veiz, cinc veiz, sis veiz*, and so on, to > *deux fois, trois fois, cinq fois, six fois*, and the like. Meyer-Lübke however says this theory is "unwahrscheinlich" (*REW*, 9307). While the final consonant of the numbers in such combinations today is supposed to be silent, many people say "cinq livres [sẽk li:vr], six livres [sis li:vr]."

---

153. For assimilation of Sardinian articles to nouns, see chap. 4, sec. 1.

Very good examples of the effect of anticipation, or umlauting, from vowels in following syllables, can be seen in derivatives of two Latin numbers: VĪGĬNTĬ (= twenty) and TRĪGĬNTA (= thirty):

VIGÍNTI > [vijínte] > *vint(e)* or *vinti*, with the original final *-i* preserving (or restoring) the initial vowel: Sard. *vinti*, P. *vinte*, C. Pr. vint, Fr. vingt; but It. *venti*, Sp. *veinte* [< venti, vejnte]; cf. Engad. *vainch*

TRIGÍNTA > [trejenta] > *treinta* or *trenta*, with final *-a* lowering both initial and medial vowels: It. C. Pr. Engad. *trenta*, Sp. *treinta*, Fr. *trente;* but Sard. *trinta*, P. *trinta*

A very special case of anticipation is found in Portuguese, where the final vowel of adjectives and pronouns (as well as nouns) determines the quality (that is, open or closed) of a preceding vowel:

nôvo (m.) [nóvu], *nova* (f.) [nɔ́va]
isto [íštu] (< L. ĬSTU(D)) = this (neuter)
êste [éšte] (< L. ĬSTE) = this (masculine)
esta [ɛšta] (< L. ĬSTA) = this (feminine)

Dissimilation, the opposite process, is a tendency to make like sounds more dissimilar, or to exchange one sound for another which may resemble the first in some way. That is, the sound may keep its position but change its manner of articulation, and so on. Sometimes, both processes (assimilation and dissimilation) are involved, as in FĒCĬ > Sp. *hize. L* and *r* are two letters that frequently interchange or dissimilate, one to the other.
Examples of dissimilation:

VEXÍCA > Rm. *bǎṣicǎ* (this may be merely a relaxing, or slurring of both *e* and *a,* an assimilation) (e̜ > ə?)
ÚLMU > Fr. *orme* (Sp. *olmo,* etc.) (*l* > *r*)
GÚLA > Rm. *gurǎ* (*l* > *r*)
ERÍCIU > P. *ouriço* (o̜ for e̜)
WILHÉLM- > Sp. *Guillermo* (*l* > *r*)
ANTENÁTU > *ANNATU > Sp. alnado (*n* > *l*)
PAVÓRE > Pr. *pagor* (*v* > *g*)
CERÉSIA > It. *ciliegia* (*r* > *l, sj* > *ĝ*)
LUSCINIÓLU > Sp. *ruiseñor,* P. *rouxinol,* Fr. *rossignol* (*l* > *r*)
TRÉMERE > OFr. *criembre* > Fr. *craindre* (This is double, i.e., *tr* > *cr* and *-mbr-* > *-ndr-*)
VÉTULU > VEC'LU > Sard. *vricu* (*l* > *r*, with metathesis)

Which of the following are cases of assimilation, which dissimilation?
PALÚMBU > Rm. *porumb*
CATHÉDRA > Fr. *chaise*, OFr. *chaire*
ÁRBORE > Sp. *árbol*, It. *albero*
ÁNIMA > Sp. *alma*
FÉMINA > Sp. *hembra*, Fr. *femme*
*ARÁMINE > Sp. *alambre*
SÓMNU > Fr. *somme*, Sp. *sueño* (< *suenno*)
GEMÉLLU > Fr. *jumeau*
VÍMINE > Sp. *mimbre*
FÍLU > Rm. *fir*
ÁNGELU > Rm. *înger*
LIMITÁRE > Sp. *lindar*
PAPILIÓNE > It. *padiglione*
GÉNERU > Sard. *benneru*
LÍLIU > It. *giglio*, Sard. *lizu*, Sp. *lirio*, C. *lliri*
CÚBITU > It. *gomito*
TÍTULU > Fr. *titre*
ARÁTRU > Sp. *aladro*, P. *alaire*, C. *aladre;* cf. Sp. P. *arado*, C. *arada*, Pr. *araire*,
   Sard. *aradu*
CHRISTÓPHORU > Sp. *Cristóbal*, C. *Cristófol*
TENÉBRAS > Sp. *tinieblas*
PLUS > Sard. *prus*
BÚRSA > S. *bolsa*, P. *bôlsa*
VIGÍNTI > Sp. *veinte*
SCÁLA > P. *escada*
VÚLPE > Sard. *gurpe*
MÁRMORE > Sp. *mármol*, Fr. *marbre*
CÁELU > Rm. *cer*
Í(N)SULA > P. *ilha*, C. *illa*
PRÓPRIU > It. Sp. *propio*, C. *propi;* cf. P. *proprio*, Fr. *propre*
RÉGULA > P. *regra*
PULMÓNE > Sard. *prumone*
SIMILIÁRE > It. *somigliare*
ÁMITA > *ÁNTA > Fr. *tante* (*ATÁMITA, Wartburg. See Meyer-Lübke, *REW*
   424)
DÉBERE > It. *dovere*
CAPÍTULU > Fr. *chapitre*
ÁNCHORA > Sp. *ancla*
PAPÝRU > Sp. P. *papel*
FRÁTRE > Sp. *fraile*
ARBÍTRIU > Sp. *albedrío*
VÁDU > Sard. *gual*
IULIO > It. *luglio*, Engad. *lügl*
Note that the workmen regularly employed in maintenance of Saint Peter's in Rome are
called *sampietrini* (< *San Pietro*): why the *-m-*?
Note also that the Sassarese dialect of Sardinian regularly dissimilates both *r* and *s* to *l:*
viltu (< VÍSTU), *altilta* (< ARTÍSTA!).

Metathesis

One of the commonest phenomena of language change is that called metathesis, which involves the shifting of sounds (usually consonants, or a combination of consonant and vowel) within words. Two adjacent sounds may reverse positions, or two consonants exchange syllables, or one sound shift from one end of a word to the other. A very frequent shift in Medieval Spanish, and even in the Siglo de Oro period and later, produced such interesting verb forms as *dandos* for *dadnos*[154] and *dejaldos, llevalda* for *dejadlos, llevadla*,[155] forms which have disappeared in Modern Spanish. Greater ease in pronunciation accounts for many such shifts.

Examples of metathesis in Romance are widespread:

FÉM(I)NA > fem'ra > Pr. *frema* (⟵ *r*)
MIRÁC(U)LU > Sp. *milagro* (*r* ⟷ *l*)
PARÁB(O)LA > Sp. *palabra*, P. *palavra* (*r* ⟷ *l*); cf. Fr. *parole*, It. *parola*
PERÍC(U)LU > Sp. *peligro* (*r* ⟷ *l*); but P. *perigo* (< *perigoo*) and Fr. *péril*
PÓP(U)LU > pop'lo > plopo > It. *pioppo*, Gal. Sp. *chopo*, C. *xop* (⟵ *l*)
PIGRÍTIA > P. *preguiça* (⟵ *r*) (Cf. Sp. *pereza*)
VÉNERIS (DIES) > VÉN'RES > Sp. *viernes* (*nr* > *rn*); but Fr. *vendredi*
FÍCATU > *FÍTICU(?) > Pr. *fetge*, OFr. *fege, feie*, Fr. *foie*[156] (*c* ⟷ *t*); cf. Sp. *hígado*, P. *fígado*.
PULMÓNE > Rm. *plamân* (⟵ *l*), Sard. *prumone* (*ul* > *ru*)
PÉRSICA > Sp. *prisco*, P. *presega* (*er* > *re*); but Fr. *pêche*
CÁPRA > Pr. *craba* (one of several forms) (⟵ *r*)
VET'LU > *VECLU > vecru > Sard. *uricu* (⟵ *r*)

As can be seen from the above examples, *r* and *l* seem to be most apt to metathesize.

---

154. "Dandos del agua, si vos vala el Criador" (Give us water, so help you God [*Poema del Cid*, 2798]).

"Dejaldos; que estoy cansado" (Lope de Vega, *Fuenteovejuna*, 2256); and "Llevalda, y haced que guarden su persona diez soldados" (*Fuenteovejuna*, 1641–42).

155. See note 154 above.

156. See Rohlfs 33.

One of the most interesting examples is a case of triple metathesis. The word FÁBRICA produced a number of variant forms, of which *fabrique* (Fr.), *fabbrica* (It.), *fabrega* (Pr.), and *fábrica* (Sp. P.) are learned, while the Sp. *forja* is borrowed from Fr. *forge* or Pr. *forga, farga*. The Standard Spanish derivation would have been *forga* (< fabr'ga) like the Pr. variant *faurga*. But, in both Spanish and Portuguese, FÁBRICA gives the popular derivative *fragua*, through the stages FÁBR'GA > FAÚRGA > FRÁUGA > FRÁGUA. Analogy, or popular etymology may also have been a factor through the root FRANG, FRAG- (*frangir, frágil*) = "break(able)."

Account for the changes in the following, that is, which are cases of metathesis?
FORMÓSU > Rm. *frumos*, Sp. *hermoso*, P. *formoso*
OBLITÁRE > Fr. *oublier*, C. *oblidar*, Sp. P. *olvidar*
CREPÁRE > Rm. *crapa*, Sp. P. *quebrar*, Fr. *crever*, Pr. *crebar*
CREMÁRE > Pr. *cremar*, Sp. *quemar*, OFr. *cremer*, P. *queimar*
SPÁTULA > It. P. *espádua*, Fr. *épaule*, Sp. *espalda*
CÓRVU > Sp. *cuervo*, It. *corvo*, Sard. *crobu*, Rm. *corb*

Extra examples of metathesis:
ÁGUILA > C. *àliga* (+ reg. *àguila*)
GÉNERU > Sp. *yerno*; but P. *genro*, Fr. *gendre*
GLYCYRRHÍZA[157] > Sp. *regaliz*, Fr. *réglisse*, C. *regalissia*
SIBILÁRE > Sp. *silbar*, P. *silvar*, cf. C. *siular, xiular*
TÍTULU > Sp. *tilde*, P. *til*, Pr. *tiltre*, but Fr. *titre*
CAPÍTULU > Sp. *cabildo*, Fr. *chapitre* shows dissimilation, It. *capicchio* regular T'L > C'L development, and P. *cabido* is probably semilearned via *cabidolo* > *cabido(o)*
MÓDULU > Sp. P. *molde*, but Fr. *moule*, C. *mottle*, Pr. *motle*
MIRÁCULU > Sp. *milagro*, P. *milagre;* but Fr. *miracle*
BIBERÁTICU > Sp. *brebaje*, Fr. *breuvage*
GÉNUCULU > P. *joelho* (*e* ⟷ *o*)
MÉRULU > P. *melro*

Analogy

This is a type of assimilation, a process by which words which are somewhat similar to other words are altered in sound and spelling to conform even more closely to the pattern of the other words. Examples are

157. Meyer-Lübke (*REW*) lists a much reduced "Latin" etymon, LIQUITITIA (5079), but this ultimately goes back to the Grk. "sweet root." Cf. Arab-Spanish *orozuz*, and Sp. *paloduz* (= *palo dulce*).

many. The Spanish-Portuguese form *cinco* is probably due to analogy with other numbers ending in -*o*: *cuatro* (*quatro*), *ocho* (*oito*), while Italian has the regularly derived form *cinque*. A similar example is the -*o* ending in Portuguese for the months *setembro, outubro, novembro, dezembro*, based on the pattern of *maio, junho, julho, agôsto*, and so on. (Sp. *septiembre, octubre, noviembre, diciembre*.) Analogy plays a great role in verb patterns, for example, OSp. *lievo, lievas, lieva, levamos, levades, lievan* > Modern Spanish *llevo, llevas, lleva, llevamos, lleváis, llevan*. Also, the preterite of verbs such as *saber:* OSp. *sope, sopiste, sopo, sopimos, sopístedes, supieron* > Sp. *supe, supiste, supo*, all with the phonologic *u* of the third plural! Other languages have similar cases.

Another term often applied to analogical phenomena is "contamination." This is evident in a mixing or crossing of prefixes, as in EXÁGIU > Sp. *ensayo*, P. *ensaio* (EN-), but C. *assaig* (AD-?), and Fr. Pr. *essai* (EX-). It. *saggio* shows loss of initial syllable.

A special type of analogy goes under the heading of folk etymology (or "false etymology") which plays an important part in altering word forms to fit "more acceptable" patterns, a kind of "mental assimilation." Examples in English are *island* (< AS. *igland*) by analogy with *isle* (< OFr. *isle*), and *aisle* (<Fr. *aile*), also by analogy with *isle*! Compare also the rustic English "sparrow grass" for *asparagus*. Other English examples are "Sea Willow" for the Spanish geographical *Cíbola* in the U.S. Southwest, "Rotten Row" in London from the French *Route du Roi*, and "Key West" from the Spanish *Cayo Hueso*.

The Spanish conquistadores in Mexico transformed the Nahua place name Cuauhnahuacan into *Cuernavaca* with a more familiar sound. Italian changed MELANCHÓLIA into *malincuore* ("sickness in the heart"). The *d* in modern French *poids* is due to the mistaken notion (on the part of early grammarians!) that it came from L. PÓNDUS. Compare the correct derivation in English *avoirdupois*. In *coeur*, French has restored the *o* of L. COR, which gave OFr. *cuer*, enabling the word to be spelled with original *c*- instead of *queur*.

An excellent example of contamination is the crossing of STÉLLA x ÁSTRU > Sp. *estrella*, P. *estrêla*.

The seemingly inconsistent usage in French of *au* and *en* with different countries, such as *au Japon, en Chine* (with either possible in *au Portugal, en Portugal*) is easily explained as a logical phonological development of OFr. *en le* through the forms *en l', el, eu, ou*, and then by analogic crossing with *au* (< *a + le, al* > *au*). The feminine combination *en la* never did go through this change, although the article is not used nowadays: hence the difference in usage by gender. It. *a Roma*, and Fr. *à Paris* have the original L. AD.

Analogy even extends to shifting of accent. A good example is REGÍNA > *reína > Sp. *reina* by analogy with *rey*.

Synthesis

Synthesis is the process of combining elements or whole words, to produce a new word. This may also be called compounding, as when two nouns, or a noun and verb, and so on, are combined as one unit. There are many examples of both:

HOC + ÍLLE > OFr. *oïl*, Fr. *oui* (whereas Pr. used only HOC, hence Pr. is also known as Langue d'oc)

HAC + HÓRA > Sp. *ahora*, P. *agora*, C. *ara* (?) (See Meyer-Lübke, *REW*, 4176.)

DE ÚBI > It. *dove*, Sp. *do*

DE ÚNDE > Sp. P. *donde*

DE-IN-ÁNTE > Sp. *delante*, P. *diante*

AD HÚNC > Sp. *aún*, C. *adhuc*[158]

HOC ÁNNO > Sp. *ogaño*, P. *aganho*, Sard. *occannu*, C. *anguany*, OFr. *ouan*

ECCE HÓC > It. *ciò*, OFr. *ceo* > Fr. *ce*, etc. (Sard. *custu* < ÉCCU ÍSTU)

PER HÓC > It. *però*, Sp. P. *pero*, etc.

APUD HÓC > Fr. *avec* (See Meyer-Lübke, *REW*.)

ACCU + ÍLLO > Sp. *aquel(lo)*, Fr. *quel*, It. *quello*, etc.

ACCU + ÍSTE > OSp. *aqueste*, It. *queste*, etc.

Latin, like Greek but to a somewhat lesser extent, had the ability to combine or compound nouns, nouns and verbs, preposition-adverbs and verbs, etc. In the modern Romance tongues, however, this process has been largely replaced by an analytical approach using prepositions. For instance, the Latin LUCIFER (= light-bearer) would have to be rendered literally in Spanish as *portador de luz*. Nevertheless, Spanish has such modern formations as *portaféretro* (= pallbearer or coffin carrier). Compare Fr. *porte-monnaie* (= purse) and Italian *reggi-pancia* (= belt, lit., "belly supporter").

Examples of Latin compounds in Romance, and new formations are:

---

158. Diez gives this derivation, Meyer-Lübke (*REW*) suggests AD UNUM. However, the Catalan form seems to support Diez.

MANU + OPERÁRE > Fr. *manoeuvrer*, Sp. *maniobrar*, P. *manobrar*
MANU + TENÉRE > It. *mantenere*, Fr. *maintenir*, Sp. *mantener*, etc.
AD + ROTULÁRE > Sp. P. *arrojar*, C. *arruxer*

Older formations existing in Classical Latin times were numerous and have come down into the modern languages without much change:

AVE (bird) + SPEC- (= look) > AUSPÍCIU (= divination) > Sp.
   auspicio, P. *auspício*, C. *auspici*
NAVE (boat) + ÁGERE, *AGÁRE (= drive) > NAVIGÁRE
   (= sail) > Sp. P. C. *navegar;* but Fr. *nager* (= swim)

Compounding continues to be popular today, producing such combinations as Sp. *de a de veras, un timbre de a cinco,* and so on.

§7. Latin Cases, Gender, etc.

Because of blurring of case endings in Vulgar Latin, most of the case distinctions in Romance disappeared, to be replaced by prepositional constructions that governed one basic form; for example, LÍBER PÉTRI > It. *il libro di Pietro*, and FÍLIO ÍLLUM LÍBRUM DAT > Sp. *Da el libro al hijo.* The basic case form surviving in the majority of instances was the accusative, or a generalized form similar to it. In Old French, however, distinction between nominative and other cases continued until well into the fourteenth century; that is, Old French had a nominative case and an oblique case, the latter functioning for all but subject and predicate uses. Examples of this distinction follow:

OFr. (nom.) *Li reis est morz.* (Fr. *le roi est mort.*)
         Li rei sont mort. (Fr. *les rois sont morts.*)
OFr. (obl. -acc.) *Amons le rei.* (Fr. *Nous aimons le roi.*)
         Amons les reis. (Fr. *Nous aimons les rois.*)
OFr. (obl. -gen.) *La fille le rei* (Fr. *La fille du roi*)[159]
         Les filles les reis (Fr. *Les filles des rois*)

The characteristic masculine declension in Old French was:

(nom. sg.) *li reis*   (nom. pl.) *li rei*
(obl. sg.) *le (lo) rei*   (obl. pl.) *les reis*

159. Old French could also express the same idea of possession by *La fille al rei* (Mod. Fr. *La fille au roi*). Modern Romanian has a similar construction, with a preposition derived from AD + ÍLLE: *al mamei* (= of the mother).

The feminine nouns were more regular, and like modern forms:

(nom. sg.) *la fille*   (nom. pl.) *les filles*
(obl. sg.) *la fille*   (obl. pl.) *les filles*

Remnants of the use of the oblique case are still found in modern French, such as *L'église Saint Étienne*, that is, "The church *of* St. Stephen."

Old Provençal also kept the same case distinctions, for example, *amics* (*amix*) (nom. sg. and acc. pl.), *amic* (acc. sg. and nom. pl.). Other examples of varying masculine declensions are:

Nom. Sg.	Acc. Sg.	Nom. Pl.	Acc. Pl.	
cels	*cel*	*cel*	*cels*	(< *CÁELUS, CÁELU, etc.)
cans	*can*	*can*	*cans*	(< CÁNIS, CÁNE, etc.)
coms	*comte*	*comte*	*comtes*	(< CÓMES, CÓMĬTE, etc.)

Feminine nouns and adjectives, as in Old French, were "regular":

domina (sg. nom. and acc.)   *dominas* (pl. nom. and acc.)
maire (< MÁTER, MÁTRE . . .)   *maires* (pl. nom. and acc.)

Romanian has kept case endings in its postfixed articles, with one form for nominative-accusative, and another for genitive-dative:

MASCULINE
(*domn*, "gentlemen")

Nom. -Acc.	*domnul* the gentleman	*domnii* the gentlemen
Gen. -Dat.	*domnului* of, to the . . .	*domnilor* of, to the gentlemen

(*frate* "brother")

Nom. -Acc.	*fratele* the brother	*frații* the brothers
Gen. -Dat.	*fratelui* of, to the . . .	*fraților* of, to the brothers

FEMININE
(*casă* "house")

Nom. -Acc.	*casa* the house	*casele* the houses
Gen. -Dat.	*casei* of, to the house	*caselor* of, to the houses

In the nominative-accusative forms listed above for Romanian, it can be seen that the plural is also the Old Latin nominative.

Because of the loss of final -*s*, Italian chose to keep the nominative of most of its nouns as the basic form, particularly in the plural. Examples:

uomo (man) < L. HÓMO (nom. sg.), *uomini* (men) < L. HÓMĬNES (nom. pl.)

libro (book) < L. LÍBRU(M) (acc.), *libri* (books) < L. LÍBRI
(nom. pl.)
tavola (table) < L. TÁBŬLA(M) (nom. or acc. sg.), *tavole* (*tables*) <
L. TÁBŬLAE (nom. pl.)

The possibility of an alternate derivation for the Italian and Romanian
forms (other than Latin nominative) is stated by Rebecca Posner (p. 137),
but see Grandgent, *From Latin to Italian*, secs. 163–64.
Compare the parallel Spanish, Portuguese, and Catalan forms:

Sp. *hombre*	(< HÓMINE, acc. sg.)	*hombres*	(< HÓMINES, acc. pl.)
P. *homem*		*homens*	
C. *home*		*homes*	
Sp. *libro*	(< LÍBRUM, acc. sg.)	*libros*	(< LÍBROS, acc. pl.)
P. *livro*		*livros*	
C. *llibre*		*llibres*	
Sp. *tabla*	(< TÁBULA(M))	*tablas*	(< TÁBULAS, acc. pl.)
P. *tábua*		*tábuas*	
C. *taula*		*taules*	

Occasionally one finds examples of "doublets" from both nominative
and accusative Latin case forms, for example:

It. *drago* (dragon) < L. DRÁCO (nom. sg.)
It. *dragone* (dragon) < L. DRACÓNE(M) (acc. sg.)

Vestiges of all the case forms in Latin do still exist but, except for the
forms in Romanian cited above, have largely lost their original value.

Nominative singular in -*s*:

Sard. *sitis* (< SÍTIS); but Sp. *sed*, It. *sete*, P. *sêde*, etc.
Sp. *Dios*, Sard. P. *Deus* (< DÉUS); but It. *Dio*, C. *Déu*
Sp. *Carlos*, C. *Carles*, Fr. *Charles* (< CÁROLUS); but It. *Carlo*
OSp. *huebos*, OFr. *ues* (< ÓPUS, both nom. and acc.)

Genitive singular in -s:

Sp. *martes*, C. *dimarts* (< MÁRTIS, "day of Mars"); but It. *martedì*,
Fr. *mardi*
Sp. *jueves*, C. *dijous* (< JÓVIS, "day of Jove"); but It. *giovedì*, Fr.
jeudi[160]

160. The French and Italian forms are in the oblique case, but with no genitive -*s*
ending. In *Lündeschdi*, Engadinian seems to have for "Monday" a form with analogic -*s*
like that of Spanish *lunes* (< *LUNIS?). Other Engadinian days of the week show no trace
of -*s*.

Dative singular:

Sp. *me, te, se* (< MÍHI, TÍBI, ÍLLI, and SÍBI) as in *me lo, te lo, se lo* = atonic pronouns "to me," "to you," etc.; also It. *glielo,* "(it) to him," Sard. *li, ddi*

Accusative singular: see basic forms discussed above.

Ablative singular:

Sp. *hoy,* Fr. *hui (aujourd'hui),* It. *oggi,* Sard. *oe,* P. *hoje,* C. *avui,* etc. (< HÓDIE = "on this day"); cf. Engad. *hoz*
Sp. *ogaño,* OFr. *ouan,* Sard. *occanno* (< HŌC ÁNNŌ)
Sp. *ahora,* P. *agora* (< HĀC HŌRA)

Plural Cases

The one case (besides Italian and Romanian nominatives and the regular *-s* accusatives) which has left distinctive forms in the plural is the genitive ending -ÓRUM, -ÁRUM, in the Italian and French possessives *loro* and *leur* and in Romanian *-lor* endings cited above. There are also geographical names retaining this ending in a fossilized form, as in *Francourville* (FRANCÓRUM VILLA) near Chartres, and also the name of a liturgical feast, Fr. *la chandeleur,* It. *la candelara* (< FÉSTA CANDELÁRUM).[161] Spanish has *candelaria.*

Neuter plurals in -A persisted in Italian and Rhetian (see below) and occasionally passed into the other languages as feminine singulars. Examples:

SĬGNA (signs) > Sp. *seña* (sg.), P. *senha,* C. *senya*
ŎPERA (pl. of ÓPUS) > Sp. P. *obra,* Sp. *huebra,* It. *opera,* etc.[162]

The Modern French form of masculine nouns and adjectives ending in *-eau* does not come from the singular oblique case, but rather is a generalized (i.e., "analogic") form based on the oblique plural (with support from the nominative singular). The Old French declension of this type of noun and adjective and the modern derivation can be seen in figure 10.[163]

---

161. Rohlfs 149–50.
162. Cf. Gender below.
163. The *-x* pl. ending, as stated above is due to confusion of an odd manuscript form of *-s* which was mistakenly read as *-x.* A few exceptional plurals end in *-s,* however, such as *bal, bals.*

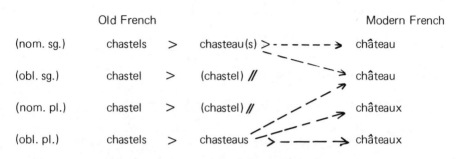

10. *Case evolution from Old French to Modern French*

Gender

Many nouns either had two genders in Latin, or were of indeterminate declension endings and became confused in Romance, in some cases producing doublets. The Latin neuter accusative plural, for example, was in most cases mistaken for a feminine singular. Some instances in Italian of a neuter plural ending -*a* still exist, but are treated as feminine plurals of a masculine noun, for example, *il braccio* (m. sg.), but the plural *le braccia* (f. pl.); *il dito* (m. sg.), *le dita* (f. pl.); *l'ovo* (*uovo*) (m. sg.), *le ova* (f. pl.); *l'osso* (m. sg.), *le ossa* (f. pl. = bones in a living being). For the last an alternate m. pl. *gli ossi* exists, referring to bones not in a living being! Throughout the Romance-speaking world the neuter gender as such was absorbed into the other two genders; hence a difference in classification and treatment in the various languages:

> SPÍCU (n.) > Fr. *épi* (m.), SPÍCA (f.) > It. *spiga*, Sp. *espiga* (f.)
> STÉLLA (f.) > C. *estel*, Sard. *isteddu* (m.) (< *STÉLLU)[164]
> COLÓRE (m.) > Sp. *color* (m.), Fr. *couleur* (f.)
> MÁRE (n.) > Fr. *mer* (f.), Sp. *mar* (m. and f.)

A vestige of the old plural meaning remains in some nouns which have a collective sense, for example:

> LÍGNU > It. *legno*, Sp. *leño*, P. *lenho* (= log), and *legna*, *leña*, *lenha* (= firewood)

---

164. This last cited by Meyer-Lübke (*REW*), but there are also the regular feminine forms (i)*stella*, *iltella*. Sardinian also has kept some fifth declension feminine nouns, e.g., *sa domo* (= *the house*).

This word was used in Classical Latin almost exclusively in the plural, in the modern collective sense, whereas some derivatives refer to the basic material rather than to a single piece of wood: Romanian *lemn* (= wood). The Italian *legna* is both singular and plural feminine. A further extension of the *-o* form to mean "ship" is found in Italian, Spanish, Portuguese, Catalan (*lleny*), Provençal (*lenh*), and Old French (*lein*). This meaning is usually listed as poetic.

MATÉRIA (f. sg.) (= matter, wood) on the other hand has produced a modern masculine singular in *-o*, referring to a single log or beam: Sp. *madero*, P. *madeiro;* cf. the modern fem. sg. Sp. *madera*, P. *madeira* (= wood).

SÍGNU (n. sg.), SÍGNA (n. pl.) have given two modern singulars of different genders: Sp. *signo*, *sino* and *seña;* Rm. *semn*, It. *segno*, Sard. *sinnu*, Fr. *seing* (all masc.); C. *signe* and *senya*, P. *signo*, *sino*, and *senha*. Several of the masculine forms have the specialized meaning of "bell" (i.e., a special kind of "sign" or "signal"!): P. *sino*, OFr. *seing*, Pr. *senh*, C. *seny*.

A similar case is that of FÓLIU (sg.), and FÓLIA (pl.) which have given modern Italian *foglio* (= sheet of paper) and *foglia* (= leaf); cf. Sard. *folu*, OFr. *fueil*, C. *full*, P. *folho* and Sard. *foza*, Fr. *feuille*, Rm. *foaie*, Pr. *fulha*, C. *fulla*, Sp. *hoja*, P. *folha*. Such doublets are not unusual.

Engadinian has a number of duplicate plurals, with the *-a* (feminine singular) forms (< Latin neuter plurals) listed as "irregular" or "collective" plurals.[165] Examples:

	Regular Plural	Collective Plural
bratsch (arm)	*ils bratschs*	*la bratscha*
bös-ch (*tree*)[166]	*ils bös-chs*	*la bos-cha*
öss (*bone*)	*ils öss*	*la ossa* (bone structure)
daint (*finger*)	*ils daints*	*la dainta*
fögl (*leaf*)	*ils fögls*	*la föglia* (foliage)
ram (branch)	*ils rams*	*la ramma* (group of branches)

True neuters can be seen in modern pronominal forms such as Sp. *esto*, *eso*, *aquello*, *ello*, P. *isto*, *isso*, *aquillo*, It. *esso;* also Sp. *lo que*, P. *o que*, Sard. *su chi*, which are used only in the singular with no reference to any masculine-feminine noun. The same is true of the It. *ciò* (*cioè* = "that is")

---

165. See Schlatter 10.
166. Pronounced [bǿšč]. The cognates of this word in French (*bois*), Italian (*bosco*), Sp. *bosque*, etc., all have the collective sense of "woods." Akin to Eng. *bush*, Scot. *bosky, boskey*. The French form also refers to the material, "wood."

and the Fr. *ce* (OFr. *ço*) in such phrases as *c'est vrai, qu'est-ce que c'est.* Combinations with prepositions and adverbs have produced such forms as Rm. *însa* ("but"), OIt. *lunghesso, sovresso,* and so on. The last is still used poetically.

Semantic Shift

Through the course of centuries, words change not only in their form and pronunciation, but also in their meaning in many cases. The meaning may become more specialized or restricted, and vice versa. It may be applied to part of the original object, to adjacent elements, or to the whole of which the original was a part. All kinds of semantic shifts are possible and do occur. Examples:

TRÁHERE (to draw, pull) > Fr. *traire* (= to milk), Sp. *traer* (= to bring, carry); cf. Sp. *ordeñar,* P. *ordenhar,* "to milk," < ORDINIÁRE (to prepare, set in order)

FAÚCE (upper throat, jaw) > It. *foce,* P. *foz* (= mouth of river), Sp. *hoz* (= ravine)

ZÓNA (belt, girdle) > It. Sp. P. *zona,* Fr. *zone* (= zone, as well as original girdle, belt; It. also = "the shingles")

MEDICÍNA (medicine, surgery) > C. *metsina* (poison)

POTIÓNE (drink) > Fr. *poison* (= poison); cf. Germ. *Gift* (= poison, i.e., "what is given")

ÁVICA (small or large bird) > It. Sp. *oca,* Fr. *oie,* Rm. *auca* (= goose)

AVICÉLLU (small bird) It. *uccello,* Fr. *oiseau* (= bird, but also very early in both languages became a slang word for penis!)

MATÉRIA (matter, material) > Sp. *madera,* P. *madeira* (= wood)

FORMÁTICU (moulded [cheese]) > Fr. *fromage,* It. *formaggio* (= cheese)

AURÍCULA (ear lobe) > Sp. *oreja,* P. *orelha,* Fr. *oreille,* etc. (= ear)

GÁUDIA (joys) > Sp. *joya* (= jewel)

FÚRCA (pitchfork) > Sp. *horca* (= gallows)

PACÁRE (appease) > It. *pagare,* Sp. P. C. Pr. *pagar,*[167] Fr. *payer* (= to pay)

COLLOCÁRE (to place) > Sp. *colgar* (= to hang), Rm. *culca,* Fr. *coucher* (= to lay down)

RÚGA (furrow, rut) > Sp. *ruga* (wrinkle), P. Pr. *rúa,* Fr. *rue* (= street)

CANÍCULA (little dog) > Fr. *chenille* (= grub caterpillar)

---

167. Also, Sp. *Pagarse(de)* = "to be pleased (with)."

CATHÉDRA (seat, chair) > Sp. *cadera* (= hip)

DELICÁTU (delightful, charming) > Sp. P. *delgado*, Fr. *délié* (= slim), and It. *delicato*, Fr. *délicat* (= delicate)

SALÚTE (greeting) > Rm. *sărut* (= kiss)

RÚBEU (red) > Rm. *roib* (= chestnut colored horse, fox, See Meyer-Lübke, *REW*, 7408); cf. Fr. *roux*

CALMÁRE (to calm, cease) > Fr. *chômer* (= be idle, cease work)

FÓLLICA (foolish good time) > Sp. *huelga* (= strike)

NAVIGÁRE (to sail, navigate) > Fr. *nager* (= to swim)

MERCÉDE (reward) > Fr. *merci* (= Thanks!); cf. E. "mercy"

VERMÍCULU (little worm) > Fr. *vermeil*, Sp. *bermejo*, etc. (= vermilion color)

TÁBULA (board, plank) > Fr. *table*, etc. (= table)

FÓCU (hearth) > It. *fuoco*, Sp. *fuego*, Fr. *feu*, etc. (= fire)

DÍCTA (things said) > Sp. *dicha* (= fortune, good luck)

ROTÉLLA (little wheel) > Sp. *rodilla* (= knee, kneecap)

MÚTTU (mutter, grunt) > Fr. *mot* (= word)

COLLÉCTA (things gathered) > Sp. *cosecha* (= harvest)

LABORATÓRE (worker, laborer) > Sp. *labrador* (= farmer)

MÍTTERE (to send) > It. *mettere*, Sp. P. *meter*, C. Pr. *metre*, Fr. *mettre* (= to put)

FÚNDERE, *FUNDÍRE (pour out, melt) > Sp. *hundir* (= sink) (Analogy with *fondo*?)

FOCÁRIA (pertaining to the hearth) > Sp. *hoguera* (= bonfire)

FORMÓSU (shapely) > Sp. *hermoso*, P. *formoso*, Rm. *frumos*, C. *formos* (= beautiful)

APPREHÉNDERE (to apprehend) > It. *apprendere*, Sp. P. *aprender*, Fr. *apprendre* (= to learn)

NATÍVU (original, native) > Fr. *naïf* (= naive)

PÓDIU (elevated place) > It. *poggio*, Fr. *puy* (= hill): Sp. *poyo* (= stone bench)

CÓDEX, CÓDICE (block, manuscript, writing) > Engad. *cudesch* (= book)

SAGÍTTA (arrow) > Engad. *sajetta* (= lightning); cf. It. *saeppola* (< SAGÍTTULA, small arrow) same meaning

Frank. BUSK (forest) > Fr. *bois* (wood, woods), Engad. *bös-ch* (= tree)

(Arab.) ZAGAL (bold, brave) > Sp. *zagal* (= shepherd)

PERFÍDIA (treachery) > Sp. *porfía* (stubbornness, resistance), P. *porfia* (= dispute)

RÉGIA (royal) > It. *reggia* (= palace)

VULTÚRE (vulture) > Rm. *vultur* (= eagle)

CAÉLU (sky, heaven) > Rm. *cerul (gurei)* ("roof" — of mouth)

AVIÓLU (little grandfather) > Fr. *aïeul* (ancester)

PÍLA (pillar) > Sp. *pila*, P. *pia* (= fountain, basin)

PÁLA (spade, shovel) > Fr. *pale* (= oar blade)

SALÍRE (to leap, jump) > It. *salire* (= to rise), Fr. *saillir* (= jut, gush), Sp. *salir*, P. *sair* (= depart, go out)

TRÍFOLU (3-leafed clover) > It. *trefolo* (= tangle of thread)

SALUTÁTE (greeting) > P. *saudade* (= longing)

CÁLCE (heel) > It. *calce* (foot — of page), Pr. *cautz* (= foot — of mountain), Sp. *coz*, P. *couce, coice* (= kick)

CÁLICE (cup) > Sp. *cauce* (= riverbed)

SÁLTA (jump, leap) > Sp. *jota* (= a dance)

CÁLIDU (hot) > Sp. *caldo* (= broth)

(IN)SÚLSU (unsalted) > Sp. *soso* (= tasteless)

PALPÁRE (to stroke, caress) > P. *poupar* (= save, economize)

CANÁLIA (pertaining to dogs) > Fr. *canaille* (= rabble)

AERÁMEN, -MINE (copperware) > Sp. *alambre*, P. *arame* (= wire)

RÚPTA (broken) > Fr. *route* (< RÚPTA VÍA) (= route)

GÚTTA (drop of liquid) > It. *gotta*, Fr. *goutte* (= gout)

TRANSPASSÁRE (to pass over) > Fr. *trépasser* (pass away, die)

MANSIÓNE (staying, dwelling) > Sp. *mesón* (= inn)

SÉNSU (sense, feeling) > Sp. *seso* (= brain, judgment), Corsican *sensi* (= temple — of head)

TRANSVÉRSU (crosswise) > Sp. *travieso*, P. *travesso* (= naughty, mischievous)

SÍGNU (sign) > Fr. *seing* (= signature)

INSIGNÁRE (to show) > Fr. *enseigner*, Sp. *enseñar*, P. *ensinar* (= to teach, or show)

COGNÁTU (related) > Sp. *cuñado*, P. *cunhado*, C. *cunyat*, Rm. *cumnat* (= brother-in-law)

CÓGNITU (known) > OFr. *coint* (= pleasing, pretty > English *quaint*)

TAM MÁGNU (so big) > Sp. *tamaño*, P. *tamanho* (= size)

GÚLA (throat) > Rm. *gură* (= mouth)

OBSTÁRE (thwart) > Fr. *ôter* (= take away)

ORATIÓNE (speech) > Sp. *oración* (= prayer, sentence)

VÓTA (vows) > Sp. P. C. *boda* (= wedding)

COGITÁRE (to think) > Sp. P. C. *cuidar* (= take care of, mind)

PÚLLU (young animal) > It. *pollo* (= fowl), Rm. *puiu* (= cub, whelp), Sp. *pollo*, C. *poll* (= chicken, young bee)

CIVITÁTE (citizenship, state) > It. *città*, Sp. *ciudad*, P. *cidade*, Fr. *cité*, etc. (= city, town); Rm. *cetate* (= fortress)

RACÉMU (bunch, cluster) > Fr. *raisin* (= grape)

LICÉRE (to be permitted) > Fr. *loisir* (= leisure)

MÚSCULU (muscle, "little mouse") > Sp. *muslo* (= thigh; cf. Sp. *cadera*), C. *muscle* (= shoulder), P. *bucho* (= upper arm, animal stomach), Sard. [mušu] (= rope)

DESPÉCTU (contempt) > Sp. *a despecho de*, Fr. *en dépit de* (= in spite of)

PÍNNA (feather) > Sp. *peña* (= cliff. Cf. Engl. "pinnacle")

MÁSSA (mass, lump, lot) > C. *massa* (= too much)

Í(N)SULA (island) > Sard. [isča] (= swamp — between hills)

*MUCCULÁCCULU (snotty little one) > Sp. *muchacho* (= boy).[168] Meyer-Lübke (*REW*, 5791) says < *mocho* MÚTILU, "stubby"; but cf. It. *moccolone*, Sard. *muccunozu* (= snotty kid)

APOTHÉCA (storehouse) > Fr. *boutique*, Engad. *butia* (= shop), Sp. *botica* (= pharmacy, drugstore), Sp. *bodega*, P. *adega* (= wine cellar)

LÍMPIDU (limpid, transparent) > Sp. *limpio* (= clean), *lindo* (= lovely)

MÁGIS (more) > Fr. *mais*, P. *mas* (= but); cf. Sp. *mas* (= but), a variation of *más*, and P. *mais*, < MÁGIS

SĪC (thus, so) > It. Sard. Sp. C. Pr. Fr. *si*, *sí*, P. *sim*, Engad. *schi* (= yes), Rm. *și* (= and); cf. OFr. *si* = and)

APRÍCU (sunny) > Sp. P. *abrigo*, C. *abric*, Fr. *abri* (= shelter)

SATIÓNE (sowing time) > Sp. *sazón*, Fr. *saison*, etc. (= season)

VENÁTU (hunting) > Sp. *venado* (= deer)

SPÉCIE (appearance, kind) > It. *spezie*, Engad. *spezcha*, Fr. *épice* (= spices)

CALCEÁRE (to kick) > Sp. *calzar*, Fr. *chausser* (= to shoe)

MAXÍLLA (jawbone) > Sp. *mejilla*, Engad. *massella* (= cheek), Rm. *măseà* (= milk tooth)

ARTÍCULU (joint) > It. *artiglio* (claw), Sp. *artejo* (= knuckle), P. *artelho* (= foot knuckle), Fr. *orteil* (= big toe)

Exercise: Look up the meaning of MFr. *hâbler* (< FABULÁRE), Rm. *vită* (< VITA, "life").

---

168. This etymon is one suggested by the late Hayward Keniston as a possibility which phonologically fits the modern development.

Diminutives (and Augmentatives)

Many Classical Latin words seem to have been popularized in Vulgar Latin in a diminutive form which in time often displaced the original basic one. Examples are legion:

Basic Latin	Diminutive	
SÓROR (sister)	= SORORÍLLA	> It. *sorella*
FRÁTRE (brother)	= FRATÉLLU	> It. *fratello*
SÓLE (sun)	= SOLÍCULU	> Fr. *soleil*
VAS (vessel)	= VAXÍLLA	> Sp. *vajilla*, P. *baixela*, C. *vaixell*, Fr. *vaisselle*, etc.
AÚRE (ear)	= AURÍCULA	> It. *orecchio* (m.), Sp. *oreja*, P. *orelha*, Fr. *oreille*, etc.
ÁVE (bird)	= ÁVICA	> It. Sp. *oca*, Rm. Pr. *auca*, OFr. *oue*, Fr. *oie*, Vegl. *yauca*, Engad. *ocha*, Friul. *auke*
ÁVE (bird)	= AVICÉLLU	> It. *uccello*, C. *ocell*, Fr. *oiseau*, etc.[169]
ÓVE (sheep)	= OVÍCULA	> Sp. *oveja*, P. *ovelha*, C. *ovella*
CÓNCHA (shell)	= CÓNCHULA	> Sp. P. *concha* (The original etymon CÓNCHA > Sp. *cuenca*.)

Extra Diminutives:

AVIÓLU (little grandfather) > Sp. *abuelo* (grandfather)

SOMNÍCULU (little sleep) > Fr. *sommeil* (= sleep)

CULTÉLLU (small knife) > Sp. *cuchillo*, It. *coltello*, Fr. *couteau* (= knife)

ÁPE, dim. APÍCULA (= little bee) > It. *pecchia*, Sp. *abeja*, Fr. *abeille*,[170] etc. (= bee)

ÁCU, dim. ACÚCULA (needle) > Sp. *aguja*, P. *agulha*, etc.

VÉTUS (old), dim. VÉTULU > It. *vecchio*, Sp. *viejo*, Fr. *vieil*, etc.

PAR (equal), dim. PARÍCULU > It. *parecchio*, Fr. *pareil*, etc.

VÉRME (worm), dim. VERMÍCULU > It. *vermiglio*, Sp. *bermejo*, Fr. *vermeil*, etc.

GÉNU (knee), dim. GENÚCULU > It. *ginocchio*, Sp. *hinojo*, C. *genoll*, etc. [171]

---

169. This word illustrates why diminutives or other variants from a basic form often became the chosen form. L. ÁPE and ÁVE by normal derivation both > *éf* in Old French, leading to confusion in meaning.

170. See note 169 above.

171. Latin itself had numbers of diminutives, e.g., the word PUÉLLA (= girl), in origin a diminutive of PUER (= boy), also had a diminutive PUELLULA.

Early Romance had a wide variety of diminutive (and augmentative) endings, traces of almost all of which can be found in each of the modern tongues. Yet individual languages seem to have had their favorite types of endings. French, for instance, became very fond of *-et, -ette*, as evidenced in the many words ending thus, such as *cabinet, clarinette, allumette*, and so on. Italian also has its *-etto, -etta* formations, for example, *libretto, canzonetta*, and in addition many in *-ino, -ina: cartolino, Giannina, signorina.* Compare Sp. *oficina*, P. *senhorina, menino, cafèzinho* (with *-z-*). Spanish, however, preferred *-ito, -ita* (with variants *-cito, -cita*): *señorito, señorita, Pepito, Pepita.* This ending was even extended to adverbs and other parts of speech, such as *ahorita* (= just now, pretty soon), *a solitas* (= all alone, by oneself), *prontito* (= right away), and so on. The ending often carries a note of affection — *viejecito* (= "nice" little old man). Portuguese also participates in this extension to other parts of speech and variety of nuances: *cedo* (= early), *cedinho* (= pretty early); *devagar* (= slow, slowly), *devagarzinho* (= slow and easy); *só* (= alone), *sózinho* (= all alone); *culpado* (= guilty), *culpadinho* (= somewhat to blame).

Akin to the diminutives are those augmentative endings indicating largeness (or a pejorative, unattractive quality), for example Fr. *cabochon* (< *caboche*), Sp. *cabrón* (< *cabra*), *grandote* (< *grande*). Sp. *hombrón* means "big fellow," while *hombrona* refers to a coarse, masculine-type woman.

For Catalan, Joan Gili lists several suffixes with diminutive (*-et, -eta*), augmentative (*-às, -assa*), and pejorative (*-ot, -ota*) meanings. Examples are:

	Dim.	Aug.	Pej.
gat (= cat)	*gatet*	*gatàs*	*gatot*
peu (= foot)	*peuet*	*peuàs*	*peuot*
dona (= woman)	*doneta*	*donassa*	*donota*
mà (= hand)	*maneta*	*manassa*	*manota*[172]

The wide range of usage can be well illustrated with the basic Sp. *casa* (= house), which has given birth to *casita* (= little house, "mistress"), *caseta* (= bath house), *casilla* (= cabin, post-office box, voting booth, etc.), *casal* (= country place), *casalicio* (= house, building), *casarón*, *caserón* (= large tumbled-down house), *casería* (= country house), *caserío* (= country house, group of houses, hamlet), *casillero* (= filing cabinet), *casón* (= large house), *casucha, casucho, casuca* (= shack, shanty). *Casino* was borrowed from Italian. Diminutives can also have diminutives: It. *fratellino*, Sp. *pobrecito, pobrecitillo* (poor little fellow). A violin (< It.

---

172. Gili 35–36.

violino), is a little viol, whereas a *violoncello* or *cello* is a "big little viol." And so the list goes on.

Rhetian also has diminutive endings, such as *-et*, *-etta* and *-in*, *-ina:* *cudesch* (= book), *cudeschet* (= little book), *cudeschin* (= nice little book); *duonna* (= lady), *duonnetta* (= little lady), *duonnina* (= sweet little lady). Others are *-un*, *-una*, *-ada:* *hom* (= man), *homun* (= big guy), *badigl* (= shovel), *badigliada* (= shovelful).[173]

The chief Italian suffixes are:

Diminutives

1. *-ino*, *-ina*, *-ello*, *-ella*, *-etto*, *-etta*, denoting smallness and grace: *una stanzina* (= a pretty little room), *una vecchietta* (= a nice little old lady); note *Quella ragazza è bellina* (= That girl is rather pretty, pretty cute), *Canta benino* (She sings fairly well), *una casa grandetta* (= a somewhat large house).

2. *-uccio*, *-uccia*, *-uzzo*, *-uzza*, smallness and endearment, often disparagement: *un monelluccio* (= a cute little rascal), *Carluccio* (= Dear Charles), *pagliuzza* (= bit of straw).

3. *-olo*, *(-uolo)*, *-ola* *(-uola)*, *-occhio*, etc.; *figliuolo* (= son), *figliola* (= daughter), *figliolaccia* (= ill-mannered child), *tovagliolo* (= napkin < *tovaglia*, tablecloth), *Pinocchio* (= pine seed, no-good little pine tree < *pino*, pine).

Augmentatives

1. *-one*, *-ona*, denoting extraordinary size: *uno stradone* (= a very large street), *casalone* (= a ruined castle), *peperone* (= big pepper) — note *peperoncino* (= big little pepper!), *un fenestrone* (= a big window < *fenestra*), *boccona* (= large mouth, cannon wad).

2. *-otto*, *-otta*, "middling large": *una ragazzotta* (= a sturdy young girl).

3. *-accio*, *-accia*, conveys disdain or scorn, worthlessness: *un tempaccio* (= some terrible weather), *una pennaccia* (= a lousy pen), *un ragazzaccio* (= an awful, nasty kid).

4. *-astro*, *-astra*, not quite what it should be: *un poetastro* (= a would-be poet), *giallastro* (= yellowish).

As in Spanish, a basic word may take a variety of suffixes: It. *casa* > *casetta, casettina, casettuccia, casale, casino, casalone;* cf. also *pioggia* (= rain) > *pioggerella, pioggerellina, pioggeretta, pioggerettina* (all = drizzle).

Although Spanish has more and a greater variety of these endings than the other languages, Italian, Portuguese, and Catalan, as we have seen, also have a goodly stock of them. In all[174] the Romance tongues, the capacity to form new diminutives and augmentatives is still very strong and active.

173. Schlatter 56–57.
174. An example of diminutives in Sardinian is *craba* > *crabitta; crabu* > *crabiolu* (Cagliaitan).

Engendered, or Transitional Sounds

Certain combinations of consonants, and occasionally of vowels, seem to produce automatically another sound that helps in the transition from one to the other. That is, an -ML- generally produces a -B-, as in TREMULÁRE > Fr. *trembler*, while an -NR- > -NDR-, as in TÉNERU, which gives Fr. *tendre* by loss of the weak syllable. The transition sound may be avoided, however, by metathesis: Compare Sp. *tierno* from TÉNERU (but *vendré* (Sp.) and (Fr.) *viendrai*, both from VENIR + *AI > VEN'RAI, etc.).[175] In the case of vowels, hiatus often produces a transitional *yod*, for example, SÍNU > *seo > P. *seio*. Further examples are:

FÁM(I)NE > Sp. *hambre* (< *FÁM'RE); but Fr. *faim*
NÓM(I)NE > Sp. *nombre* (but Fr. *nom* and P. *nome* < NÓMEN)
FÉM(I)NA > Sp. *hembra;* but Fr. *femme*[176]
NÚM(E)RU > Fr. *nombre;* but Sp. *número*, a learned form
MÓL(E)RE > Fr. *moudre*, C. *moldre* (-L'R- > -LDR-; but Sp. *moler*
    by shift of accent to MOLÉRE)
GÉN(E)RU > Fr. *gendre;* but Sp. *yerno* by metathesis
CÉ(N)A > P. *ceia*
TÉ(L)A > P. *teia*
VÉ(N)A > P. *veia*
CÚLM(I)NE > Sp. *cumbre*

Doubling

With a few exceptions, double consonants in Latin have been reduced to single consonant sounds in Romance. They have been retained in a number of languages, however, as a spelling device, for example, -*ss*- in French and Portuguese, to distinguish from the single *s* voiced variety. In Spanish and Catalan *ll* represents a separate consonant sound. In most languages -*rr*- is longer and stronger than -*r*-. Not in French, however,

---

175. Assimilation may also avoid transitional sounds: DÁMNU > Sp. *daño* (OSp. *danno*), and SÓMNU > Sp. *sueño*.

176. See note 175 above.

where it is merely a question of spelling: *terre* [tɛ:r] (with a trilled or uvular *r*) instead of *tère*. *Mère* is spelled with (ˋ) and single *r*. Romanian -*rr*- has been reduced to -*r*-: *țara* < TÉRRA.

Italian is the main exception to the above statement.[177] This language, through a tendency toward intensified stress on tonic syllables, doubled many a single consonant, while preserving original doubles. In some cases, this newly produced checked syllable prevented diphthongization, as in FÉBRE > It. *febbre*. Compare Fr. *fièvre*, Sp. *fiebre*.

Examples of doubling in Italian are numerous:

FÉMINA > It. *femmina*
PÓPULU > It. *pioppo* (metathesis: *PLÓPO > *pioppo*)
EXÁGIU > It. *saggio*
CÁPULU > It. *cappio* (but Fr. Sp. *cable*)
FÁBRICA > It. *fabbrica*
RÉGIA > It. *reggia*

Diphthongization (*in Portuguese*)

Diphthongization of open vowels (ę, ǫ) rarely took place in Portuguese. So-called "exceptions" may be borrowings from Spanish. On the other hand, diphthongs did develop in Portuguese for other reasons (some already mentioned), as illustrated below:

1) Hiatus due to loss of medial *l*, *n* or other consonant. The *yod* that is engendered is a transitional or "helping" sound. (See Engendered Sounds above.)

CÉNA > P. *ceia*
ARÉNA > P. *areia*
TÉLA > P. *teia*
FOÉDU > P. *feio*

2) Transposition (metathesis):

VENÁRIU > P. *vieiro* (also with loss of *N*)
BÁSIU > P. *beijo*
ÁPIU > P. *aipo*
CÓRIU > P. *coiro, couro*

177. Plus Sardinian. For examples, see sec. 5.

3) Vocalization of a consonant (usually in a checked position):

ÁLTRU > P. *outro*
ÓCTO > P. *oito*
ÁCTU > P. *auto* (cf. Spanish)
FÁCTU > P. *feito*

4) Shifting (or lifting) of L. AU diphthong to *ou, oi:*

AÚRU > P. *ouro, oiro*
AUSÁRE > P. *ousar*

5) Confusion of root or prefix: ERÍCIU > *ouriço*

Then of course there are the many nasal diphthongs of varying origins:
-ão (-am), -ui (in *muito*), *-em, ões, -ães.*

Chapter 4

Morphology and Syntax

These areas of linguistic interest are much too broad to treat adequately in this text. However, a few items do merit attention and are touched upon slightly in the following pages. For more special treatments, consult grammars and studies in specific languages, as well as Posner for a general overall view (chaps. 5 and 6).

§1. Definite Articles and Pronouns

Unlike Greek, Latin had no definite article. The noun VIR carried the meaning of "man," "the man," or "a man."[1] In Romance, however, the felt need for the article produced an array of forms derived from the Latin demonstratives ÍSTE and ÍLLE (= that), and ÍPSE (= the same).[2] These also furnished third person personal pronouns (subject and object). The list of derivatives is a long one. (See Posner 142–43.) A few samples here should suffice:

Articles

ÍPSE, ÍPSA, ÍPSU > C. *es, sa,* Sard. *su, sa, s'*
ÍPSOS, ÍPSAS > C. *ets, ses,* Sard. *sos, sas, is*
ÍLLE, ÍLLA, ÍLLU, etc. > Rm. *-le, -l, -a,* It. *il, lo, la,* Pr. Sp. *el, lo,*
  la, P. *o, a,* C. *el, l', lo, la,* Fr. *le, l', la,* Rh. *il, igl, el, la,* etc.

---

1. Cf. Russian, which says "man sick" for "the man is sick."
2. Latin HIC (= this) seems to have disappeared almost entirely, except in combined forms such as HAC HÓRA > Sp. *ahora,* P. *agora,* APUD + HOC > Fr. *avec,* PER + HOC > Sp. P. *pero,* It. *però* (Meyer-Lübke, *REW,* 4158). Note that English *the* is a form related to, if not derived from, the A.S. demonstrative *thaet,* just as *a* is an unstressed form of *an* or *one.* Also, the German article *der* has an identical stressed form meaning "that," as in *der Mann* (= the man) and **der** *Mann* (= that man).

ÍLLI, ÍLLAE, ÍLLOS, ÍLLAS, etc. > Rm. *-i, -le, -li, -le (-lele, -ile),* It. *i, gli, le,* Sp. Pr. *los, las,* P. *os, as,* C. *els, los, les,* Fr. *les,* Rh. *ils, las,* etc.

Sardinian Articles and Nouns[3]

	Singular	Plural
M.	(bridge)	
	su ponti [su bónti]	is pontis(i) [ispóntis, ispóntizi]
	(man)	
	s'ommi [sómmi]	is ommis(i) [isómmis, isómmizi]
F.	(stone)	
	sa perda [sabérda]	is perdas(a) [ispérdas, isperdaza]
	or	
	sa pedra [sabédra]	is pedras(a) [ispédras, ispédraza]
	(ear)	
	s'origa [soríga]	is origas(a) [isorígas, isorígaza]

When preceding a noun beginning with a nasal consonant, the final *-s* of the plural form of the article is assimilated to the nasal either by voicing to [z], or (in popular usage) completely to [m] or [n]. Note examples:

M.	(wall)	
	su muru [sumúru]	is murus(u) [izmúrus, izmúruzu]
		im murus(u) [immúrus, immúruzu]
	(mountain)	
	su monti [sumónti]	is montis(i) [izmóntis, izmóntizi]
		im montis(i) [immóntis, immóntizi]
	(nose)	
	su nasu [sunázu]	is nasus(u) [iznázus, iznázuzu]
		in nasus(u) [innázus, innázuzu]
F.	(mother)	
	sa mamma [sa mamma]	is mammas(a) [izmámmas, izmámmaza]
		im mammas(a) [immámmas, immámmaza]

Pronouns (and Adjectives)

ÍPSE, ÍPSA, ÍPSU, ÍPSI, ÍPSAE, ÍPSOS, ÍPSAS > It. *esso, essi, esse,* Sard. *isse, issu, issa, issos, issas,* Sp. *eso, ese, esa, esos, esas,* P. *isso, êsse, essa, êsses, essas*

---

3. This table of article-noun combinations in Cagliaitan, with phonetic transcription, was furnished by Maria Ibba, a native of Sardara, and does not serve for Logudorese, which has plural articles in *sos, sas,* or the other dialects (Sassarese, Tempiese) with forms derived from ÍLLE, ÍLLA, etc.

ÍLLE, ÍLLA, ÍLLU, ÍLLOS, ÍLLAS, etc. > Rm. *el, ea, ei, ele,* It.
egli, ella, eglino, elleno, lei, loro, Sp. *él, lo, le, se, ella, la, ellos,*
ellas, los, las, les, P. *êle, o(lo), ella, a(la), lhe, lhes, êles, os (los),*
as (las), elas, C. *ell, ella, el, l', 'l, lo, la, li, hi, ho, els, 'ls, los, les,*
Fr. *il, elle, le, l', la, ils, elles, les, lui, leur,* Rh. *el, ella,* etc., Pr.
el, ilh, ella, la, li, lui, lei, etc., Sard. *ddi, dda, li, la,* etc.

The Latin demonstrative ÍSTE replaced HIC as a first person "this"
in a number of languages, and was itself replaced by ÍPSE as the second
person "that-near-you." Examples are Sp. *este (esta,* etc.), P. *êste (esta,*
etc.), Rm. *ăst, asta,* etc. As seen above, ÍLLE, ÍLLA, etc. continued with its
third person "that yonder," "that-near-him" force it had in Latin. All of
these forms frequently combined with *ÁCCU- (< ÉCCE) as in C. *aquest,*
aqueix, aquel, aquesta, aqueixa, aquella, etc., It. *questo, quello, questa,* etc.,
Rm. *acest, cest, acel, cel,* etc., Rh. *quel, tschel, quaist, quaista,* etc., Sard.
iccude, cuddu, cudda, custe, custu, custa, OSp. *aqueste, aquesse,* Sp. *aquel,*
aquella, etc., Pr. *aquel, aquela, aquest, aquesta, cella, cel, aicel,* OFr. *icest,*
cest, icel, cel, MFr. *ce, cet,* etc. (There are many such derivatives.)

Complete sets of subject and object pronouns had best be sought in
individual grammars of the various languages. Two rather odd plural
forms, however, do deserve some comment: the Italian unstressed object
forms *vi* and *ci* (= you, us). The first had a logical phonological development from the proclitic use of *voi dico* (= I tell you), helped along by
analogy with *mi, ti (voi > vo > ve > vi).* Then, because this *vi* was identical
with the adverb *vi* from ÍBI (= there), an analogic form *ci* came into being
for the first person plural "us" (= "here" < ECC'ÍC < ÉCCE HIC).[4]
Examples: *vi prego* (you're welcome, lit., I beg you), *Arrivederci* (= so
long, see you later, lit., to seeing us [each other] again).

Prepositions and Adverbs

Prepositions and adverbs combine with many phrases to produce a
variety of idioms that differ from language to language. Their list is endless
and too complex for any kind of comparative grouping. They often defy
rules of logic and must be learned by rote. For instance, the use or nonuse of
prepositions to govern infinitives requires years of compilation in some
languages (notably Spanish and Portuguese), and the nonnative can never
be sure of complete mastery. A simple illustration of the difference in
prepositional phrases is the translation of "at home." In Spanish and
Portuguese it is *en casa, em casa* respectively, in French *chez (+ moi, toi,*

4. Grandgent 136.

lui, etc.), in Italian *da casa,* in Rhetian (Sursilvan) *a casa* (*Negin era a casa* = No one was at home), Catalan *a la casa,* Romanian *acasa,* and so on.

§2. Verbs

As stated elsewhere, many Latin verbs shifted conjugations in Romance or were regularized and simplified, but as a whole the conjugation of the various tenses continued in forms patently derived from the original mother tongue, and with many of the same functions, uses, and meanings. Some were lost, or changed, and there were some new formations.

Of the indicative mood, the following tenses continued in modern form to fulfill functions similar to those in Latin: present, imperfect, past perfect (pluperfect), and perfect. (See Posner 146 ff.) The last, however, came to refer to a state or specific act in past time of limited duration, as contrasted to the imperfect. In its perfect sense (= "I have done") it was replaced by periphrastic constructions. The past perfect, or pluperfect, underwent changes in meaning and function in some languages and was itself largely replaced by a new compound formation. Other tenses (future, future perfect) disappeared in favor of new combinations. Some subjunctive tenses continued, but with restricted uses, others changed in function and meaning or were replaced by different modes of expression.

New Tense Formations

Compound Past

In most Romance languages a new compound past grew up and took over the "I-have-done" aspects of the Latin PERFECTUM. It developed from such phrases as CÉNAM PREPARÁTAM HÁBEO, that is, "I have supper prepared," lit., "in a having-been-prepared state." Early medieval examples regularly show agreement between noun and adjective, as in OFr. *Vedutes avons les dous serors* (= We have seen the two sisters) and OSp. *Auemos ueidas las dues hermanas.* Modern French, and to a certain extent Italian and Catalan, still show agreement when the noun or pronoun precedes the verb: Fr. *Je les ai vues* (= I have seen them), but *J'ai vu les deux soeurs* without agreement.[5] Interestingly enough, in colloquial French

---

5. Provençal also shows agreement in such cases: *E lauzet Dieu e'l grazi que l'avia la vida sostenguda* (= And he praised God and thanked him that he had sustained his life). For further examples, see any grammar of the individual languages.

this *passé composé* tense has itself replaced the original simple perfect or *passé défini* now reserved for formal speech and literature, thus coming linguistically full circle. Rhetian also uses the compound form as a simple past: *El ha quietau el cun* (= He hushed the dog).

Auxiliaries

The Iberian peninsula hesitated for a long time between HABÉRE and TENÉRE as the correct auxiliary to be used in this compound tense, Spanish finally settling on HABÉRE, and Portuguese TENÉRE: (Sp.) *Hemos preparado la cena,* (P.) *Temos preparado a ceia.* However, Spanish still uses *Tenemos preparada la cena* in the original sense of "We have the supper all ready, all cooked," with adjectival agreement of the past participle.

Since the original Classical Latin past participle was a perfect passive one, such a phrase as EST TERMINATUS (-UM) meant "It is having-been ended," or "It has been ended." An intransitive verb like VENÍRE obviously could not have a passive aspect, hence the past participle VÉNTUS, and its regularized Romance (= Vulgar Latin?) formations VENÍTUS, VENÚTUS had to mean "having come." For this reason the Medieval derivatives of EST VENÍTUS (-ÚTUS) (= is having come) came to mean "has come." Old Spanish and Old Portuguese, for example, at first participated in this development — *es venido (-a), e vindo (-a)* — but gradually settled for HABÉRE and TENÉRE respectively for all active forms of the compound tense: Sp. *ha venido, ha tomado,* P. *tem vindo, tem tomado* (= he has come, he has taken). French still uses the old construction for many intransitive verbs of motion and the like, likewise Italian and Rhetian: Fr. *Il est venu,* It. *è venuto.* These must show agreement: *elle est venue, è venuta* (= she has come). Italian wavers, however, using either *essere* or *avere* with some verbs, that is, *è salito, ha salito* (= he has gone up), whereas French would always say *il est monté.* But Italian does say *siamo stati* (= we have been), with agreement, while French says *nous avons été* (no agreement). Old Provençal also allowed some variation, such as *ac anat* (= he had gone) with *avere,* but in these examples with *venire,* the verb *essere* is used, and there is agreement: *Suy be vengutz?* (= Am I welcome?), *Cazutz sui en mala merce* (= I have fallen into (the) ill graces), *Girarz se levet, la n'es vengutz* (= Giraurt got up and came there). Because of the case system, which paralleled Old French, the agreement is not apparent in the following plural form: *Quant al monestier son vengut, amdui s'en intreron el cor* (= When they came to the monastery, both entered into the courtyard). Engadinian, like Italian, says *essans stos*

(= we have been), with verb "to be," and like both French and Italian shows agreement with a noun or pronoun object preceding a transitive verb: *l'avains visa*. Some Sursilvan examples are these: *Sia mumma ei vegnida immediat* (= His mama came [has come] at once), *Cu eis el vegnius miers?* (= How did he get [come] bitten?).[6] French and Italian also use the verb "to be" with all reflexive verbs: Fr. *Je lui ai dit que non* (= I told her no); It. *Avevi promesso di scrivermi* (= You had promised to write me); but Fr. *Je me suis dit que non* (= I told myself no); and It. *Mi ero promessa di scriverti* (= I had promised myself to write you). Spanish, Portuguese, Catalan, and Romanian do not participate in this usage. For Sardinian, see below.

Catalan has a still different periphrasis very commonly used instead of the simple preterite. It consists of the present indicative of the verb *anar* (= to go) plus the infinitive of the basic verb of action: *vaig cantar* = "I sang," *vam treballar* = "we worked," *van dir* = "they said" (lit., "I go to sing," "we go to work,"). When the preposition *a* precedes the infinitive, the whole becomes the usual approximate future, just as in the other languages: "we are going to work," and so on.

Spanish and Portuguese not only have two verbs "to have," as shown in examples above, but also two verbs for "to be" from Latin ÉSSE x SEDÉRE (= to be, to sit) and STÁRE (= to stand). They have a variety of uses based on the distinction of "permanence, inherent quality, action," as opposed to "temporariness, state, or position." The two languages are not always parallel, yet a few examples should suffice to illustrate some of the differences: Sp. *El rey fué muerto por los insurgentes* (= The king was killed by the rebels [action]), and *El rey ya estaba muerto al llegar los insurgentes* (= The king was already dead when the rebels arrived [state]); Sp. *El tejado está cubierto con tejas* and P. *O telhado é coberto com telhas* (= The roof is covered with tiles [note difference]); but Sp. *El tejado está cubierto de nieve* and P. *O telhado está coberto de neve* (= ... covered with snow [same auxiliary]). Spanish does say, however, as in first example (*El rey ...*) above, *El tejado fué cubierto con tejas*, indicating the action of covering rather than the state. For place or position, whether temporary or not, Spanish will use *estar*, Portuguese usually *ser* if thought of as permanent: Sp. *¿Dónde está la biblioteca?* P. *Onde é a biblioteca?* (= Where is the library [located]?) Older Spanish said *Pablo es muerto* (= Paul is dead), nowadays *Pablo está muerto* (considered as a state, the result of the action of dying). Today, *Pablo es muerto* means "Paul is a dead man," that is, *muerto* is a noun. There are many other special distinctions, too numerous to go

6. For further Rhetian examples, see Posner 160.

into here, such as *ser* for all passives, *estar* with present participles (both languages), and so on. Besides *essere*, Italian also has *stare*, with similar uses to the above, but much more restricted and less common: *Sta cantando* (= She is singing), *Sta bene!* (= OK!) See grammars of these languages.

Other auxiliaries are commonly used as substitutes of verbs "to be," particularly when motion is indicated: Sp. *Viene cantando* (= He is singing); *Don Pablo andaba luchando con todos* (= Don Pablo went about [was] fighting with everybody); *Ya queda hecho* (= It's already done). In Rhetian, for example, the passive voice (or state) may use *star*, *essere*, or *gnir* (Engadinian), as in *Illa Biblia sta que escrit* (= In the Bible it is written), *Il cudesch füt escrit* (or *gnit escrit*) *sainza agüd de ningün* (= The book was written without anyone's help).

Sardinian also has compound tenses with auxiliaries "to have" and "to be," as well as past participial agreement like that in the preceding examples from other languages. A few samples of usage should suffice.

Luke 2:6, 7, 16 (Cagliaitan):

1. Maria, sa femina chi ddi *fiat estetia* sposada [Note agreement of *estetia*].
2. E *fiat suççediu* [And it "was" happened], mentras fiant [they were] inni, chi si *fiat cumpliu* [refl.] su tempus de partoriri.
3. E issa *hiat partoriu* [gave birth = pluperf. "had"?] su fillu suu primigeniu.
4. E *fiant andaus* [were gone: agreement] de pressi et *hiant agatau* [had found: no agreement] a Maria e a Giuseppi e a su pipieddu.

Matt. 2:2, 10, 18 (Logudorese):

1. *Hamus bidu* s'istella sua in s'oriente, et *semus bennidos* a lu adorare [have seen — no agreement; are come — agreement].
2. Bidende pero s'istella, *si sunt allegrados* cum gosu meda mannu [reflexive with "to be" and agreement].
3. E totus si *fiant maravigliaus* de is cosas chi fianta nadas a issus [refl. with "to be" and agreement].

Pluperfect

Based on the same compound perfect, a new pluperfect (past perfect) was formed throughout most of the Romance area. It is composed of the imperfect of the auxiliary HABÉRE or TENÉRE, plus the past participle. Spanish, French, Provençal, Italian, Catalan use HABÉRE, whereas Portuguese also has TENÉRE (*ter*)*: Sp. *No lo había sabido*, Fr. *Je ne l'avais pas su*, Pr. *Non l'avia saüput*, It. *Non l'avevo saputo*, C. *No l'havia* *sabut*, P. *Não o tinha sabido* or *Não o havia sabido* (= I had not known it). Portuguese also has the direct descendant from the Latin pluperfect in the simple form, that is, *Não o soubera* (< VL. *SAPÚERAM). Either of the compound tenses, however, is preferred to the simple form, the one with *ter* being the colloquial favorite. Old Spanish also had this simple pluperfect form, but it had early become an alternate simple past equivalent to *supe*, the preterite, namely, *supiera*, "I knew, I learned." In time, because of its frequent use in conditional sentences, it became the equivalent of the imperfect subjunctive (< L. pluperfect subjunctive) and even the new conditional tense itself (see below). Today it is recognized and classified as an imperfect *-ra* subjunctive alternate to the *-se* form. The old preterite use, however, is still found, particularly in South America. Catalan also has this *-ra* as well as the *-se* subjunctive form. Romanian differs from the other languages in having retained a simple form of the pluperfect indicative apparently derived from the Latin pluperfect subjunctive: *cântasem* (= I had sung).[7]

Future

The Classical Latin future indicative, for one reason or another, was also replaced by various periphrases which in some cases coalesced into simple forms. The commonest was a combination of HABÉRE and the infinitive, as HÁBEO CANTÁRE, "I have to sing" (= I will sing), sometimes in conjunction with a preposition, as HÁBEO AD CANTÁRE, HÁBEO DE CANTÁRE. In most of the Romance territory, the word order regularly adopted was CANTÁRE HÁBEO, so that the forms eventually combined into one unit based on the infinitive stem, plus an abbreviated set of endings: It. *canterò* Sp. C. *cantaré*, P. *cantarei*, Fr. je *chanterai*, Rh. *c(h)antero*, *c(h)antera*, Pr. *cantarai*. Both Old Spanish and Old Portuguese regularly divided the two elements with an intervening atonic pronoun object, and Portuguese still does so today: OSp. *cantar-lo-e*, P. *cantâ-lo-ei*. Nowadays, the object pronoun *must* (and in Portuguese *may*) precede the future verb, as *lo cantaré*, *o cantarei*. An alternate choice of *he de cantar*, *hei-de cantar* still retains some of the original "must" flavor, but in its sense of strict necessity has been supplanted by Sp. P. *tengo que . . . , tenho que cantar*, and P. *tenho de cantar* (= I have to sing). Sardinian also has adopted "must" constructions for its future: *deppo cantare*. (= I must

7. An alternate past perfect, variously called *preterite perfect, past anterior*, etc. developed as a parallel construction, using the preterite of the auxiliary. Its usage is very much restricted today. Examples are: Pr. *ac anat, ac dich*, Sp. *hubo ido, hubo dicho*, Fr. *il fut allé, il eut dit* (= he had gone, he had said), etc.

sing) and *ap (hapo) a cantare* (= I have to sing). The *a* is sometimes missing: *Custu . . hat essiri su signali: heis agatai a su pipiu . . .* (This will be the sign: you will find the child . . .).

Another very widespread periphrasis, often called the "approximate future," is the English-type phrase "I am going to . . ." which in Catalan, as we have seen, expresses a past event. Other languages have *Je vais chanter* (Fr.), *voy a cantar* (Sp.), *vou cantar* (P.), *vo a cantare* (It.).[8] Rhetian also can say *Nus giain* (inf. *ir*) *a chantar* (Engadinian) (= We are going to sing), but more commonly uses the verb "to come" in this construction: *Eu gnarà a chantar* (= I will be coming to sing); *Eu vegn a chantar* (= I am coming to sing) (Engadinian); and *Jeu vengel a cantar* (Sursilvan). On the other hand, Romanian (like English) adopted the verb "to want, wish" for its standard future: *voiu cântà* (L. VÓLO CANTÁRE),[9] and also has a subjunctive construction, *am sa cînt* (*cânt*) (= I have that I [should] sing).

Conditional

Throughout most of the western Romance territory, a new tense — the conditional, or past future — was formed, using the future as a model, but with imperfect indicative endings: Fr. *chanterais*, Sp. P. C. Pr. *cantaría* = "I should (would) sing." Like the future, this tense could often be divided in Old Spanish and still can today in Portuguese, *cantar-lo-ia, cantá-lo-ia*, as well as be expressed with *había (havía) de* + infinitive. For this tense Italian differs, adding to the future stem a special set of endings taken from the preterite (past definite) of *avere: -ei, -esti, -ebbe, -emmo, -este, -ebbero*. Romanian differs still further in the formation of its conditional by using a periphrasis derived probably from two past subjunctive tenses of HABERE: *aş, ai, ar, am, aţi, ar* + the infinitive, as for example *aş face* (= I would do . . .). Compare Engadinian, which uses pluperfect subjunctives in both parts of conditional sentences: *Scha eau avess . . . schi dessi . . .* (= If I had . . . , I would give . . .). In most of the Romance languages, compound tenses of the conditional also exist in "I would have sung" forms.

Conditional Sentences

Conditional sentences have developed along different lines in individual languages, with most of them using the new conditional tense in the apodosis

8. Catalan can also say *vaig a cantar*, with preposition. Not to be confused, however with the preterite *vaig cantar!* (See sec. 2.)

9. Cf. English "I will sing."

or conclusion, and various forms of the subjunctive in the protasis (= if clause or condition), in contrary to fact sentences. The complete set of combinations (future more vivid, future less vivid, and so on) is too involved to treat adequately in a short space. For individual languages, see specific grammars. A few samples of one type of condition (contrary to fact in present time) will serve to illustrate the wide range of possibilities:

1. English: If I had enough money, I would buy it.
2. French: Si j'*avais* assez d'argent, je l'*achèterais* (imperfect indicative + conditional).
3. Spanish: Si *tuviese* (*tuviera*) bastante dinero, lo *compraría* (*comprara*) (-*se* or -*ra* imperfect subjunctive + conditional or -*ra* subjunctive).
4. Portuguese: Se *tivesse* bastante dinheiro, *comprá-lo-ia* (*comprava-o*) (imperfect subjunctive + conditional or imperfect indicative).
5. Italian: Se *avesse* abbastanza dinaro, lo *comprerei* (imperfect subjunctive + conditional).
6. Romanian: Dacă *aş avea* destul bani, *aş cumpăra-*o (conditional + conditional).
7. Catalan: Si *tingués* bastant diner, ho *compraria* (imperfect subjunctive + conditional).
8. Rhetian (Sursilvan): (a) Sch'il buob *havess* da murir . . . (= If the boy were to die , , , [future less vivid type, conclusion unexpressed]); (b) Ella *havess* bein saviu proteger il buob . . . (= *She* would sure have known how to protect the boy . . . [contrary to fact type, condition unexpressed] imperfect subjunctive in both types of clauses.[10]

Subjunctives

The Latin subjunctive has continued to the present day as a highly useful mood in Romance, with many of the same functions. In the Medieval stages, usage throughout the entire area was remarkably consistent, but the modern tongues have diverged somewhat from each other, and Romanian has even increased subjunctive use at the expense of the infinitive.[11]

One new function of the subjunctive is the expression of emotion in subordinate clauses, a use that had its origin in Latin clauses of fear, < TÍMEO NE (= I fear lest . . .) and other verbs of the type. The vestige of the Latin construction is seen in the pleonastic *ne* still used occasionally

---

10. Note that both clauses use subjunctive, as in this Engadinian sentence: *Eu füss gnü, sch'eu avess pudii* (= I would have come, if I had been able). See Conditional discussion above.

11. Cf. modern Greek, where the infinitive has been entirely displaced.

in French *Je crains qu'il (ne) meure* (= I am afraid he will die [may he not do so!]). From fear, the subjunctive came to express any emotion (or attitude), even when dealing with facts: Fr. *Je regrette que vous soyez malade* (= I am sorry that you are sick), Sp. *¡Qué buena suerte que ella no se haya caído!* (= How lucky she didn't fall!), Rm. *Bine au făcut să-i scrie* (= They did well to write him), P. *Fico contente que não venha* (= I'm glad he isn't coming), and so on.

Wishes and commands, doubt and uncertainty, are regularly expressed in the subjunctive, although there are some national differences: Sp. *Dudo (quiero) que llueva*, P. *Duvido (quero) que chova*, It. *Dubito (voglio) che piova* (= I doubt it will rain, I want it to rain); but the verb "to hope" governs the subjunctive in Spanish and Italian, the future indicative in French and (usually) in Portuguese: Sp. *Espero que llueva*, It. *Spero che piova;* Fr. *J'espère qu'il pleuvra*, P. *Espero que choverá*. Compare also Rm. *Sper că va veni* (= I hope he will come [ind.]).[12]

Some examples of various Rhetian subjunctive uses are: *Jeu vuless veser in' autra stanza* (= I'd like to see another room) (Sursilvan), *Meis bap voul ch'eu finischa mia lecziun* (= My father wants me to finish my lesson) (Engadinian), *Id ais necessari cha tü scrivast subit a teis frar* (= You must write your brother right away) (Engadinian), *Jeu havevel tema che la vipra hagi miers mei* (= I was afraid that the snake would bite me) (Sursilvan), *Pover Marco nu savaiva sch'el stuvesse crider u surrir* (= Poor Marco did not know whether he should laugh or cry) (Engadinian).

Time clauses referring to the future fall under the category of uncertainty. In French, Catalan, Italian they take the future indicative: Fr. *Quand tu y arriveras, sois sûr de m'écrire*, (= When you arrive there, be sure to write me), C. *Quan arribaràs . . .* , It. *Quando arriverai . . . .* The other languages use subjunctives: Sp. *Cuando llegues*, P. *Quando chegares* (future subjunctive), and so on. The future subjunctive, used by Portuguese here and in other types of clauses, has largely disappeared elsewhere. Yet when referring to actual events or situations, these time clauses regularly use the indicative, for example, Sp. *Cuando llegaron, fueron en seguida al hotel* (= When they arrived, they went immediately to the hotel). One type of temporal conjunction, however, is almost invariably followed by the subjunctive: Fr. *avant que*, Sp. P. *antes que*, It. *prima che*, Pr. *ans que*, all meaning "before." Rhetian seems to be an exception, as in this Sursilvan example: *Savessen ins buca far enzatgei avon ch'il miedi arriva?* (= Isn't

---

12. This probably uses indicative to make the "wish" more likely. Cf. the subjunctive of *Sper să fiu aicea mâine* (= I hope he will be here tomorrow [less probably?]). Romanian normally expresses uncertainty and emotion with subjunctive, but note indicative of *Îi păru rău că s'a făcut de râs* (= He regretted he had made himself the butt of laughter.)

there anything to do [we can do] before the doctor arrives [indicative]?).[13] Standard subjunctive constructions are like these: Fr. *Ils s'en sont allés avant que je sois arrivé pour les aider* (= They left before I arrived to help them), Sp. *No me dijeron nada antes que tú llegaras* (= They told me nothing before you arrived). Compare indicative of Sp. *hasta que tú llegaste* (= until you arrived). Examples from Provençal show both subjunctive and indicative: *E'n Guilhems no poc far ne dir tant qu'el pogues tornar en la grasia de madon' Alamanda* (= And Don Guilhems could do or say nothing until he could return into the favor of Milady Alamanda), *E lauzet Dieu e'l grazi que l'avia la vida sostenguda tro qu'el l'agues vista* (= And he praised God and thanked him that he had sustained his life until he had seen her), but compare *lo melhor trobador del mon tro que venc Guirautz de Bornelh* (= the best troubador in the world until along came Guirautz de Bornelh). The first example rightly has a subjunctive referring to a desired but as yet unfulfilled event, but the second (with subjunctive) refers to an accomplished fact, as does the third. Perhaps the emotional force of *lauzet* and *grazi* carries over into the subordinate clause. For other examples, see various grammars.

Sardinian shows some dialect differences in use of subjunctives, as illustrated by the following examples:

1. (Luke 2:1 [Cagl.]) . . . un edittu de Cesari Augustu, chi si *fazzesit* (impf. subj.) su contu de totus is abitantes de sa terra (expression of command).

2. (Luke 2:10 [Cagl.]) *Non timais* ("Be not afraid" — present subj. [negative command]).

3. (Matt. 2:8 [Log.]) *Andade* et *dimandade . . .* (impv. affirmative command; all dialects agree on use of impv.]).

4. (Matt. 2:8) Time and purpose clauses. Note that the two northern dialects (Sassarese and Tempiese) use the future indicative in the time clauses, the others (Logudorese and Cagliaitan) subjunctives, with all using subjunctives in the purpose clauses:

(Log.) . . . et da chi lu *dezis* incontrare, faghidemilu (impv.) ischire, a tales qui eo *ande* pro lu adorare.

(Cagl.) . . . e candu dd'*hapais* incontrau, feimiddu (impv.) sciri, po chi deu *bandi* a dd'adorai.

(Sass.) . . . e da chi l'*incuntrareddi*, feddimilu (impv.) sabbè, a tali chi eju puru *andia* par adurallu.

(Temp.) . . . e candu l'*aareti incuntrata* (= la criatura — note agreement), fetimillu (impv.) sapè, attalichì eu ancora *andia* par adorallu.

13. But, since the first conjugation of present indicative in Rhetian (Engadinian, at least,) is identical to subjunctive in third person (as in French), this is probably subjunctive, after all!

Contrary to expressions of doubt and uncertainty, verbs of certainty and affirmation (saying, thinking, believing, and the like) regularly take the indicative. In the older stages of the languages, however, many of them governed either mood, depending on the degree of certainty involved. A good example is this excerpt from the Old French romance, *Perlesvaus:* "Missire Gauvains esgarda le Graal, et li senble q'il *voie* [= subj.] une chandoile dedenz . . . et voit la pointe de la lance . . . , et li senble qu'il *voit* [= ind.] ·ii· angres . . ." (= Milord Gawain looked at the Grail, and he thinks he sees a candle therein [but he is not sure] . . . and he sees the point of the lance . . . and he thinks he sees two angels . . . [this time he is sure of it]).[14] Modern Italian preserves this distinction today with verbs of thinking and believing: *Credo que sia vero* (= I believe it is true [but I am not sure]). Rhetian (Engad.) has a similar construction after verbs of this type: *Il vestí da la giuvna, laschaiva supponer che eir ella saja turista* (= The clothing of the young girl led one to suppose that she also was [be] a tourist). As in this example just quoted, Rhetian (Engad.) may have been influenced by German in employing subjunctives in many subordinate clauses where indicatives would normally appear in other Romance languages — *Ingün nu savaiva dingionder ch'ella gniss e che ch'ella vuless* (No one knew whence she came or [and] what she wanted). Compare Fr. *Personne ne savait d'où venait-elle ni ce qu'elle voulait,* Sp. *Nadie sabía de dónde venía ella, ni lo que (qué) quería.* But, in the absence of a conditional tense in Rhetian, are we to accept these subjunctives as equivalent to the conditional of probability, namely, Fr. *viendrait, voudrait,* Sp. *vendría, querría* (= might she possibly be coming, might she possibly be wanting)? Note also that Spanish *-ra* subjunctive and *-ría* conditional are practically interchangeable, *¿Qué quisiera?* (What would you like?) being more common than *¿Qué querría?*

There are many other types of subjunctive uses, as in adjective phrases expressing uncertainty (a type, or characteristic) and nonexistence of a type (negative antecedent). A few samples will suffice: Pr. *Non troban cella ni cellui que non lur diga: "Deus vos sal!"* (= They do not find anyone [male or female] who does not say to them: "God keep you!"); Sp. *Lo que quieran, no me importa* (= Whatever they want doesn't matter to me [Cf. *Lo que quieren . . .* = What they really do want . . . (a definite thing, no uncertainty)]); Fr. *Nous cherchons un emploi qui nous fournisse occasion de voyager* (= We are looking for a job which will give us a chance to travel); Engad. *Eu nu cugnosch in quaist pajais ingün che sapcha il rumantsch* (= I am

14. *Le Haut Livre du Graal: Perlesvaus* (Chicago: University of Chicago Press, 1932), vol. 1, p. 119, vv. 2429–31. For a general overall view of subjunctive uses in Old French, see Davis.

unacquainted with anyone in this country who knows Rumantsch); *Muossa'm ün let, ingio che possa durmir* (= Show me a bed where I can sleep).

One peculiarly unique phrase in French which has long puzzled many philologists may not be a subjunctive at all: the traditional sentry's challenge *Qui vive?* (= Who goes there?). It has been suggested that this phrase came from contact with Italian soldiers during military campaigns and is a Gallicized version of Italian *Chi vi va?* (Ind. = Who there goes?).

Infinitives

The popular tendency has been to substitute other constructions for the subjunctive wherever possible, especially the infinitive. A Frenchman would be very unlikely to say today *Je crains que je ne puisse pas le faire* (= I fear I cannot do it), when he can say *Je crains ne pas pouvoir le faire;* nor will a Spaniard state *Quiero que lo haga yo* for *Quiero hacerlo* (= I want to do it). The same is true of all the Romance languages except Romanian, which has veered in the opposite direction. It says *Prefer să mă duc acasă* (= I prefer to go home); *Nu poate să facă astă* (= he cannot do this); *El vrea să vorbească* (= He wants to talk); and *Începuse să ningă* (= It began to snow) — all subjunctives. And yet Romanian says *Sper că va veni* (= I hope he will come) and *Cred că are dreptate* (= I believe he's right) with indicative.[15] The other Romance languages even prefer the infinitive in such "normally" indicative clauses as Sp. *Creí morir* (= I thought I would die); Fr. *Elle croyait s'évanouir de faim* (= She thought she would faint from hunger); It. *Credo l'avere trovato!* (= I believe I have found it!). And many expressions of command, permission, prohibition, and the like use an infinitive in lieu of the equally correct subjunctive: *No me permite hacerlo* instead of *No permite que lo haga* (= She does not allow me to do it); Fr. *Nous lui avons dit de revenir bientôt* for *Nous lui avons dit qu'il revienne bientôt* (= We told him to come back soon).

One special use of the infinitive is that expressing a command or wish. It is so used extensively in advertisements or public announcements, as in the Spanish *No fijar carteles* (= Post No Bills), *Dirigirse al apartado 259* (= Address Box 259). It is less personal than the imperative or subjunctive, and may be a shortened form of *Favor de no fijar*, and the like. Other languages can employ the infinitive for commands, notably Rhetian (Engad.), in which negative commands are regularly so expressed: Compare *Va a chasa!* (impv.), and *Ch'El giaja a chasa!* (polite, with subjunctive) (both = Go home!); but *Nun ir a chasa!* (= Don't go home! [inf.]).

15. See Posner 201, Seiver 79.

In addition, Portuguese has a so-called "personal infinitive," derived from the Latin imperfect subjunctive, with special endings for all persons except the first and third singulars. It is used to avoid ambiguity, as in *Ao chegarmos à cidade, veio uma tremenda chuvarada* (= As we reached the city, there came a tremendous downpour). Spanish handles this situation by adding a subject pronoun to the infinitive — *Al llegar nosotros a la ciudad, vino un tremendo chaparrón.*

In English a limited number of verbs take an infinitive without a preceding preposition (can, may, must, should, had better, dare not, need not, etc.). All the rest require *to* before the infinitive. In Romance it is not so simple: in French and Italian there is a long list of verbs using no preposition (such as "can," "wish," and the like), a longer list using *à* (*a*), and the rest using *de* (*di*, or *da*), with *pour* and *per* expressing "in order to" in purpose clauses. In Romanian, only a very few govern an infinitive directly, the remainder require *a*, sometimes combined with *de*. Catalan, like Sardinian, also has some without, others with *a*. On the other hand, both Spanish and Portuguese use a variety of prepositions, depending on the basic idea of the governing verb. Spanish particularly is very consistent, however, in using (with a few minor exceptions) the same preposition which would be used with a noun or pronoun, since the infinitive is in function essentially a verbal noun. English has another verbal noun, the gerund, which follows prepositions other than "to" (fond *of* fishing, determined *on* going [as well as determined *to* go]. But the Romance languages must depend on the infinitive for all such uses. There are no complete lists available for Spanish or Portuguese, although some very useful ones are found in Spaulding and Leonard, *Spanish Review Grammar;* and Ramsey-Spaulding, *A Textbook of Modern Spanish* (See Bibliography). The great Colombian philologist, Rufino José Cuervo, had begun an exhaustive study in Spanish, entitled *Diccionario de construcción y régimen,* a project cut short by his untimely death in 1911, so that only two volumes of this badly needed work were published. Some representative examples of government of infinitives follow:

French

Je ne *veux* pas y aller (= I don't want to go there).
It *faut* rentrer vite (= It is necessary to return quickly).
On *peut* le faire, oui (= They can do it, yes).
Nous *allons* acheter une maison (= We are going to buy a house).
Elle *a réussi à* trouver l'objet perdu (= She succeeded in finding the lost object).

Jean *a appris à* patiner (= John has learned to skate).

Il est très *difficile de* patiner (= It is very hard to skate).

Ce livre est très *difficile à* lire (= This book is very hard to read).

Les soldats ne leur *permettent* pas *d'*entrer tout de suite (= The soldiers do not allow them to go in at once).

Je *disais* aux enfants *de* fermer toujours la porte (= I was telling the children always to close the door).

Italian

Basta dirlo una volta (= It's enough to say it once).

Dovrò sorridere del alleviamento che senti (= He must have smiled at the relief he felt).

Già *sapeva* nuotare (= She already knew how to swim).

Voglio insegnarmi a nuotare (= I want to teach myself how to swim).

Finalmente, Carlo *arrivò a* studiare la musica (= Carlo finally got to study music).

Vi *prego di* aspettare (= I beg you to wait).

Mi *tocca di* finire il lavoro oggigiorno (= It is up to me to finish the work right today).

Impariamo a parlare inglese (= We are learning to speak English).

Romanian

Știĭ clădi casele? (= Do you know how to build the houses?)

N'*avea* cum scrie (= He had no way to write).

A început a ploua (= It started to rain).

Eștĭ *gata de a* asculta? (= Are you ready to listen?)

Au stat cu *gândul de a* mânca acuma (They have stayed with the idea of eating now).

Provençal

En Guilhems no *poc* far ne dir . . . (= Don Guilhems could do or say [nothing]). . . . per lo mal que la reina n'*auzi* dire (= . . . because of the evil which the queen heard about him).

Carles, lo reis, le *fez* a gran honor recebre (= Charles the King had him received with great honor).

E lo *fait a* saber a la comtessa Eleonore (= And he informed the Countess Eleanor of it).

La prumiera ley demostra a qui ha sen e raczon, ço *es a* conoiser e servir a Dio (= The first law shows [this] to him who has sense and reason, that is to know and serve God).

La segonda ley, que Dio done a Moysent, nos *ensegna a* temer Dio e servir lui (= The second law which God gives to Moses teaches us to fear God and serve him).

Mas la tercza ley nos *ensegna* amar Dio de bon cor (= But the third law teaches us to love God with good heart. Note lack of *a*).

Autra ley d'ayci enant non *deven* plus aver (= No other law henceforth shall they [must they] have further).

Spanish

No *queremos comenzar a* trabajar hasta mañana (= We don't want to start working until tomorrow).

Carlota *ha decidido* quedarse un rato (= Carlota has decided to remain a while).

Si Ud. *logra* conseguirlo, ¡bueno! (= If you succeed in getting it, fine!)

¡*Se me olvidó* decírselo! (I clean forgot to tell him so!)

Vamos a escoger un sitio nuevo (= Let's choose a new site).

No *se atreverían a* mencionarlo (= They wouldn't dare mention it).

Estamos *dispuestos a ayudarles a* colocarse (= We are ready to help them find a job).

No *deje de* visitar a Paris (= Don't fail to visit Paris)

Los dos *se olvidaron de* cambiar su dinero (= They both forgot to exchange their money).

Le *prometo tratar de* consultar un médico cuanto antes (= I promise you to try to consult a doctor as soon as possible).

Está para llover (= It's about to rain).

Quedan muy *impacientes por* conocerles (= They are very impatient to meet you).

La dama *insistió en* pagar la cuenta (= The lady insisted on paying the bill).

Siempre *soñé con* hacerlo y *cuento con* hacerlo, ¡cueste lo que cueste! (= I have always dreamed of doing it and I am counting on doing it, whatever the cost!)

Portuguese

Esperamos ir à lua um dia (= We hope [expect] to go to the moon some day).

Não *podem contar* fazê-lo sem dinheiro (= They cannot count on doing it without money).

O homem *desejou* falar com o senhor (= The man wanted to speak to you).

Sempre *receava* cair dum edifício alto (= I was always afraid of falling from a high building).

Você *vinha* ajudar-me? (= You were coming to help me?)

O trem *tardava a* chegar (= The train was late in arriving).

Lhes *convidamos a* (*para*) tomar algo (= We invite you to have something).

A aeromoça *appressou-se a* tranqüilizar os passageiros (= The stewardess hastened to calm the passengers).

Canso-me de reiterá-lo tantas vezes (= I'm tired of repeating it so many times).

Prefiro não *acusar*-lhe *de abrir* o pacote (= I prefer not to accuse him of opening the package).

As crianças *gostam de* brincar (= Children love to play).

Maria *esqueçou-se de* darnos a chave (= Mary forgot to give us the key).

Essa menina *acabará por* matar-se! (= That girl will end by killing herself!)

O jovem *hesitava em* interromper a conversa (= The young man hesitated to interrupt the conversation).

Senhor, *pedimos*-lhe *para* considerar ao menos uma alternativa (= Sir, we ask you to consider at least one alternative).

Catalan

Van caure (= They fell) (the periphrastic preterite).

La teva germana, l'*he sentida* cantar (= I've heard your sister sing).

Li *faré* lliurar les dues xicotes (= I'll make him set the two girls free).

Haig de sortir (= I have to leave).

Pensi a dir-ho de tant en tant (= Remember to say it from time to time).

En Pinotxo *començou a* correr com gos boig (= Pinocchio began to run like a crazy dog).

Què *deu anar a* fer? (= What do you suppose he's [must he be] going to do?).

Anaven allà *per a* interrogar-lo (= They were going there to question him).

Rhetian

Las steilas *antschet a* svaneir (= The stars begin to disappear). (Surm.)

Üna rouda da vent *fa* girar il motor (= A windmill makes the motor turn). (Engad.)

Que *po* esser la forza d'üna maschina vapur? (= What can the power of a steam engine be?). (Engad.)

La duonna Maria *cumainzet a* crider scu ün iffaunt (= Doña Maria began to cry like a child). (Engad.)

Giusep *vegn a* veser ella questa sera (= Joseph will see her this evening). (Surs.)

El *sesprova da* star en peis (= He tries to stand up). (Surs.)

Il buob *ei per* murir (= The boy is about to die!). (Surs.)

Ella dat *segn da* haver capiu (= She gives a sign that she has understood, a sign of having understood). (Surs.)

Sia mamma voul ch'ella finischa la charta *avant co* sortir (= Her mother wants her to finish the letter before going out). (Engad.)

Jeu *vuless* veser in' autra stanza (= I'd like to see another room). (Surs.)

Sin bab *vul* buca crer (= His father refused to believe [it]). (Surs.)

Giusep *ha* auter *da* far (= Joseph has other things to do). (Surs.)

Guarda be *da* nu perder il bigliet (= Take care not to lose the ticket). (Engad.)

Noss Pover Mario nu savaiva sch'el *stuvess* crider u surrir (= Our poor Mario did not know whether he should cry or laugh [smile]). (Engad.)

Probabel *vegn* jeu *a* murir en Svizra (= I shall probably die in Switzerland). (Surs.)

Sardinian

Enide a l'adorare (= Come and [= to] adore him). (Cagl.)

Su bambinu *es nadu pro* nos liberare (= The child is born, has been born, in order to free us). (Cagl.)

Totus *andànt a* faisì registrai (= They all went to be registered). (Cagl.)

... unu gosu mannu chi *hat a* teniri totu su populu (= a great joy which shall be to all people [which all the people will have]) (Cagl.)

E custu 'nd' *hat* essiri a bosu su signali (= And this shall be the sign [of it] to you). (Cagl.)

Semus *bennidos a* lu adorare, (Log.), Seus *benius a* dd'adorai (Cagl.), Semu *giunti par* adurallu (Sass.), Semu *vinuti a* adorallu (Temp.) (= We have come to adore him [Matt. 2:2]).

Heroides demandaiat . . . ue Christus *deveret* nascher (= Herod asked where Christ was to be born). (Log.)

Faghidemilu ischiri (Log.), *Feddimilu* sabbè (Sass.) (= Let me know [it]).

Hamus a exultare, et nos *hamus* allegrare cum tegus (= We will be glad, and rejoice in thee [with thee]). (Log.)

Is mandragoras *cumenzant a* fragai (The mandrakes begin to smell, be fragrant). (Cagl.)

Special Reflexive Uses

One of the most fascinating verbal aspects is the extensive use of reflexive verbs as a substitute for the passive (or middle) voice. Spanish is of particular interest in this respect. Then there is the "indefinite *se (si)*" type, as in Sp. *Aquí se está muy bien* (= One is very comfortable here) and It. *Si sta più freschi nella casa* (= We are cooler in the house).[16] The whole topic is much too important for a cursory glance here. Highly recommended is a recent study by Sandra S. Babcock, *The Syntax of Spanish Reflexive Verbs* (The Hague: Mouton, 1970).[17] While Spanish and Portuguese use the auxiliary "to have" (*haber* and *ter*) with compound tenses of reflexive verbs, even when the verb is intransitive (e.g., *se ha ido, tem-se ido* = she has gone away), French and Italian employ the verb "to be" with all reflexives in compound tenses, in addition to its use with nonreflexive intransitives (see above): Fr. *Elle s'en est allée*, It. *Se ne è andata* (= She has gone away); and Fr. *Elles se sont lavées*, It. *Si sono lavate* (= They washed themselves). It is very possible that this construction developed in these two languages as a substitute descendant of the Latin middle voice, which was identical in form with the Latin passive. If so, the use of *être* and *essere* as the auxiliaries would have a logical explanation.

Every language has its own special tense and modal uses besides the general ones listed above. A complete comparative list would require volumes. The reader should therefore consult specific studies for each language of interest to him.

16. For such constructions, French has the indefinite *on* (< HÓMO; cf. German *man*.)

17. *Hispania* has had many articles dealing with reflexive constructions in Spanish, among them the following: T. B. Irving, "The Spanish Reflexive and the Verbal Sentence," *Hispania* vol. 35, no. 8 (Aug. 1952), 305–9; John Robert Smitz, "The *Se Me* Construction: Reflexive for Unplanned Occurrences," *Hispania*, vol. 49, no. 3 (Sept. 1966), 430–33; J. C. Davis, "The *Se Me* Construction: Some Comments," *Hispania*, vol. 50. no. 2 (May 1967), 322–23; Anthony G. Lozano, "Non-Reflexivity of the Indefinite *se* in Spanish," *Hispania* vol. 53, no. 3 (Sept. 1970), 453–57; J. C. Davis, "More on Indefinitive *Se*," *Hispania* vol. 55, no. 2 (May 1972), 312–13.

§3. Word and Sentence Order

Because of its case system, Latin enjoyed a flexible word order which permitted almost any position of elements within the sentence. The artificial sentence MATER MEA SUS MALA EST has often been quoted to show how an abnormal (but possible) sentence order could lead to confusion. Without the diacritical long mark on ĒST, the sentence seems to read "My mother is a bad pig," rather than the correct "Mother, a pig is eating my apples." Granted this is a queer sentence, even for Latin, and normally case endings easily differentiate subjects from objects. The classical order of HELÉNA PAÚLUM VÍDIT (= Helen sees Paul), the order favored by Caesar and Cicero in their writings, was replaced, however, as the "normal" word order in Romance by HELÉNA VÍDIT PAÚLUM. Hence we have (with loss of cases) Fr. *Hélène voit Paul*,[18] C. *Elena veu en*[19] *Pau*, It. *Elena vede Paolo*. But Spanish, Sardinian, and Romanian, and to a lesser extent nowadays, Portuguese, indicate the direct object noun (for animate beings) with a preposition equivalent to the old Latin accusative case: Sp. *Elena ve a Pablo*, Rm. *Elena vede pe Pavel*, P. *Elena vê* (*a*) *Paulo*. This allows for great variety in sentence order and rhythm: Sp. *A Pablo ve Elena, Ve a Pablo Elena, Ve Elena a Pablo*, and so on.

This flexible word order enjoyed by some of these languages permits emphasis upon special items by position within the sentence, or what has rightly been called rhythmic stress. The same factor holds good for adjective-noun position.[20] Most grammars ignore this basic criterion of stress and list various categories of adjective position such as "affective," "stylistic," "distinctive," "nondistinctive," "inherent," "inseparable," "quality," "literal," "figurative," and so on. All of this categorizing is unnecessary if one keeps in mind that in general "whichever is more important, for the speaker's meaning, comes last" (Robert K. Spaulding and Irving A. Leonard, *Spanish Review Grammar* [New York: Henry Holt and Co., 1945], sec. 38). There are some notable exceptions, of course, such as

18. Because of their preservation of a simplified case system, both Old French and Old Provençal could still enjoy a flexible word order.

19. *En* is the special form of *el* used as the article before a masculine name beginning with a consonant.

20. For comprehensive studies of word order, see J. C. Davis, "Rhythmic Stress in Spanish," *Hispania*, vol. 37, no. 4 (Dec. 1954), pp. 460–65; "Adjective Position in French," *University of South Florida Language Quarterly* (*USFLQ*), vol. 6, nos. 3–4 (Spring-Summer 1968), pp. 2–6; "Variability in Portuguese Word Order," *Hispania*, vol. 51, no. 3 (Sept. 1968), pp. 469–72; G. T. Fish, "Adjectives Fore and Aft: Position and Function in Spanish," *Hispania*, vol. 44, no. 4 (Dec. 1961), 700–708.

French adjectives *bon, joli*, and the like, which regularly precede, as well as specialized adjectives (numerals, demonstratives, etc.), but the general rule applies in most cases. Spanish examples:

mi amigo (my *friend*)	*amigo mío* (*my dear* friend)
una gran casa (a large *house*)	*Casa Grande* (*Big* House)
la blanca nieve (white *snow*)	*la Casa Blanca* (the *White* House)

Italian is well known for its use of the definite article with possessive adjectives, as in *la sorella mia* (= my sister; in origin "that sister of *mine*"). This was once common practice in Romance and is still a matter of choice in Portuguese: (*a*) *minha irmã*, the use with the article being rather stilted, formal style. In direct address, however, the article is not used. But, compare Sardinian in these examples from the Bible, most of them from "The Song of Songs": *sa çittadi sua* (his city, i.e., the his city), *sa binza mia* (my vineyard), *s'estimaddu meu* (my beloved); but *sorri nosta* (Cagl.), *sorre nostra* (Log.), while Sassarese and Tempiese have *la noltra suredda, la nostra suredda* (= our sister). In the samples where the possessive adjectives follow, they carry the stress.

And numerals also may follow, with increased stress: Sp. *por primera vez* (= for the first *time*) and *por vez primera* (= for the *first* time). Many similar examples can be cited for other languages. Thus, correct adjective-noun position can usually be determined (or interpreted where encountered in the foreign idiom) by the stress in English: P. *Hei perdido êsse nôvo chapéu!* (= I've lost that new *hat!*), *êsse chapéu nôvo!* (= that *new* hat). Even in the case of the specialized French adjectives *bon, joli*, and the rest, a postposition carries extra stress: *C'est là une très jolie femme* (= That's a very pretty *woman*), *C'est là une femme très jolie* (= That's a *very pretty* woman). Postposition can even turn an indefinite adjective like Spanish *alguno* (= some) into a strong negative: Sp. *En el baño no llevamos ropa alguna* (= In the bath we wear *no* clothes *at all*). Rebecca Posner states (p. 173) in regard to emotive and stylistic inversion that a change of order brings into relief the element of the sentence that is to be stressed, and she gives examples: Fr. *Vint la guerre* (= *Then* came the war); Sp. *No quiero yo el caballo* (= *I* don't want the horse); and Italian *Gran destino è il mio* (= *Mine* is a great destiny). But she misses the point when she says that "in Romance the verb tends to gravitate to the second 'strong position' in the sentence," and that "when the phrase begins with a 'strong word,' like an adverb, the subject is *relegated* (italics ours) to a postverbal position." In reality, there is a double stress in such sentences as Rm. *Aşa ere frate-mieu* (= *Thus* was my *brother*, or "*That's* what *my brother* was like) and

Sp. *Entonces se comenzó el juego* (= *Then* began the *game*), while the verb is merely a pivot (with meaning, but no real stress) about which the other elements swing. But note the unusual verbal emphasis produced by inversion of *No tiene casa* (= He doesn't have a *house*) to *Casa no tiene* (= He doesn't *have* a house) with the verb in final strong position. Professor Posner goes on to say that emphasis is not always very great or important, and cites an example heard often by her in Romania — *Bere numai avem* (= There is no beer left) — with the comment "Emphatic no doubt . . . but not of great stylistic content!" Many authorities on stylistics would disagree, notably Professor Edmund Epstein of Southern Illinois University (Carbondale), an expert in the field, who edits the journal, *Language and Style,* and believes that *any* departure from so-called "normal" style becomes a matter of stylistics.[21]

The order of atonic objective pronouns also is governed by the principle of rhythmic stress, which in Medieval times did not allow such unstressed pronouns to begin a sentence because the initial position was a strong one. This accounts for the present-day difference in word order of affirmative and negative commands: Fr. *Dites-moi, Ne me dites pas;* Sp. *Dígame, No me diga* (= Tell me, Don't tell me). Until recent times, the order *Dijéronmelo* (= They told me so) was also the normal one in Spanish and the other languages: OIt. *vedolo* (= I see it), ORm. *rogu-te* (= I beg you; archaic, but still in use today); see Grandgent, *Latin to Italian,* sec. 171. Portuguese still says *disse-lho* (= I told him so). Present participles usually require postposition: Rm. *dându-mi,* Sp. *dándome,* It. *dandomi* (= giving me), but Fr. *en me donnant* with the pronoun sheltered behind the stronger preposition *en* in initial position, resulting in a strong-weak-strong rhythm. Rules for position of pronouns which are objects of infinitives differ nowadays from language to language, but are based in origin on the same principle of rhythmic stress.

Representative samples of varying sentence word order in Sardinian are the following from the biblical *Song of Songs:*

"Thy name is an ointment poured forth" (1:2).

1. Ozu ispartu est su nomen tou. [Log.]
2. Su nomini tuu est coment'un ollu chi si ghettat appizzus. [Cagl.]
3. Ozu ilpaltu è lu to'innomu. [Sass.]
4. Ociu spaltu è lu to'innomu. [Temp.]

---

21. Inversion is a regular feature of Rhetian, particularly when an emphatic adverb begins the sentence (Germanic influence?), as in this sentence: *Alura sortit el da la chambra* (= Then he left the room [Engadinian]).

"My beloved is like a roe [or a young hart]" (2:9).

1. Simile est s'estimadu meu ad unu crabolu. [Log.]
2. S'amigu miu est simili a una craba. [Cagl.]
3. Lu me'iltimaddu è simili a un crabbolu. [Sass.]
4. Lu me'istimatu è simiddanti a un capriolu. [Temp.]

"The watchmen that go about the city found me" (3:3).

1. M'hant incontradu sas guardias, qui custodiant sa cittade. [Log.]
2. M'hanti incontrau is arundas chi costodiant sa cittade. [Cagl.]
3. M'incuntresini li patrugli, chi iltazini a gualdia di la ziddai. [Sass.]
4. M'incuntresini li sintinelli, chi stani a gualdia di la citai. [Temp.]

There are many other grammatical items of interest to the serious student, who is urged to consult various authorities in each language field. See Bibliography.

Appendixes
Selected Bibliography
Index

Appendix A

Linguistic Puzzle

This word in its original, learned form has survived in most Romance tongues (+ English), with more or less its original meaning. Italian, however — for once — went "popular" and (by apheresis) came up with *spedale*. Its shortened, popular form (< French — the French being more "hospitable" than most peoples?), with an extension of meaning and use to include all those in need or weary, not merely those seriously ill, has spread from them to other nations. Now you'll find them all around the globe. Young persons hiking or cycling through Europe are especially grateful for one in its older French form, with one more letter in its spelling.

Using the Italian word as a basis, deduce the answers to the following questions:

1) What is the Latin etymon?

2) The earlier French (and English) form?

3) The modern, universal word (5 letters)?

4) What *one* letter shows that this word is borrowed from French (that is, could not be Spanish, Italian, or Portuguese in derivation)?

5) Why did the middle consonant not voice?

Appendix B

Comparative Passages: French, Italian, Romanian, Spanish, Portuguese, Catalan

Note that in the following passages and equivalent parallel translations, constructions differ somewhat.

French Original

Aujourd'hui, nous allons à la banque. Pourquoi? N'as-tu pas assez de dollars? J'entends dire que tu as besoin d'argent. Qui n'a pas besoin d'argent? Où est située la banque? Cette banque-ci fait de bonnes affaires (= beaucoup d'affaires). Qui est cette demoiselle avec le jeune homme américain des États-Unis? Je ne sais pas. Elle est petite mais très belle, n'est-ce pas? Tout le monde (= tous) parle d'elle.

Au printemps il pleut beaucoup. En été les jours sont longs, mais en hiver, courts. Quand il fait beau temps, je vais à la campagne. Dis-moi, je te prie, ce que (laquelle) tu veux, une cravate bleue ou une cravate jaune? C'est ici la chemise de mon frère. Quel jour est aujourd'hui? Aujourd'hui est vendredi et demain est samedi. Je dois aller à l'épicerie.

Italian Version

Oggi andiamo alla banca. Perchè? Non hai sufficenza di dolari? Sento dire (Odo) che hai bisogno di danaro. Chi non ha bisogno di danaro? Dov'è situata la banca? Questa banca fa molti affari. Chi è quella signorina col giovane americano degli Stati Uniti? Non so. È piccola ma molto formosa (bella), non è ver'? Tutti parlano di ella.

Nella primavera piove molto. Nell'estate i giorni sono lunghi ma nel inverno corti. Quando fa bel tempo, vado alla campagna. Dimmi ti prego ciò che (che cosa) vuoi, una cravatta azzurra, od una cravatta gialla? Questa è la camicia del mio fratello. Che giorno (quale giorno) è oggi? Oggi è venerdì e domani è sabato. Devo andare alla spezieria.

154

Romanian Version

Astăzĭ mergem la bancă. Pentruce? Nu ai destui dolarĭ? Aud că ai nevoe de banĭ. Cine nu are nevoe de banĭ? Unde-i situată banca? Banca asta face multe afacerĭ. Cine-i domnişoara aceia cu tânărul american din Statele-Unite? Nu ştiu. E mică dar foarte frumoasă, nu-i aşa? Toată lumea vorbeşte de ea. Primăvara plouă mult. Vara zilele sunt lungĭ iar iarna scurte. Când timpu-i frumos mă duc la ţară. Spune-mi vă rog ce doriţĭ, o cravată alabastră sau o cravată galbenă? Asta e cămaşa fratelui. Ce zi e astăzĭ? Astăzĭ e vinerĭ şi mâine e sâmbătă. Trebue să mă duc la băcănie.

Spanish Original

Trayéndome el libro, él cayó. Su humor me divierte. Tu hermano te busca. Este clima es frío; no puedo acomodarme a él. Ella reía y lloraba a la vez. Cantaba bella y dulcemente. Si hace viento no saldremos. No nos veremos mañana .... ¡Mañana no nos veremos! Dile al pintor que venga.

Portuguese Version

Trazendo-me o livro, êle caiu. O seu humor me diverte. O teu irmão te procura. Êste clima é frio; não posso acomodar-me a êle. Ela ria e chorava ao mesmo tempo. Cantava bela e docemente. Se fizer vento (estiver, está ventando) não sairemos. Não nos veremos amanhã .... Amanhã não nos veremos! Dize-lhe ao pintor que venha.

Catalan Version

Tot portant-me el llibre ell va caure. El seu humor em diverteix. El teu germà et busca. Aquest clima és fret; no m'hi puc acostumar. Ella reia i plorava alhora. Ella cantava bellament i dolça. Si fa gens de vent, no sortirem. No ens veurem demà .... Demà no ens veurem pas! Digues al pintor que vingui.

Appendix C

Proverbs and Folk Sayings

Proverbs and other folk sayings are often the best source of linguistic material, since they reveal the common idiom of the people. Many are widespread, and invite comparison in various languages.

> Mătrăgună, mătrăgună
> Mărită-mă peste-o lună
> De nu 'n asta, 'n cealălaltă,
> Mărită-mă după olaltă.

> Mandragora, mandragora
> See that I'm married by this day next month,
> If you can't by then, then as soon as possible,
> Anyway, just get me a husband!

Magical verses chanted by Romanian women as they gather the mandrake root, said to have the power to arrange marriages and promote fertility, among other things.

Among some better-known proverbs are the following:

At night, all cats are grey
  La nuit tous les chats son gris (Fr.)
  De noche los gatos todos son pardos (Sp.)
  De noite todos os gatos são pardos (P.)
Crows do not peck out each other's eyes
  Les corbeaux ne crêvent pas les yeux aux corbeaux (Fr.)
  Crobu cun crobu no si tirad ogu (Sard.)
  Corvi con corvi non si cavan gli occhi (It.)
Don't look a gift horse in the mouth
  A caval donato non guardar in bocca (It.)
  À cheval donné, il ne faut point regarder à la bouche (Fr.)
  A caballo dado no le miren el diente (Sp.)
Good wine needs no bush
  El buen vino la venta trae consigo (Sp.)
  El vino bueno no ha menester pregonero (Also Sp.)

156

À bon vin, point d'enseigne (Fr.)
A buon vino non bisogna frasca (It.)
O bom vinho não ha mester ramo (P.)
No woman is ugly if she is well dressed
  Compuesta, no hay mujer fea (Sp.)
  Bem toucada não ha mulher feia (P.)
Silence lends consent
  Quien calla, otorga (Sp.)
  Qui ne dit mot consent (Fr.)
  Chi tace acconsente (It.)
Silence is golden
  Bouche serrée, mouche n'y entre (Fr.)
  En boca cerrada no entra mosca (Sp.)
  Em boca cerrada não entra mosca (P.)
  In bocca chiusa non c'entran mosche (It.)
Where there's a will there's a way
  A chi vuole, non mancano modi (It.)
  Donde hay gana hay maña (Sp.)
Who knows nothing doubts nothing (or *Ignorance is bliss*)
  Chi niente sa di niente dubita (It.)
  Nada duvida quem não sabe (P.)

Readings in Provençal, Sardinian, Catalan, Romanian

Provençal

"Guirautz de Bornelh"

Vertatz es qu'en Guirautz de Bornelh amava una domna de Gasconha, que era apelada n'Alamanda. Fort era prezada e de sen e de valor e de beutat, e sofria los precs d'en Guiraut per lo gran enansamen qu'el li fazia, e per los bos chantars qu'el fazia de lei, on ela se delechava fort per so c'om be los entendia. E ilh se defendet da lui ab paraulas e ab promesas mout cortezamen, que anc no ac da lei mas u sol gan, don el visquet lonc temps joios. Mas pois n'ac gran tristesa e dolor, car el lo perdet. E can madon' Alamanda o saup, ela lo blasmet e repres fort del gan, dizen que mal l'avia gardat e que mais no li daria alcu joi ni esper da lei alcun endrech d'amor e que tot so qu'ela li avia promes li desmandava, car be vezia que trop s'era lonhatz da so comandamen. E can Guiratz auzic lo comjat, el fo fort dolens e iratz, e venc s'en a una donsela que era apelada Alamanda atresi com sa domna. Aquesta donsela era fort corteza e savia e sabia be trobar e entendre e sabia letras. E li contet so que sa domna li avia dich, e li demandet coselh en sieu chantar qui es escritz en aquest libre e comensa aisi: "Sius quer coselh, bel' ami' Alamanda . . . ." E'n Guirautz no poc far ne dir tan qu'el pogues tornar en la grasia de madon' Alamanda, car ela era mout felona vas lui per so qu'ela si volia partir de lui, don ela li trobet l'ochaizo del gan. Don Guirautz, si tot li fo greu, s'en partic; e sapchatz que madon' Alamanda no li det comjat so per lo gan, si tot en trobet ochaizo, car ilh o fes per so que pres per so drut tal don ela fo fort blasmada, car el era om fort malvatz e crois. Don Guirautz de Bornelh remas mout tritz o dolens longa sazo per lo dan de si e per lo blasme de lei, car ilh avia fach amador de tal qui no·lh covenia.

Sardinian

"Es Nadu Su Bambinu"

Notte de gelu e custa d'ogni signu
De alegria si sente in abundare
Ca in sa gruta es nadu su bambinu
De s'inferru pro nos liberare!

Es nadu, es nadu, es nadu su bambinu,
Enide, enide, totus a l'adorare,
Enide a l'amirare,
Enide a l'adorare,
A l'amare!

[A Christmas Song][1]

Catalan

"Les Dotze Van Tocant"

Les dotze van tocant,
 ja és nat el Rei Infant,
  fill de Maria.

El Cel és estrellat
 el món és tot glaçat,
  neva i venteja.

La Verge i el Fillet
 n'estan tots morts de fred
  i el vell tremola.

Josep, a poc a poc,
 encén allà un gran foc
  i els àngels canten.

[Popular folk Christmas Song]

"La Nacionalitat Catalana"

Cada any la natura ens dóna una imatge viva del que és el renaixement d'un poble. Cada any l'hivern estronca la circulació de la vida, deixa nues de verdor les branques, cobreix la terra de neus i de gebrades.

Mes la mort és aparent. Les neus de les muntanyes es fonden, engruizint els rius que porten a la plana la força acumulada de geleres i congestes; la terra sent penetrar, per totes les seves molècules, la humitat amorosa de l'aigua que fecunda; sota la crosta de les glaçades o el gruix protector de neu i gebre, les llavors tremolen i es clivellen, obrint-se per a donar pas a la vida que revé; les velles soques dels arbres senten l'estremitud, l'esgarrifança, que anuncia la nova pujada de la saba. Després el sol allarga els dies i entebiona l'aire, reculen les neus als bacs de les altres serres; l'oreig gronxa els sembrats i les branques grosses, a punt de brotonar; creix l'esclat de moviment, de vibració, d'activitat per tota la natura; i les seves

---

1. Courtesy of Maria Ibba, a native of Sardara, Sardinia. The spellings are hers. She also lists the following phonetic indications: *notte* [ɔ], *gelu* [ʒ], *signu* [ñ], *nadu* [đ], *sente* [zénte], *enide* [đ], *totus* [đótus], *adorare* [đ].

innombrables remors canten altra vegada l'himne etern a la vida renovada (Enric Prat de la Riba, 1870–1917).

Romanian

Pământul Românesc

Legătura principală între platoul Transilvaniei și șesul Munteniei este Valea Prahovei, cunoscută prin bogăția ei în petrol. Cu Moldova de nord, numită Bucovina, muzeu de artă veche românească, legatură se face peste Măgura, ajungând în Vatra Dornei, cunoscuta stațiune balneară.

Acest cerc de munți, avansați ca o cetate în spre stepa din nordul Mării Negre, este dublat de un cerc de râuri care înconjoară cetatea cu șanțuri de apă. Nistrul, Dunărea și Tisa încercuesc șesurile din jurul cetății munților.

Această regiune se numia în antichitate Dacia Felix. Împăratul Traian a încorporat-o în Imperiul Roman și a transformat-o într'o provincie romană, în anul 106 după Christos.

The Geography of Romania

The principal connection between the plateau of Transilvania and the plain of Walachia is the Valley of the Prahovia, known for its riches in petroleum. With northern Moldavia, called Bucovina, a museum of ancient Romanian art, there is a connection across Magura (Mountain), passing by Vatra Dornei, the well-known watering place.

This circle of mountains, put forward like a fortress toward the steppe north of the Black Sea, is surrounded by a circle of rivers, which provides the fortress with moats. The Dniester, the Danube, and the Theis encircle the plains round about the fortress of mountains.

This region was known in ancient times as Dacia Felix. Emperor Trajan incorporated it into the Roman Empire and made it a Roman province in the year A.D. 106.

Items from Daily Newspapers

La 7 februarie 1974
INSULA GRENADA
VA DEVENI INDEPENDENTA

Insula Grenada, de origine vulcanică, este situată la nord de Trinidad-Tobago, făcînd parte din Arhipelagul Antilelor Mici. Ea are o suprafață de aproximativ 120 mile pătrate și o populație de circa 100,000 locuitori . . . . Insula a fost descoperită în anul 1498 de Cristofor Columb, care a denumit-o Conception. Ea a fost colonizată în anul 1650 de guvernatorul francez al Martinicăi, iar în 1674 a trecut în posesiunea coroanei Franței . . . . În timpurile moderne, Grenada a fost posesiune britanică, avînd, în ultima perioadă, împreună cu alte cinci insule din Antile, statutul de "state asociate" cu Anglia.

Grenada este primul din aceste teritorii care îşi dobîndeşte independenţa. Economia insulei este bazată în principal pe producţia agricolă, exportîndu-se în special în Anglia, cacao, nuci de cocos, uleiuri, banane, bumbac şi trestie de zahăr. Grenada şi-a dezvoltat în ultimii ani o industrie turistică, care îi aduce importante venituri.

Capitala ţării este oraşul St. George's. Insula are de-a lungul coastei cîteva oraşele foarte pitoreşti: Charlotte Town, Grand Roy, Woldford, Grenville, Victoria, Santeurs.

În ţară trăiesc circa
400 de centenari

La ora actuală în ţară trăiesc circa 400 de oameni care au atins şi au depăşit vîrsta de 100 de ani. Această cifră, raportată la numărul populaţiei, dă unul dintre celi mai mari procente din întreaga lume. După un studiu al Institutului de geriatrie din Bucureşti, reiese că indicele de longevitate cel mai ridicat există în Banat şi în Dobrogea. Şi acum citeva "recorduri" de longevitate; Ioana Rădulescu din Caracal a împlinit de curind 120 de ani, iar Ruxandra Rusu din satul Plăvăneştii Noi, comuna Andrieşeşti, judeţul Iaşi, nu mai puţin de 126 de ani! Am aflat şi că decanul de vîrstă al longevivilor noştri, Ilie Stamate, din comuna Ilovăt, judeţul Mehedinţi a decedat la vîrsta de 145 de ani.

Şahinşahul Iranului a ratificat noua
lege petrolieră

Şahinşahul Iranului, Mohammad Reza Pahlavi Aryamehr, a ratificat, marţi, noua lege petrolieră care conferă ţarii sale, pentru prima dată, "controlul deplin şi real" asupra industriei ţiţeiului şi încheie victorios indelungata luptă pentru re-cuperarea acestei bogăţii naţionale.

După semnarea documentului de 100 pagini — moment de importanţă politică şi economică remarcabilă, urmărit de milioane de locuitori la reţeaua de televiziune — Şahinşahul Mohammad Reza Pahlavi a declarat că acest eveniment reprezintă "o zi nouă în istoria iraniană."

Astăzi incepe recoltarea sfeclei
de zahăr

La 1 August, în sudul şi vestul ţarii începe recoltarea primelor parcele cultivate cu sfeclă de zahăr. Acţiunea se declanşeaza cu aproximativ 10–12 zile mai devreme fată de anul trecut. Condiţiile climatice din aceste zone — in special din luna iulie — au favorizat creşterea greutăţii rădăcinilor şi acumularea de zahăr. Desigur că specialiştii din unităţile cultivatoare vor identifica culturile mai avansate în vegetaţie, adică cele care sînt în măsură să asigure cel puţin 23–25 tone de sfeclă la hectar şi a căror rădăcini au minimum 13 la sută conţinut de zahăr.

Rhaeto-Romance Selections

Parallel Passages

The following are from various translations of Alphonse Daudet's *La Chèvre de M. Seguin*. The versions differ somewhat; all the Romansch translations are quite free ones. (*La chavretta da Sar Padruot*, trans. Cla Biert; *La tgora da Maschal Curdegn*, trans. Franzestg Schmid; *La cauretta da Mistral Gieri*, trans. Gieri Carigiet; *La tgora da Mastral Giari*, trans. Margritta Salis. Reprinted with the permission of the publishers, La Ligia Romontscha, Cuera [Chur], Switzerland.)

Ladin (*Engadinian*)

Hai, che banadida ch'ella d'eira, la chavrina da sar Padruot! Chenüna bellina, cun seis ögls chöntschs, cun sa barbetta e sas uraglinas nairas glüschaintas, las cornas stribladas e la bella mantella alba sco la naiv! E lura tant manaivla, charina, as laschond muoldscher sainza far bau, sainza far cupichar la sadella. Schi, procha üna sillina be da magliar.

Surmiran

Oh, tge bela tgorigna tgi Curdegn ò nò! — Propa ena beligna cun dus îgls mievels, ved sies misung en barbis scu en franzos, las unglas tot neiras glischaintas, dus cornas groppeidas e sies peil alv lung tgi cuatava la tgorigna scu ena mantiglia. E daple tant tgunscha, tgerigna, stat da munscher sainza far flép, na zappa betg cugls peis ainten la sadela! Gea — gl'è propa ena zilligna tg'ins pudess magler aint.

Sursilvan

O, tgei biala cauretta che mistral Gieri haveva! Propi ina amureivla cun dus egls migeivels, cun in barbis git, culs calzers resch ners e tarlischonts, ils corns menai ed il peil alv sco la neiv. E lu era ella ton dumiastia e scheva mulscher senza se-balluccar e senza derscher la sadlutta. Gie — ei era propi ina sila da magliar en.

Sutsilvan

Ah, tge banadida c'ell'eara, la tgoretta da mastral Giari. Tgenegna bealetta, cun seas ils prus, cun la barbetta gezza, cugls calzers neraglias a targlischaints, las cornas strivladas, cugl pel alf, alviras sco'gl latg c'ella scheva mulschar sainza samovar a sainza mettar igl pe an la sadeala. Ea, proppi egna Sila dad adaver bugent.

French Original

Ah! qu'elle était jolie la petite chèvre de M. Seguin. Qu'elle était jolie avec ses yeux doux, sa barbiche de sous-officier, ses sabots noirs et luisants, ses cornes zébrées et ses longs poils blancs qui lui faisaient une houppelande! et puis docile, caressante, se laissant traire sans bouger, sans mettre son pied dans l'écuelle; un amour de petite chèvre.

Although there is basically little difference between Upper and Lower Engadinian, some variation in forms is found, as in these samples, with other dialects of Rhetian listed for comparison (note: *ch* and *tg* are both spellings for the sound [č]):

Haut-Engad.	Bas-Engad.	Surs.	Suts.	Surm.	L.
eu	*eau*	*jeu*	*jou*	*ia*	ÉGO
ova	*aua*	*aua*	*ava*	*eva*	ÁQUA
chavra	*chevra*	*caura*	*tgora*	*tgora*	CÁPRA
chasa	*chesa*	*casa*	*tgeasa*	*tgesa*	CÁSA

Excerpt from "La vipra"

The following Sursilvan translation of Andri Peer's "La vipra" (*La vipra/ Fistatgs*, trans. Paulina Carduff-Vonmoos, Oeuvre Suisse des Lectures pour la Jeunesse no. 800, pp. 14–16), is reprinted with the permission of the publishers, La Ligia Romontscha, Cuera [Coire], Switzerland. (A young goatherd has been bitten by a snake. He is found by another mountaineer, taken home, and put to bed. Friends and neighbors suggest various remedies while waiting for the doctor to come. Meanwhile the boy's mother stands helpless and remorseful at the bedside of her son, Tin.)

Prender el sin schui e purtar el en quater sparuns giu en vischnaunca, clamar signur Valentin che ha telefon, el dueigi far vegnir immediat il miedi per in buob miers dad ina vipra e metter el en siu letg, pilvermo, quei ei fatg en in gienà. Negin era a casa, mo la glieud, catschada dallas marveglias, ei spertamein currida neutier.

≪Tgei eisi cun Tin? eis el sefatg mal, ha el rut la comba?≫

≪Mo veseis buc ch'el ei alvs sco in lenziel?≫

≪Para ch'ina vipra ha miers el gia da miezgi, ed el ei tuttina staus tier las cauras, pauper buob.≫

≪O Dieus, mo sch'el miera buc! Mo mirei co el ei tut pass e fa buca sun.≫

≪Savessen ins buca far enzatgei avon ch'il miedi arriva?≫

Gieri ei era leu. Il sulet che quescha en quei plonschem e berglem; el studegia, sch'el duessi buca metter sut il cavagl pil miedi. Enaquella arriva il buob da Valentin cun la nova ch'il docter seigi gia sin via e ch'ins dueigi zugliar il malsaun en cozzas e mirar ch'el stetti eri. Denton ein era auters vischins arrivai neutier, ed enzatgi ei ius per Giovannina e per Melmo. La glieud discutescha:

≪Sch'ins ha fatg nuot encunter, sa mo il miedi aunc gidar. Quel ha da quels serums, mo ins stoppi squitrar quei immediat.≫

≪Ed il vinars, quel gida era mo sch'ins beiba immediat, ed era da tagliar cul cunti ina mesaglina ella miersa e tschitschar ora il tissi . . .≫

≪Ils vegls barschavan≫, di Gieri Tarlenda, ≪sas aunc, cu miu bab era ius cun miu frar Cristoffel sin fravgia ed ei han catschau ad el in fier ardent ella carn? Quei ferdava sco dad enferrar?≫ — E suenter in mument: ≪Mo gidau ha ei!≫

Giovannina ei vegnida en tut stuida, paupretta, al capugl dil letg da siu buob, ed ussa sa ella buca tgei pigliar a mauns e bragia e sedespara da buca esser stada a casa. Ella havess bein saviu proteger il buob da quei biestg dad in um. Mo era ella ei la cuolpa cun siu hers dad ir a schurnada.

Some vocabulary helps for above passage: *buc(a)* = not; *dad* = by; *tgei* = what; *sco* = like, as; *co* = how; *enzatgei* = meanwhile; *schi* = if, whether; *sin* = on; *cu* = when.

Psalm 23 in Various Languages

Engadinian

Il Segner ais meis pastur, eu nu vegn in manguel; l'am fa star sün pas-chüra verdainta, el am maina pro auas frais-chas.

El dà rinfrais-ch a mi' orma.

El am guida sün güstas sendas per amur da seis nom.

E gess eu tras s-chüras chavorgias, eu nu tem ingün mal.

Perche tü est pro mai, teis bastun e tia bachetta, quels sun meis cuffort.

Tü'm pinast pro üna maisa davant meis fadivs; tü uondschast meis cheu cun öli e fast combel meis chalsch.

Ventüra e grazch'am cumpagnan tuot ils dis da ma vita.

Ed eu avdarà per lönch in la chasa dal Segner.

Sursilvan

Il Segner ei miu pastur, a mi cheu maunca nuotzun.

Sin pastira verda el lai mei ruassar, e lai mei maner el muletg sper las auas.

El frestgenta mi' olma.

Silla dretga via meina el mei per amur de siu num.

Sche jeu gie tras stgira val viandass, sche hai jeu buc tema dil mal; pertgei ti eis cun mei, tiu fest e bitget mei cunfortan.

Ti tegns alzau tia lontsch' avon mei encunter mes inimitgs.

Cun ieli ti unschas miu tgau, miu biher ei pleins tochen sum.

Gie, mei cumpognan ventira e grazia tras tut ils gis della veta, e jeu sai star ella casa dil Segner a semper.

Spanish

1. Jehová es mi pastor; nada me faltará.

2. En lugares de delicados pastos me hará descansar; junto a aguas de reposo me pastoreará.

3. Confortará mi alma; me guiará por sendas de justicia por amor de su nombre.

4. Aunque ande en valle de sombra de muerte, no temeré mal alguno, porque tú estarás conmigo; tu vara y tu cayado me infundirán aliento.

5. Aderezas mesa delante de mi en presencia de mis angustiadores; unges mi cabeza con aceite; mi copa está rebosando.

6. Ciertamente el bien y la misericordia me seguirán todos los días de mi vida, y en la casa de Jehová moraré por largos días.

Portuguese

1. O Senhor é o meu pastor: nada me faltará.

2. Êle me faz repousar em pastos verdejantes; leva-me para junto das águas de descanso.

3. Refrigera-me a alma. Guia-me pelas veredas da justiça por amor do seu nome.

4. Ainda que eu ande pelo vale da sombra da morte, não temerei mal nenhum, porque tu estás comigo: a tua vara e o teu cajado me consolam.

5. Preparas-me uma mesa na presença dos meus adversários, unges-me a cabeça com óleo; o meu cálice transborda.

6. Bondade e misericórdia certamente me seguirão todos os dias da minha vida; e habitarei na casa do Senhor para todo o sempre.

French

1. L'Éternel est mon berger: je ne manquerai de rien.

2. Il me fait reposer dans de verts pâturages, il me dirige près des eaux paisibles.

3. Il restaure mon âme, il me conduit dans les sentiers de la justice, à cause de son nom.

4. Quand je marche dans la vallée de l'ombre de la mort, je ne crains aucun mal, car tu es avec moi: ta houlette et ton bâton me rassurent.

5. Tu dresses devant moi une table, en face de mes adversaires; tu oins d'huile ma tête, et ma coupe déborde.

6. Oui, le bonheur et la grâce m'accompagneront tous les jours de ma vie, et j'habiterai dans la maison de l'Éternel jusqu'a à la fin de mes jours.

Romanian

1. Domnul este Păstorul meu: nu voi duce lipsă de nimic.

2. El mă paște în pășuni verzi, și mă duce la ape de odihnă.

3. Îmi înviorează sufletul, și mă povățuiește pe cărări drepte, din pricina Numelui Său.

4. Chiar dacă ar fi să umblu prin valea umbrei morții, nu mă tem de niciun rău, căci Tu ești cu mine. Toiagul și nuiaua Ta mă mîngîie.

5. Tu îmi întinzi masa în fața protivnicilor mei; îmi ungi capul cu untdelemn, și paharul meu este plin de dă peste el.

6. Da, fericirea şi îndurarea mă vor însoţi în toate zilele vieţii mele, şi voi locui în Casa Domnului pînă la sfîrşitul zilelor mele.

Provençal

Iavè qu'es mon pastor; res non me mancarà: el m'a pargat dins los verds pasturals; còsta l'aiga ont aurai sujorn el me condús, amor d'i refortir mon anma; sus dralhòls dreches el me mena, per l'amor de son nom.

Quand correguèssi ieu en comba tenebrosa, non crentariái lo mendre mal. — Estant que t'ai al ras de ieu, lo tieune gafe e'l tieu baston me bòtan en plena fisança.

Per ieu aparelhas la taula als uèlhs vesents dels mieunes enemics; d'oli m'esperfumas lo cap e mon gòt es ras que s'abronda.

Doçor e gràcia me segràn cada jorn de la mieuna vida: ma demòra es l'ostal de Iavè per tot lo manne de mos jorns.

Catalan 1

El Senyor és mon[1] pastor, i res no pot mancar-me; en una sabrosa prada ell m'ha posat.

Vers les aigües regalades m'ha portat; ha fet retornar la meva ànima.

M'ha conduit pels camins de justícia, a causa del seu nom.

Així, baldement camini per entre ombra de mort, cap mal no temeré; perquè Vós sóu amb mi.

Vostra crossa i vostre bàcul, ells m'han consolat.

Heu parada davant meu una taula, contra els que m'atribolen.

Haveu ungit amb oli el meu cap, i el meu calze embriagant quant deliciós és!

I m'acompanyará vostra misericòrdia, tots els dies de ma[2] vida.

Per tal que jo habiti en la casa del Senyor, per dies i dies.

Catalan 2

Yahuè és el meu pastor, no em manca res, en verdes prades em fa jeure; em mena a les aigües de repòs, reviscola la meva ànima.

Per viaranys de dretura em guia per causa del seu nom; fins si per 'tenebrosa' vall camino, no sento por de mal.

Car Vós vora de mi: la vostra vara i el vostre gaiató, ells m'han aconhortat.

Taula haveu parat al meu davant, de cara als meus adversaris; amb oli haveu ungit la meva testa, el meu veire sobreïx.

---

1. *Mon, ma:* these forms are somewhat colloquial nowadays, and are limited to certain set expressions, such as *mon pare*, *ma vida*, instead of *el meu pare*, *la meva vida*.
2. See note 1 above.

Si, ventura i gràcia em persegueixen tots els dies de ma[3] vida; i sojornaré en la casa de Yahuè, durant llargs dies.

Italian

L'Eterno è il mio pastore, nulla mi mancherà. Egli mi fa giacere in verdeggianti paschi, mi guida lungo le acque chete. Egli mi ristora l'anima, mi conduce per sentieri di giustizia, per amor del suo nome.

Quand'anche camminassi nella valle dell'ombra della morte, io non temerei male alcuno, perché tu sei meco; il tuo bastone e la tua verga son quelli che mi consolano. Tu apparecchi davanti a me la mensa al cospetto dei miei nemici; tu ungi il mio capo con olio; la mia coppa trabocca.

Certo, beni e benignità m'accompagneranno tutti i giorni della mia vita; ed io abiterò nella casa dell'Eterno per lunghi giorni.

Sardinian

Deus es su pastore meu, nudda mi máncata; issu mi ponet in bellas pasturas, mi yuket iss' oru 'e abbar de cossolu, recrea' s'ánima mea; mi yuket in andattar derettas pro more 'essu lumes suo. Mancari ande in badde 'e morte non timo male perunu. Tue ses kin mecus, kin su fuste ei su bácculu e custu es su cuffortu meu. Tue apparitzas sa mesa daennantis a mimme, a cara 'essor nimicor meos. Tue m'unghes sa conca kin ozu, mi prenas su cálike a cúccuru. Solu 'e benes e piakeres mi prenas in tottu sa bida mea. Dego app'istare in sa domo 'essu Sennore pro medas, medas annos.[4]

---

3. See note 1 on page 167.

4. Although some parts of the Bible have been translated into the various Sardinian dialects, the Psalms have not. This translation is through the courtesy of Prof. Massimo Pittau, of the Università di Sassari, Sardegna. Note his use of the letter *k* before front vowels (*i*), (*e*). According to Meyer-Lübke, the form *domo* is from a Latin dative or ablative, hence the *-o* ending. See *REW* 2745.

Biblical Passages in Sardinian Dialects

Luke 2:1–20

Cagliaitan, or Campidanese

1. In cuddas dis fiat istetiu pubblicau un edittu de Cesari Augustu, chi si fazzessit su contu de totus is abitantis de sa terra.

2. Custu contu fiat istetiu su primu, essendi Quiriniu proconsolu de sa Siria.

3. E totus andànt a faisì registrai, dognunu in sa çittadi sua.

4. Giuseppi puru fiat alzau de Galilea, de sa çittadi de Nazareth, a sa Giudea, a sa çittadi de David nomenada Betleem, — essendi issu de sa domu e de sa famiglia de David, —

5. Po faisì registrai cun Maria, sa femina chi ddi fiat istetia sposada, sa cali fiat pringia.

6. E fiat suççediu, mentras fiant inni, chi si fiat cumpliu su tempus de partoriri;

7. E issa hiat partoriu su fillu suu primigeniu, e dd'hiat fasciau, e dd'hiat corcau in d'una pappadroxa, essendi chi no'nci fiat logu po issus in sa locanda.

8. E in cudda contrada e totu inci fianta de is pastoris, chi aturànt in is campus e fianta fendi sa guardia de sa notti accanta a su cumoni insoru.

9. E un angelu de su Signori ddis fiat apparessiu; e sa gloria de su Signori hiat resplendiu a ingiriu de issus; e si fianta spantaus cun meda timori.

10. E s'angelu ddis hiat nau: «Non timais, poita, eccu, deu dongu a bosaturus notizia de unu gosu manu chi hat a teneri totu su populu,

11. chi oi a bosaturus est nasciu unu Salvadori, chi est Cristu su Signori, in sa çittadi de David.

12. E custu 'nd'hat essiri a bosu su signali: heis agatai a su pipiu in is pannizzus, corcau in d'una pappadroxa.»

13. A s'improvvisu inci fiat istetia cun s'angelu una multitudini de s'esercitu de su celu, chi laudanta a Deus, narendi:

14. «Gloria a Deus in is celus altissimus, paxi in terra, intre is ominis a Issu aggredessius.»

15. E fiat suççediu chi candu is angelus s'indi fianta stesiaus de issus, in su celu, is pastoris hianta nau s'unu a s'alteru: ≪Arribeus finzas a Betleem, e castieus su chi est suççediu, su chi su Signori hat fattu sciri a nosu.≫

16. E fiant andaus de pressi e hiant agatau a Maria e a Giuseppi e a su pipieddu corcau in sa pappadroxa;

17. E candu dd'hianta bistu, hianta fattu sciri sa paraula chi ddis fiat istetia nada a propositu de custu pipieddu.

18. E totus cuddus chi ddus hiant intendius, si fianta maravigliaus de is cosas chi fianta nadas a issus de is pastoris.

19. E Maria cunservàt totus custas paraulas, ponendiddas in su coru suu.

20. E is pastoris s'indi fianta torraus, donendi gloria e laudendi a Deus de totu su chi hiant intendiu e bistu, comenti ddis fiat istetiu fueddau.

Matthew 2:1-15

Logudorese

1. Essende edducas naschidu Jesus in Bethlehem de Juda in sas dies de su re Herodes, ecco qui sos magos dai s'oriente benzesint a Jerusalem,

2. Narzende: Ue est su naschidu Re de sos Judeos? hamus bidu s'istella sua in s'oriente, e semus bennidos a lu adorare.

3. Intendende però su re Herodes si est turbadu, et tota Jerusalem cum ipsu.

4. Et cungreghende totu sos principes de sos sacerdotes, et sos iscribas de su populu, dimandaiat ad ipsos ue Christus deveret nascher.

5. Ma ipsos li rispondesint: In Bethlehem de Juda: proite qui gosi est iscriptu dai su Propheta;

6. Et tue Bethlehem, terra de Juda, non ses sa minima inter sos principes de Juda: proite dai te hat a bessire su capitanu, qui hat a reggere su populu meu Israele.

7. Tando Herode, jamadu a cua sos magos, deligentemente s'informesit da ipsos de su tempus de s'istella qui lis cumparzesit.

8. Et mandadolos in Bethlehem, nesit: Andade et dimandade deligentemente de custu piccinnu: et da qui lu dezis incontrare faghidemilu ischire, a tales qui eo ande pro lu adorare.

9. Sos quales hapende intesu su re, sind'andesint: et ecco s'istella qui haiant bidu in oriente, andaat innantis finzas qui andende istesit subra, ue fit su piccinnu.

10. Bidende però s'istella si sunt allegrados cum gosu meda mannu.

11. Et intrados a sa domo incontresint su piccinnu cum Maria mama sua: et inclinendesi lu adoresint: et abbertos sos tesoros ipsoro li offerzesint regalos, oro, incensu et mirra.

12. Et hapende recidu sa risposta in su sognu de non torrare ad Herode per atera via sique torresint in su paesu ipsoro.

13. Sos quales appena partidos, ecco s'Anghelu de su Segnore cumparzesit in sognu a Juseppe, nende: Pesa, et lea su piccinnu, et i sa mama sua, et fui in Egiptu,

et firma in cuddae finzas qui ti l'hap' a narrer. Proite qui Herode est pro chircare su piccinnu pro lu perdere.

14. Su quale ischidendesi leesit su piccinu, et i sa mama sua a de nocte, et si ritiresit in s'Egiptu.

15. Et istesit in cuddae finzas a sa morte de Herode, a tales qui si cumpleret su qui est istadu nadu dai su Segnore per i su Propheta nende: Dai s'Egiptu hapo jamadu su fizu meu.

Cagliaitan

1. Essendi duncas nasciu Gesus in Betlem de Giudas a tempus de su rei Erodis, eccu chi benint a Gerusalemmi is Magus de orienti,

2. Narendi: Aund'est su, ch'est nasciu rei de is Giudeus? poita nos heus bistu sa stella sua in s'orienti, e seus benius a dd'adorai.

3. Ma su rei Erodis intendendi custu, si turbat, e cun issu totu Gerusalemmi.

4. E reunendi totu is capus de is saçerdotus, e is Scribas de su populu, ddis domandàt, aundi hiat a nasciri Cristus.

5. Custus però ddi respundint: In Betlem de Giudas: poita chi aici est scrittu de su profeta:

6. E tui o Betlem de Giudas, no ses sa prus pitica in is prinçipaus de Giudas: poita de tui hat a bessiri su cumandanti, ch'hat a guvernai su populu miu de Israeli.

7. Insaris Erodis, hendi zerriau a parti is Magus, cun diligenzia s'informat de issus, in cali tempus sa stella ddis fiat cumparta:

8. E mandendiddus a Betlem, ddis narat: Baxi, e informaisì cun diligenzia de custu pipiu: e candu dd'hapais incontrau, feimiddu sciri, po chi deu bandi a dd'adorai.

9. Issus, hendi intendiu a su rei, si'nd'andant. I eccu chi sa stella, ch'hianta bistu in s'orienti, ddis andàt innantis, finzas chi benit a si firmai asuba de aundi fiat su bambinu.

10. Biendi però sa stella si fiant allirgaus cun grandu cuntentu.

11. E intrendi a sa domu, incòntran a su bambinu cun Maria mamma sua, e ingenughendisì dd'orant: e aberendi is tesorus insoru dd'offressinti po arregalu oru, incensu, e mirra.

12. I hendi tentu risposta in sonnu de no torrai aund' Erodis, si'ndi fiant torraus a su paisu insoru de un'aturu camminu.

13. Candu issus fianta partius, eccu chi s'angiulu de su Signori cumparit in sonnu a Giuseppi, e ddi narat: Pesatindi, e piga su bambinu, e sa mamma sua, e fuitindi in Egittu, e aturadì innì, finzas chi ti dd'hap'a nai deu. Poita depit acontessiri, chi Erodis circhit a su pipiu po ddu sperderi.

14. Issu si'ndi pesat, pigat su pipiu cun sa mamma a de notti, e si'ndi fuit in Egittu.

15. E s'aturat innì finzas a sa morti de Erodis: po chi aici s'accumplessit su, chi fiat stetiu nau de su Signori po mesu de su profeta narendi: De s'Egittu hapu zerriau a fillu miu.

Sassarese

1. Sendi dunca naddu Gesù in Betlem di Giuda in li dì di lu re Erodi, eccu chi li Magi dall' orienti vinisini a Gerusalem,[1]

2. Dizendi: Und' è naddu lu re di li Giudei? Abemu viltu la so' iltella in l' orienti, e semu giunti par adurallu.

3. Intindendi chiltu lu re Erodi, si è tulbaddu, e tutta Gerusalem cun eddu.

4. E riunendi tutti li prinzipi di li sazzeldoti, e l' Ilcribi di lu pobbulu, dimandaba a eddis, undi Criltu dibissi nascì.

5. Ma eddi rilpundisini: In Betlem di Giuda: palchì cussi è iltaddu ilcritu da lu profeta:

6. E tu Betlem, terra di Giuda, no sei la minima tra li prinzipali di Giuda: palchì da te debi iscì lu capitanu, chi gubernarà lu me' pobbulu Israeli.

7. Allora Erodi, ciamaddi a cua li Magi, diligentementi s' infulmesi da eddis, in ca tempu li fussi cumparsa l'iltella.

8. E abendili mandaddi in Betlem, dizisi: Andeddi, e dimandeddi diligentementi di chiltu pizzinnu: e da chi l' incuntrareddi, feddimilu sabbè, a tali chi eju puru andia par adurallu.

9. Li quali abendi intesu lu re, si n' andesini. Ed eccu l'iltella, chi abiani viltu in l' orienti, li andaba innanzi, finza chi giunta sobbra lu loggu, inui era lu pizzinu, si filmesi.

10. Videndi però l'iltella si sò alligraddi assai.

11. E intraddi in casa, incuntresini lu pizzinu cun Maria mamma soja, e incinendisi l' aduresini: e abbelti li so' tisori li prisintesini regali, oru, inzensu, e mirra.

12. E abendi rizzibiddu la rilpolta in sonniu di no turrà da Erodi, si zi turresini par altra via in lu so' paesi.

13. Appena li quali paltiddi, eccu l' agnilu di lu Signori cumparisi in sonniu a Giuseppi, dizendi: Pesa, e piglia lu pizzinnu, e la so' mamma, e fuggi in Egittu, e fèlmaddi inchiddà, finza chi ti l'aggiu a dì. Palchì Erodi ha a zilcà lu pizzinnu pal fallu murì.

14. Lu quali isciddendisi pigliesi lu pizzinnu, e la so' mamma a di notti, e si ritiresi in l' Egittu.

15. E iltesi inchiddà finza a la molti di Erodi: a tali chi si cumplissi lu chi è iltaddu dittu da lu Signori pa lu profeta, chi dizi: Dall' Egittu aggiu ciamaddu lu me' figliolu.

Tempiese

1. Essendi addunca natu Gesù in Betlemmi di Giuda, rignendi lu re Erodi, eccu chi li Magi arriesini da l' orienti a Gerusalemmi,

---

1. Note article *li, lu* in both this and Tempiese dialects instead of *sos, su* (etc.) of southern dialects.

2. Dicendi: Und' è natu lu re di li Giudei? giacchì aemu vistu la so' stella ill' orienti, e semu vinuti a adorallu.

3. Aendi intesu chistu lu re Erodi, si tulbesi, e tutta Gerusalemmi cu iddu.

4. E aendi congregatu tutti li prinzipi di li sazeldotti, e li Scribi di lu populu, li pricuntesi, undi Cristu diia nascì.

5. Iddi li rispundisini: In Betlemmi di Giuda: giacchì cussì è istatu scrittu da lu profeta:

6. E tu Betlemmi tarra di Giuda, no se' la minima intra li prinzipi di Giuda: palchì da te de' iscì lu capitanu, ch' ha a guvernà lu me' populu d' Israeli.

7. Tandu Erodi aendisi chiamatu sigrettamenti li Magi, s' infulmesi cun primura da iddi, in ca tempu li fussi cumparuta la stella:

8. E mandendili a Betlemmi, li disi: Andeti, e feti pricunta cun diligenzia di chista criatura: e candu l'aareti incuntrata, fetimillu sapè, attalichì eu ancora andia par adorallu.

9. Iddi aendi intesu lu ch' aia dittu lu re, paltisini. Ed eccu chi la stella, ch' aiani vistu in orienti, l' andaa a innanzi, tiachì arriata supr' a lu locu, undi staghia la criatura, s' arristesi.

10. E vista la stella si n' alligresini assai.

11. Ed essendi intrati illa casa, incuntresini la criatura cun Maria mamma soja, e inghinucchiendisi l' adoresini: e aend' abbaltu li so' tisori, l' offersini in donu oru, inzensu, e mirra.

12. Ed essendi stati in sonniu avviltuti di no turrà a passà und' e Erodi, par altu caminu si ni turresini a lu so' paesu.

13. Paltuti chi fusini li Magi, l' agnuli di lu Signori cumparisi in sonniu a Giuseppa, e li disi: Pesatinni, pidda la criatura, e la so' mamma, e fugghitinni in Egittu, e felmati chindi tiachì eu t' aghiu a avvisà. Palchì Erodi ha a cilcà la criatura pal falla ammazzà.

14. E Giuseppa sciutatusi piddesi a di notti la criatura, e la mamma, e si ritiresi in Egittu.

15. E si ni stesi chindi tia a la molti d' Erodi: attalichì si cumplissi lu ch' era statu dittu da lu Signori pal mezzu di lu profeta, chi dici: Aghiu chiamatu lu me' fiddolu da l' Egittu.

The Song of Songs

Italian (for Comparison)

1:1–17

1. Il Cantico de' cantici di Salomone.

2. Mi baci egli de' baci della sua bocca! . . . poichè le tue carezze son migliori del vino.

3. I tuoi profumi hanno un odore soave; il tuo nome è un profumo, che si spande; perciò t' aman le fanciulle!

4. Attirami a te! Noi ti correremo dietro! Il re m' ha condotta ne' suoi appartamenti; noi gioiremo, ci rallegreremo a motivo di te; noi celebreremo le tue carezze più del vino! A ragione sei amato!

5. Io son nera ma son bella, o figliuole di Gerusalemme, come le tende di Chedar, come i padiglioni di Salomone.

6. Non guardate se son nera; è il sole che m' ha bruciata; i figliuoli di mia madre si sono adirati contro di me; m' hanno fatta guardiana delle vigne, ma io, la mia vigna, non l' ho guardata.

7. O tu che il mio cuore ama, dimmi dove meni a pascere il tuo gregge, e dove lo fai riposare sul mezzogiorno. Poichè, perchè sarei io come una donna sperduta, presso i greggi de' tuoi compagni?

8. Se non lo sai, o la più bella delle donne, esci e segui le tracce delle pecore, e fa' pascere i tuoi capretti presso alle tende de' pastori.

9. Amica mia io t' assomiglio alla mia cavalla che s' attacca ai carri di Faraone.

10. Le tue guance son belle in mezzo alle collane, e il tuo collo è bello tra i filari di perle.

11. Noi ti faremo delle collane d' oro con de' punti d' argento.

12. Mentre il re è nel suo convito, il mio nardo esala il suo profumo.

13. Il mio amico m' è un sacchetto di mirra, che passa la notte sul mio seno.

14. Il mio amico m' è un grappolo di cipro delle vigne d' En-ghedi.

15. Come sei bella, amica mia, come sei bella! I tuoi occhi son come quelli dei colombi.

16. Come sei bello, amico mio, come sei amabile! Anche il nostro letto è verdeggiante.

17. Le travi delle nostre case sono cedri, i nostri soffitti sono di cipresso.

7:1–14

1. ....
....
Perchè mirate la Sulamita
come una danza a due schiere?

2. Come son belli i tuoi piedi ne' loro calzari, o figliuola di principe! I contorni delle tue anche son come monili, opera di mano d' artefice.

3. Il tuo seno è una tazza rotonda, dove non manca mai vino profumato. Il tuo corpo è un mucchio di grano, circondato di gigli.

4. Le tue due mammelle paion due gemelli di gazzella.

5. Il tuo collo è come una torre d' avorio; i tuoi occhi son come le piscine d' Heshbon presso la porta di Bath-Rabbim. Il tuo naso è come la torre del Libano, che guarda verso Damasco.

6. Il tuo capo s' eleva come il Carmelo, e la chioma del tuo capo sembra di porpora; un re è incatenato dalle tue trecce!

7. Quanto sei bella, quanto sei piacevole, o amor mio, in mezzo alle delizie!

8. La tua statura è simile alla palma, e le tue mammelle a de' grappoli d' uva.

9. Io ho detto: "Io salirò sulla palma, e m' appiglierò ai suoi rami." Siano le tue mammelle come grappoli di vite, il profumo del tuo fiato, come quello de' pomi,

10. e la tua bocca come un vino generoso, che cola dolcemente per il mio amico, e scivola fra le labbra di quelli che dormono.

11. Io sono del mio amico, e verso me va il suo desiderio.

12. Vieni, amico mio, usciamo ai campi, passiam la notte ne' villaggi!

13. Fin dal mattino andremo nelle vigne; vedremo se la vite ha sbocciato, se il suo fiore s'apre, se i melagrani fioriscono. Quivi ti darò le mie carezze.

14. Le mandragole mandano profumo. e sulle nostre porte stanno frutti deliziosi d' ogni sorta, nuovi e vecchi, che ho serbati per te, amico mio.

Logudorese

1:1–16

1. Mi baset cum d' unu basu de sa bucca sua: proite sas tittas[2] tuas sunt mezus de su binu,

2. Fragantes de unguentos optimos. Ozu ispartu est su nomen tou: pro cussu sas jovaneddas t' istimant.

3. Trazami: hamus a currere infactu de sos unguentos tuos. Su re m' hat introduidu in sas dispensas suas: hamus a exultare, et nos hamus allegrare cum tegus, ammentendenos de sas tittas[3] tuas subra su binu: sos justos ti amant.

4. So niedda, ma donosa, fizas de Jerusalem, comente sos tabernaculos de Cedar, comente sas peddes de Salamone.

5. Non querfedas considerare, qui sia bruna, proite m' hat iscoloridu su sole: sos fizos de mama mia hant gherradu contra ad mie, m' hant postu a tentadora in sas binzas: sa binza mia non hapo tentadu.

6. Inzitami cuddu, qui istimat s' anima mia, inue pascas, inue factas su mesudie, proite non ande vaghende infactu ad sos masones de sos cumpagnos tuos.

7. Si tue non l' ischis, o bellissima inter sas feminas, intra, et beni infactu ad sas istigas de sos cumones, et pasche sos crabittos tuos affacca ad sos tabernaculos de sos pastores.

8. Ti hapo assimizadu ad sa cavalleria mia in sos coccios de Faraone, o amiga mia.

9. Bellas sunt sas massiddas tuas comente de turture, su tuju tou comente collanas.

---

2. Instead of "breasts" (in all Sardinian versions), English and most of the Romance tongues have "love," with Italian and Romanian using "caresses" (*carezze, desmierdarile*).

3. See note 2 above.

10. Ti hamus a fagher collaneddas de oro, incrastadas de prata.

11. Mentras su re fit sezzidu ad mesa, su nardu meu hat dadu sa fragantia sua.

12. Unu mattulu de myrrha est ad mie s' istimadu meu, in mesu de sas tittas mias si det reposare.

13. Unu budrone de cypru est ad mie s'istimadu meu, in sas binzas de Engaddi.

14. Ecco tue ses bella, amiga mia, ecco tue ses bella, sos ojos tuos sunt de columbas.

15. Ecco tue ses bellu, o istimadu meu, et donosu. Su lectu nostru est plenu de flores:

16. Sas traes de sas domos nostras sunt de cedru, sos salajos sunt de cypressu.

7:1–13

1. Ite des bidere in sa Sulamitide, si non sos choros de sos exercitos? Quantu sunt bellos sos passos tuos in sa calzamenta, fiza de principe! Sas juncturas de sas coscias tuas, comente collanas, qui sunt factas dai manu de artifice.

2. S' imbiligu[4] tou comente tazza facta ad torinu, qui non mancat mai de biiduras. Sa matta tua comente unu muntone de trigu, inghiriadu de lizos.

3. Sas tittas tuas, comente duos fedos de crabola copiolos.

4. Su tuju tou comente una turre de avoriu. Sos ojos tuos comente pischinas in Hesebon, qui sunt in sa porta de sa fiza de sa multitudine. Su nare tou comente sa turre de su Libanu, qui mirat contra ad Damascu.

5. Sa conca tua comente su Carmine: et i sos pilos de sa conca tua, comente purpura de su re ligada a canales.

6. Quantu ses bella, et quantu ses donosa, carissima, in mesu sas delicias!

7. S' istatura tua est assimizada ad sa palma, et i sas tittas tuas ad sos budrones.

8. Nesi: Hap' alzare ad sa palma, et hap' arregoglier de sos fructos suos: et dent esser sas tittas tuas comente fructu de sa binza: e i s' odore de sa bucca tua comente de mela.

9. Su tuju tou comente binu optimu, dignu ad s' istimadu meu a biere, et ad sas laras suas, et ad sas dentes suas pro remuzare.

10. Eo ad s' istimadu meu, et ad mie sa mirada sua.

11. Beni istimadu meu, bessamus in sa campagna, et alloggemus in sas biddas.

12. Dai manzanu bessamus ad sas binzas, miremus, si sa binza hat fioridu, si sos flores hant battidu fructu, si hant fioridu sas melas granadas: incuddae ti hap' a dare sas tittas mias.

13. Sas mandragoras desint sa fragrantia. In sas jannas nostras sunt totu sas melas: noales et bezzas, istimadu meu, hap' arribbadu ad tie.

---

4. Italian and French here have "breast" (*seno*, *sein*), while English agrees with the others (= "navel").

Cagliaitan, or Campidanese

1:1–16

1. Chi mi basit puru cun sa bucca sua: poit' is tittas tuas sunti mellus de su binu.

2. Tenint fragu de is prus bonas pumadas: su nomini tuu est coment' un ollu chi si ghettat appizzus: e po cussu is piccioccas t' hanti stimau.

3. Tiramì: nosaterus heus a curri avatu túu a su fragu de sa pumada tua. Su re m' hat fattu intrai in is appartamentus suus: nos' heus allirgai, i heus a fai festa cun tui, arregordendinosì de is tittas tuas prus che de su binu: is tetterus ti amant.

4. Seu murena ma bella, o fillas de Gerusalemmi, coment' is tendas de Cedar, coment' is tappetus de Salomoni.

5. No mireis chi seu niedduzza poita m' hat fertu su soli: is fillus de mamma mia m' hanti fattu gherra, m' hanti postu castiadora de bingias: deu no hapu castiau sa bingia mia.

6. Naramì, tui chi s' anima mia stimat, aundi bogas a pasciri, aundi fais s' appustiprangiu, po no mi fai curri avatu a is cumonis de is cumpangius tuus.

7. Si no ddu scis, o tui sa prus bella tra totu is feminas, bessi, sighi s' arrastu de is brebeis, e ghett' a pasci is crabittus tuus accanta de is tendas de is pastoris.

8. Deu t' hapu assimbilau, o amiga mia, a is eguas de su carru de Faraoni.

9. Is trempas tuas sunti bellas coment' is turturis e su zugu tuu coment' is cannaccas.

10. Nosu t' heus a fai prendas di oru, e aderezzus de plata.

11. Candu su rei fiat in su cumbidu, su nardu miu hat ispartu su fragu suu.

12. Su stimau miu est comenti unu mazzu de mirra; issu hat aturai in mesu de su sinu miu.

13. Su stimau miu est coment' unu gurdoni de cipru in is bingias d' Engaddi.

14. Tui ses sa bella, tui ses sa bella, o amiga mia: is ogus tuus parint de columbas.

15. Tui ses su bellu, o stimau miu e allirghia mia. Su lettu nostu est plenu de floris.

16. Is bigas de is domus nostas sunti de sidru, is apusentus nostus de cipressu.

7:1–13

1. Ita has a biri in Sulamiti si no duas filas de squadronis? Cantu sunti bellus is passus tuus, o filla de principi candu andas calzada! Is giunturas de is cambas tuas comenti prendas fattas de manu de un artista.

2. Su biddiu tuu est comenti una tassa fatta a turnu chi no mancat mai de licori. Sa brenti tua comenti unu muntoni de trigu ingiriau de lillus.

3. Is duas tittas tuas comenti duus crabittus de una propriu brenti.

4. Su zugu tuu comenti una turri de avoriu: is ogus tuus comenti piscinas de Hesbon chi sunt in sa porta de sa filla de su populu: su nasu tuu comenti sa turri de su Libanu chi mirat facci a Damascu.

5. Sa conca tua comenti su monti Carmelu: e is pilus de sa conca tua comenti purpura reali accappiada in is canalis.

6. Cantu ses bella, e cantu ses graziosa, o carissima, in mesu a is delizias!

7. Sa statura tua est simili a una palma e is tittas tuas a is gurdonis.

8. Deu hapu nau: hap' alziai asuba de sa palma e hap' afferrai sa frutta: e hant essiri is tittas tuas comenti is gurdonis de sa bingia: e su fragu de sa bucca tua comenti fragu de mela.

9. Su gutturu tuu comenti su mellus binu dignu di essiri bistu de su stimau miu, e de is dentis e de is murrus suus po ddu mazziai.

10. Deu a su stimau miu, e issu furriau facci a mei.

11. Beni, o carignu miu, bessaus a su campu, firmeusnosì in is casinus.

12. Peseusnosinddi de bonu mangianu, e biaus si sa bingia est in flori, si s' arenada hat postu flori: innì t' hap' a donai su sinu miu.

13. Is mandragoras cumenzant a fragai: is fruttas sunt in is portas nostas: is noas e is beccias, o stimau miu, ch' hapu stuggiau po tui.

Sassarese

1:1–16

1. Mi basgia cun lu basgiu di la so' bocca: palchì li to' titti sò megliu di lu vinu,

2. Chi ilpirani odori d' ottimi unguenti. Ozu ilpaltu è lu to' innomu: pal chissu li giubaneddi t' hani iltimadu.

3. Traggimi fattu a te: curraremu all' odori di li to' unguenti. Lu re m' intruduzisi in li so' dilpensi: esultaremu e z' alligraremu in te, ammintèndizzi di li to' titti megliu di lu vinu: li giulti t' iltimani.

4. Soggu niedda, ma bedda, o figlioli di Gerusalemmi, cumenti li tendi di Zedar, cumenti li padiglioni di Salamoni.

5. No vògliaddi cunsiderà, chi sia bruna, palchì m' ha ilculuriddu lu soli: li figlioli di mamma meja ghirresini contra di me, mi punisini a gualdia in li vigni: la vigna meja no aggiu cultudiddu.

6. Fammi sabbè, cal' iltima l' anima meja, lu loggu di li to' palculi, lu loggu, undi colchi a mezzudì, palchì no prinzipieggia a vagà fattu a li cumoni di li to' cumpagni.

7. Si tu no lu sai, o beddissima tra li femmini, esci, e anda fattu all' imprenti di li cumoni, e pasci li to' crabbitti approbbu a li pinnetti di li paltori.

8. A li me' cabaddi di li cocci di Faraoni t' aggiu assimigliaddu, o amigga meja.

9. Beddi sò li to' cavani cumenti di tultura: lu coddu toju cumenti li cuddani.

10. Ti faremu mureneddi d' oru, incraltaddi a pratta.

11. Mentri lu re iltazìa in la so' taula, lu me' naldu desi lu so' odori.

12. Un mazzuleddu di mirra è pal me lu me' iltimaddu: tra li titti mei s' ha a trattinì.

13. Lu me' iltimaddu è pal me un buddroni di zipru di li vigni d' Engaddi.

14. Tu sei veramenti bedda, o amigga meja, veramenti bedda: l' occi toi sò di culombi.

15. Tu sei veramenti beddu, o me' iltimaddu, e graziosu. Lu lettu noltru è fiuriddu.

16. Li trabi di li noltri casi sò di chiddru, l' intauladdi di zipressu.

7:1–13

1. Chi cosa vidarai in la Sulamiti, si no cori militari? Cantu sò beddi li to' passi in li to' ilcappi, figliola di prinzipi! Li giunturi di li to' fianchi, cumenti li cuddani, chi sò frabbigaddi da manu d' altilta.

2. Lu to' umbìliggu una tazza torinada, mai mancanti di cosi di bii. La to' panza cumenti un muntoni di triggu, inghiriaddu di lizi.

3. Li dui titti toi, cumenti dui anniggi coppioli d' un crabbolu.

4. Lu to' coddu cumenti una torra d' aboriu. Li to' occi cumenti li pilchini in Hesebon, chi sò in la polta di chilta figliola di li pobbuli. Lu to' nasu cumenti la torra di lu Libanu, chi dazi in faccia a Damalcu.

5. Lu to' cabbu cumenti lu Calmelu: e li peli di lu to' cabbu, cumenti la pulpura di lu re tulzinadda in li canali.

6. Cantu bedda sei tu, e cantu graziosa, o carissima, in li to' dilizj!

7. La to' iltatura è simili a la palma, e li to' titti a li buddroni.

8. Dizisi: Alzaraggiu sobbr' a la palma, e pigliaraggiu li so' frutti: e li to' titti sarani cumenti li buddroni di la vigna: e l' odori di la to' bocca cumenti l' odori di meli.

9. La to' gola comu ottimu vinu, dignu d' essè biiddu da lu me' iltimaddu, e di li so' labbri, e di li so' denti pa rimulzallu.

10. Eju soggu di lu me' iltimaddu, e eddu è vultaddu a occi a me.

11. Veni, o iltimaddu meju, iscimu in campu, e iltèmuzzi in li biddi.

12. Iscimu lu manzanu a li vigni, e vegghiami si la vigna è fiuridda, si li fiori pruduzini lu fruttu, si li meligranaddi sò in fiori: inchiddà ti daraggiu li me' titti.

13. Li mandragori ilpirani odori. In li noltri gianni sò tutti li meli: li nobi e li vecci, o iltimaddu meju, l' arribesi a te.

Tempiese

1:1–16

1. Mi basgia cu lu basgia di la so' bucca: palchì li to' titti sò meddu di lu vinu,

2. Chi ispirani odori d' ottimi unguenti. Ociu spaltu è lu to' innommu: palchì li cioaneddi t' hani amatu.

3. Tirami infattu a te: noi em' a currì a l' odori di li to' profumi. Lu re m' intresi in drentu a li so' appusenti: aemu a esultà, e ci demu alligrà in te, ripinsendi a li to' titti meddu di lu vinu: li giusti t' amani.

4. Socu nieda, ma bedda, o fiddoli di Gerusalemmi, com' e li tendi di Cedar, com' e li padiglioni di Salamoni.

5. No vodditi mirammi, chi sia bruna, palchì lu soli mi fesi cambià di culori. Li fiddoli di la me' mamma mi fesini gherra, mi desini li vigni a valdialli: la me' vigna no fusi da me valdiata.

6. Fammi sapè chiddu, chi stima l' anima mea, lu locu di li to' pasculi, lu locu, aundi lu mezzudì ti riposi, palchì eu no cumencia a andà inghiriendi infattu a li taddoli di li to' cumpagni.

7. Si tu no lu sai, o la più bedda tra li femini, esci, e anda infattu a li pidiati di li taddoli, e pasci li to' capritti accultu a li pinnetti di li pastori.

8. A li me' cabaddi di li cocci di Faraoni eu t'assimiddu, o la me' istimata.

9. Sò beddi li to' cavani com' e di tulturella, lu to' coddu com' e cuddani.

10. T' aemu a fà cuddaneddi d' oru, pintarinati di pratta.

11. Mentri lu re staghia pusatu a mesa, lu me' nardu desi lu so' odori.

12. Un mazzuleddu di mirra è pal me lu me' istimatu, si starà illu me' sinu.

13. Lu me' istimatu è un brutoni di cipru di li vigni d' Engaddi.

14. Eccu chi bedda se' tu, o amica mea, eccu sì chi se' bedda, li to' occhi sò di culumbuli.

15. Tu sei veramenti beddu, o me' istimatu, e pienu di grazia. Lu lettu nostru è fiuritu.

16. Li trai di li nostri casi sò di cedru, li sulaghi di cipressu.

7:1–13

1. Chi cosa tu hai a vidè illa Sulamitidi, si no cori d' eselziti? Cantu sò beddi li to' passi illi calzari, o fiddola di prinzipi! Li giunturi di li to' fianchi com' e ghiun- chigli trabaddati da mani d' orifizi.

2. Lu to' biddicu una tazza fatta a turnu, chi no manca mai di bevanda: la to' mazza com' e un muntoni di tricu, inghiriatu da lici.

3. Li dui titti toi, com' e dui tennari caprioli cupiuli.

4. Lu to' coddu com' e turra d' avoriu. Li to' occhi com' e li pischini d' Hesebon, chi sò illa polta di la fiddola di la multitudini. Lu to' nasu com' e la turra di lu Libanu, ch' è in faccia a Damascu.

5. Lu to' capu com' e lu Carmelu: e li pili di lu to' capu, com' e la pulpura di lu re liata a canali.

6. Cantu bedda se' tu, e cantu splendida illi dilizii, o carissima!

7. La to' statura è simiddanti a la palma, e li to' titti a li brutoni.

8. Eu disi: Aghiu a alzà supr' a la palma, e aghiu a accapità li so' frutti: e li to' titti sarani com' e brutoni di la vigna: e l' odori di la to' bucca com' e l' odori di li meli.

9. La to' gula com' e ottimu vinu, dignu d' esse bitu da lu stimatu meu, e di li so' labbri, e di li so' denti pa rumiallu.

10. Eu socu di lu me' istimatu, e a me la so' mirata.

11. Veni, o istamatu meu, andemucinni fora a la campagna, punimu la nostra abitazioni illi casini.

12. A la matinata iscimucinni a li vigni, osselvemu, si la vigna è fiurita, si li fiori bocani li frutti, si li meli granati sò in fiori: chindi t' aghiu a dà li me' titti.

13. Li mandragori mandan' odori. Illi nostri polti sò tutti li meli: li noi, e li vecchi aghiu cunselvati pal te, o me' istimatu.

Selected Bibliography

No attempt is made here to list all the works in the Rhetian, Romanian, and Sardinian bibliographies.

There are many excellent periodicals in the field of Romance philology, of which one of the oldest and most respected is *Zeitschrift für Romanische Philologie* (Halle and Tübingen 1877–), especially good for bibliography. In addition, general publications (periodicals) in specific languages (e.g., *Hispania*, in Spanish and Portuguese) have presented over the years thousands of articles and linguistic notes upon special phases of Romance linguistics. Since adequate coverage would be impossible, there are no listings of these below, beyond a few which are cited in the central portions of this text.

General Romance Philology

Auerbach, E. *Introduction to Romance Languages and Literatures*. Translated by G. Daniels. New York: G. P. Putnam's Sons, 1961.

––––––. *Introduction aux études de philologie romane*. 3d ed., rev. Fr. Schalk. Frankfurt a. Main: Klostermann, 1965.

Bahner, Werner. *Kürze Bibliographie für das Studium der romanischen Sprachwissenschaft*. Halle (Saale): Max Niemeyer, 1962.

Bal, Willy. *Introduction aux études de linguistique romane, avec considération spéciale de la linguistique française*. Paris: Didier, 1966.

Battaglia, Salvatore. *Introduzione alla linguistica romanza*. Naples: Liguori, 1967.

Bec, Pierre. *Manuel pratique de philologie romane*. Vol. I. *Italien, provençal, catalan*. Paris: Picard, 1970.

––––––. Octave Nandris, and Žarko Muljačić. *Manuel pratique de philologie romane*. Vol. 2, *Français, roumain, sarde, rheto-frioulan, francoprovençal, dalmate, phonologie*. Paris: Picard, 1971.

Bourciez, Edouard. *Eléments de linguistique romane*. 5th ed., rev. Edouard Bourciez and Jean Bourciez. Paris: Klincksieck, 1967.

Boyd-Bowman, P. *From Latin to Romance in Sound Charts*. Kalamazoo College, Mich., 1954.

Diez, Friedrich. *Etymologisches Wörterbuch der romanischen Sprachen.* 5th ed. Bonn: Marcus, 1853.

———. *Grammaire des langues romanes.* Translated from 3rd rev. and enl. edition by A. Brachet, G. Paris, and [A. Morel-Fatio]. 3 vols. Paris: Vieweg, 1874–76.

———. *Grammatik der romanischen Sprachen.* 5th ed. 3 vols. Bonn: Weber, 1882.

Elcock, W. D. *The Romance Languages.* London: Faber and Faber; New York: MacMillan, 1960.

Gröber, Gustav et al. *Grundriss der romanischen Philologie.* 2 vols. Strasbourg: Trübner, 1888–1906.

Hall, Robert A. *An External History of the Romance Languages.* New York: American Elsevier, 1974.

Iordan, Iorgu and John Orr. *An Introduction to Romance Linguistics,* London, 1937.

——— and Maria Manoliu. *Introducere în lingvistica romanică.* Bucharest: Ed. Didactică si Pedagogica, 1965.

——— and Rebecca Posner. *An Introduction to Romance Linguistics, Its Schools and Scholars.* Revised, with a Supplement: *Thirty Years On.* Oxford: Blackwell, 1970.

Kuhn, Alwin. *Romanische Philologie.* Vol. I. *Die romanischen Sprachen.* Bern: Francke, 1951.

Lausberg, Heinrich. *Romanische Sprachwissenschaft.* 4 vols. Berlin: De Gruyter, 1956–67.

———. *Lingüística Románica.* Translated by J. Pérez Riesco and E. Pascual Rodríguez. Madrid: Gredos, 1964.

———. *Linguistica romanza.* Milan: Feltrinelli, 1971.

Mendeloff, Henry. *A Manual of Comparative Romance Linguistics. Phonology and Morphology.* Washington, D.C.: Catholic University Press, 1969.

Meyer-Lübke, Wilhelm. *Grammatik der romanischen Sprachen.* 4 vols. Leipzig: Reisland, 1890–1902.

———. *Grammaire des langues romanes.* Translated by E. Rabiet and Georges Doutrepont. 4 vols. Paris: Welter, 1890–1906.

———. *Einführung in das Studium der romanischen Sprachwissenschaft.* 3d ed. Heidelberg: Carl Winter, 1920.

———. *Introducción a la lingüística románica.* Translated and revised by A. Castro. Madrid, 1926.

———. *Romanisches etymologisches Wörterbuch.* 3d ed. Heidelberg: Carl Winter, 1935.

Millaudet, G. *Linguistique et dialectologie romanes: problèmes et méthodes.* Montpellier, Paris, 1923.

Monteverdi, Angelo. *Manuale di avviamento agli studi romanzi: le lingue romanze.* Milan: Vallardi, 1952.

Palfrey, T. R., J. G. Fucilla, and W. C. Holbrook. *A Bibliographical Guide to the Romance Languages and Literatures.* 6th ed. Evanston, Ill.: Chandler's, 1966.

Posner, Rebecca. *The Romance Languages: A Linguistic Introduction.* Garden City, N.Y.: Doubleday, 1966.

Rohlfs, Gehrhard. *Romanische Philogogie*. 2 vols. Heidelberg: Carl Winter, 1950–52.
_____. *Die Lexicalische Differenzierung der romanischen Sprachen*. Halle, 1952.
_____. *Einführung in das Studium der romanischen Philologie*. Heidelberg: Carl Winter, 1966.
Rohr, Rupprecht. *Einführung in das Studium der Romanistik*. Berlin: Schmidt, 1964.
Stepanov, G. V. *Romanskaia Filologija*. Leningrad: Izd. Leningradskogo Universiteta, 1961.
Tagliavini, Carlo. *Le Origini delle lingue neolatine*. 4th ed. Bologna: Pàtron, 1964.
Vàrvaro, Alberto. *Storia, problemi e metodi della linguistica romanza*. Naples: Liguori, 1968.
Vidos, B. E. *Handboek tot de Romaanse Taalkunde*. 's-Hertogenbosch: Malmberg, 1956.
_____. *Manuale di linguistica romanza*. Translated and revised by G. Francescato. Florence: Olschki, 1959.
_____. *Manual de lingüítica románica*. Madrid: Aguilar, 1963.
_____. *Handbuch der romanischen Sprachwissenschaft*. Munich: Huber, 1968.
Wartburg, Walther von. *Les Origines des peuples romans*. Translated by C. Cuénot de Maupassant. Paris: Presses Universitaires, 1941.
_____. *Die Ausgliederung der romanischen Sprachräume*. Bern: Francke, 1950.
_____. *Die Entstehung der romanischen Völker*. 2d ed. Tübingen: Niemeyer, 1952.
_____. *La Fragmentación lingüística de la Romañia*. Translated by M. Munoz Cortés. Madrid: Gredos, 1953.
_____. *La Fragmentation linguistique de la Romania*. Translated by J. Allieres and Georges Straka. Paris: Klincksieck, 1967.
Zauner, Adolf. *Romanische Sprachwissenschaft*. 2 vols. Berlin: De Gruyter, 1921.

Italian Philology

Dictionaries

Battisti, C., and G. Alessio. *Dizionario etimologico italiano*. 5 vols. Florence: Barbèra, 1950–57.
Devoto, G. *Avviamento alla etimologia italiana*. Florence: F. LeMonnier, 1968.
Migliorini, B., and A. Duro. *Prontuario etimologico italiano*. Turin: Paravia, 1958.
Olivieri, D. *Dizionario etimologico italiano concordato coi dialetti, le lingue straniere e la topo-onomastica*. Milan: Ceschina, 1961.
Prati, A. *Vocabolario etimologico italiano*. Milan: Garzanti, 1951.

Historical Grammars and Texts

Battaglia, S., and V. Pernicone. *La grammatica italiana*. Turin: Loescher, 1960.
Bertoni, Guilio. *Italia dialettale*. Milan: U. Hoepli, 1916.
Cortelazzo, M. *Avviamento critico alla dialettologia italiana*. Pisa: Pacini, 1969.

De Mauro, T. *Storia linguistica dell'Italia unita*. Bari: Laterze, 1970.

Devoto, G. *Profilo di storia linguistica italiana*. Florence: La Nuova Italia, 1960.

Dionisotti, C., and C. Grayson. *Early Italian Texts*. Oxford: Blackwell, 1965.

Grandgent, C. H. *From Latin to Italian*. Cambridge, Mass.: Harvard University Press, 1927.

Hall, R. A. *Bibliography of Italian Linguistics*. Baltimore, 1941.

————. *Descriptive Italian Grammar*. Ithaca: Cornell University Press, 1948.

————. *Bibliografia della linguistica italiana*. Florence: Sansoni, 1958.

Hall, Robert A., Jr. *La struttura dell'italiano*. Rome: Armando Armondo, 1971.

Jaberg, K., and K. Jud. *Sprach- und Sachatlas Italiens und der Südschweiz*. 8 vols. Zofingen; Ringier, 1928–40. Index. Bern: Stämpfli, 1960.

Lazzeri, G. *Antologia del primi secoli della letteratura italiana*. Milan: Hoepli, 1954.

Meyer-Lübke, W. *Grammatica storica della lingua italiana e dei dialetti toscani*. Translated by M. Bartoli and G. Braun. Turin Loescher, 1927–67.

Migliorini, Bruno. *Storia della lingua italiana*. *Florence:* Sansoni, 1966.

———— and G. Folena. *Testi non toscani del trecento*. Modena: Società tipografica modenese, 1952.

———— and G. Folena. *Testi non toscani del quattrocento*. Modena: Società tipografica modenese, 1953.

———— and T. G. Griffith. *The Italian Language*. London: Faber and Faber; New York: Barnes and Noble, 1966.

———— and I. Baldelli. *Breve storia della lingua italiana*. Florence: Sansoni, 1967.

Monaci, E. *Crestomazia italiana dei primi secoli, con prospetto grammaticale e glossario*. New ed., rev. and enl. by F. Arese, with an Introduction by A. Schiaffini. Rome: Società Editrice Dante Alighieri, 1955.

Monteverdi, A. *Testi volgari italiani dei primi tempi*. 2d ed. Modena: Società Tipografica Modenese, 1948.

Muljačic, Ž. *Fonologia generale e fonologia della lingua italiana*. Bologna: Molino, 1970.

————. *Introduzione allo studio della lingua italiana*. Turin: Einaudi, 1970.

Pei, M. *The Italian Language*. New York: Columbia University Press, 1961.

Prati, A. *Storia della lingua italiana*. Pisa: Libreria Goliardica, 1951.

Pulgram, E. *The Tongues of Italy: Prehistory and History*. Cambridge, Mass.: Harvard University Press, 1958.

Regula, M., and J. Jernej. *Grammatica italiana descrittiva su basi storiche e psicologiche*. Bern: Francke, 1965.

Rohlfs, G. *La struttura linguistica dell'Italia*. Leipzig: H. Keller, 1937.

————. *Grammatica storica della lingua italiana e dei suoi dialetti*. Vol. 1, *Fonetica;* Vol. 2, *Morfologia;* Vol. 3, *Sintassi e formazione delle parole*. Translated by T. Franceschi and M. C. Fancelli. Turin: Einaudi, 1966–69.

Ruggieri, R. M. *La filologia romanza in Italia*. Milan: Marzoratti, 1969.

Saltarelli, Mario. *A Phonology of Italian in a Generative Grammar*. The Hague: Mouton, 1969.

Ugolini, F. A. *Testi antichi italiani*. Turin: Chiantore, 1942.

Viscardi, A., B. and T. Nardi, G. Vidossi, and F. Arese. *Le origini. Testi latini, italiani, provenzali e franco-italiani.* Milan and Naples: Ricciardi, 1956.

Wartburg, W. von. *La posizione della lingua italiana nel mondo neolatino.* Florence: Sansoni, 1940.

_____. *Raccolta di testi antichi italiani.* Bern: Francke, 1946.

Wiese, Berthold. *Altitalienisches Elementarbuch.* 2d ed. Heidelberg: Carl Winter, 1928.

Portuguese Philology

Barros, Fernando de Araujo. *Língua portuguêsa — origens e história.* Oporto, 1942.

Boléo, Manuel de Paiva. *Introducão ao estudo da filologia portuguêsa.* Lisbon: Ed. "Revista de Portugal," 1946.

Bueno, Francisco da Silveira. *Estudos de filologia portuguêsa.* São Paulo, 1946.

_____. *A formação histórica da língua portuguêsa.* 3d ed. Rio de Janeiro: Livraria Acadêmica, 1962.

Câmara, Jr., Joaquim Mattoso. *Estrutura da língua portuguêsa.* Petrópolis, 1970.

_____. *The Portuguese Language.* Translated by Anthony J. Naro. Chicago: University of Chicago Press, 1972.

Coelho, F. A. *A língua portuguêsa: noções de glotologia geral e especial portuguêsa.* 2d ed. Lisbon: Magalhães and Moniz, 1887.

Coutinho, Ismael de Lima. *Pontos de gramática histórica.* 5th ed. Rio de Janeiro: Livraria Academica, 1962.

Entwistle, W. J. *The Spanish Language, together with Portuguese, Catalan, and Basque.* London: Faber and Faber, 1936.

Huber, Joseph. *Altportugiesisches Elementarbuch.* Heidelberg: Carl Winter, 1933.

Leão, Duarte Nunes de. *Origem da língua portuguêsa.* 4th ed. Lisbon, 1945.

Lorenzo, Ramón. *Sobre cronologia do vocabulário galego-português (anotações ao "Dicionário Etimológico" de José Machado).* Vigo: Editorial Galáxia, 1968.

Machado, José Pedro. *Dicionário etimológico de lingua portuguesa.* 2d ed. 2 vols. Lisbon: Editorial Confluência, 1956–59.

_____. *As origens do português (ensaio).* 2d ed. Lisbon: Emprêsa Contemporánea de Edicões, 1967.

Magne, Augusto. *Dicionário da lingua portuguêsa, especialmente dos períodos medieval e clássico.* 2 vols. Rio de Janeiro: Instituto Nacional do Livro, 1950–54.

Melo, Gladstone Chabes de. *Iniciação à filologia portuguêsa.* 3d ed. Rio de Janeiro: Livraria Acadêmica, 1967.

Mendonça, Renato. *A influência africana no português do Brasil.* 2d ed. São Paulo, 1935.

Monteiro, Clóvis. *Português da Europa e português da América — Aspectos da evolução do nosso idioma.* 2d ed. Rio de Janeiro, 1952.

Neto, Serafim da Silva. *Textos medievais portugueses e seus problemas.* Rio de Janeiro: Ministerio da Educação e Cultura, 1956.

_____. Manual de filologia portuguêsa. 2d ed. Rio de Janeiro, 1957.

————. Histórica da língua portuguêsa. 2d ed. Rio de Janeiro: Livros de Portugal, 1970.

Nogueira, Rodrigo de Sá. *Curso de filologia portuguêsa.* Part 1, *Noções gerais de fonética histórica.* Lisbon, 1932.

Nunes, José Joaquim. *Compêndio de gramática histórica portuguêsa: fonética — morfologia.* 6th ed. Lisbon: Livraria Classica, 1960.

————. *Crestomatia arcaica; excerptos da literatura portuguêsa . . . acompanhados de introdução gramatical, notas e glossário.* 6th ed. Lisbon: Livraria Classica, 1967.

Nunes de Figueiredo, J., and A. Gomes Ferreira. *Do latim ao português e a línqua como expressão literária.* Lisbon, n.d.

Pereira, Eduardo Carlos. *Gramática histórica.* 9th ed. São Paulo, 1935.

Said Ali, Manuel. *Gramática histórica da língua portuguêsa.* 6th ed. São Paulo: Edoções Melhoramentos, 1966.

Silveira, A. F. Sousa da. *Fonética sintáctica.* Rio de Janeiro, 1952.

————. *Lições de português.* 6th ed. Rio de Janeiro, 1960.

Vasconcelos, Carolina Michaëlis de. *Licões de filologia portuguêsa.* Lisbon: Ed. "Revista de Portugal," 1961.

Vasconcelos, José Leite de. *Estudos de filologia portuguêsa.* Rio de Janeiro: Livros de Portugal, 1961.

————. *Licões de filologia portuguêsa.* 4th ed. Rio de Janeiro: Livros de Portugal, 1966.

Vazquez Cuesta, Pilar, and Maria Albertina Mendes da Luz. *Gramática portuguêsa.* 3d ed. 2 vols. Madrid: Editorial Gredos, 1971.

Williams, Edwin B. *From Latin to Portuguese; Historical Phonology and Morphology of the Portuguese Language.* 2d ed. Philadelphia: University of Pennsylvania Press, 1962.

Catalan, Mallorcan, and Valencian Philology

Dictionaries

Albert Torrellas, A. *Diccionari català-castellà y castellà-català.* 2 vols. Barcelona: Arimany, 1959–60.

Alcover, Antoni. *Diccionari català-valencià-balear.* Palma de Mallorca, 1935.

Bassols de Climent, U. *Glossarium mediae latinitatis cataloniae: voces latinas i romances documentados en fuentes catalanas del año 800 al 1100.* Barcelona, 1960–62.

Balari y Jovany, J. *Diccionari balari.* Barcelona, 1926.

Escrig y Martínez, José. *Diccionario valenciano-castellano.* 3d ed., rev. and enl., with an essay on Limousin-Valencian orthography by D. Constantino Llombart. Cuaderno 14–48. Valencia: P. Aguilar, 1890.

Fabra, Pompeu. *Diccionari ortografic abreujat.* Barcelona: Barcino, 1926.

————. *Diccionari general de la llengua catalana.* Barcelona: Lopez-Llansàs, 1968.

Gulsoy, J. *El diccionario valenciano-castellano de Manuel Joaquín Sanelo*. Edición, estudio de fuentes y lexicología. Castellón de la Plana: Sdad. Castellonense de Cultura, 1964.

Laberia y Esteller, P. *Diccionari de la llengua catalana ab la correspondencia castellana*. Barcelona: Expasa y Companya, 1889–90.

Moll, F. de B. *Diccionari català-valencià-balear*. Palma de Mallorca, 1961–62.

Sanelo, M. J. *El diccionario valenciano-castellano*. Castello de la Plaha, Castellonense de Cultura, 1964.

Vallès, E. *Pal·las, diccionari català il·lustrat amb etimologies i equivalències en castellà, francès i anglès*. Barcelona: Massenés, 1962.

Historical Grammars, Bibliographies, and Texts

Amade, J. *Bibliographie critique pour l'étude des origines et des premières manifestations de la renaissance littéraire en Catalogne au XIXᵉ siècle*. Toulouse: Privat, 1924.

————. *Origine et premières manifestations de la renaissance litteraire en Catalogne au XIXᵉ siecle*. Toulouse: Privat and Didier, 1926.

Badia-Margarit, A. M. *Gramática histórica catalana*. Madrid, 1951.

————. *Gramática catalana*. 2 vols. Madrid: Gredos, 1962.

————. *Llengua i cultura als països catalans*. Barcelona, 1964.

Ballot y Torres, Joseph Pau. *Gramática y apologia de la llengua catalana*. Barcelona: J. A. Piferrer, 1814.

Barral i Altet, Xavier. *L'ensenyament del català a Europa i Amèrica del Nord*. Barcelona, 1971.

Capdevila, J. M. *Coms'ha d'escriure una carta en català?* Barcelona: Barcino, 1928.

Corominas, Joan. *Lleures i converses d'un filòleg*. Barcelona: Club Editor, 1971.

Crowley, W. Irving. *A Modern Catalan Grammar*. New York, 1936.

Entwistle, W. J. *The Spanish Language together with Portuguese, Catalan, and Basque*. London: Faber and Faber, 1936.

Estorch y Sigues, Pablo. *Gramática de la lengua catalana*. Barcelona: Imprenta de los Herederos de la viuda Pla, 1857.

Fabra, Pompeu. *Grammaire catalane*. Paris: Belles Lettres, 1946.

————. *Introducció a la gramàtica catalana*. Barcelona, 1968.

Folch i Capdevila, R. *Gramàtica popular de la llengua catalana*. Barcelona, 1954.

Foulché-Delbosc, R. *Recueil consacré à l'étude des langues, des littératures et de l'histoire des pays castillans, catalans et portuguais*. New York: Revue Hispanique, The Hispanic Society of America, 1911.

Gili, Joan. *Introductory Catalan Grammar*. Oxford: Dolphin, 1967.

Griera, A. *Gramàtica històrica del català antic*. Barcelona, 1931.

————. *Dialectologia catalana*. Barcelona, 1949.

————. *División dialectal de lengua catalana*. Biblioteca de autotes Españoles 37. N.p., 1961.

————. *Gramática catalana*. Madrid, 1962.

Lleó, Concepción. *Problems of Catalan Phonology.* Seattle, Wash.: University of Washington Press, 1970.

Llobera i Ramon, J. *El català bàsic.* Barcelona, 1968.

Marva, J. *Curs superior de gramàtica catalana.* Barcelona, 1968.

Meyer-Lübke, W. *Das Katalanische: seine Stellung zum Spanischen und Provenzalischen, sprachwissenschaftlich und historisch dargestellt.* Heidelberg: Carl Winter, 1925.

Moll, F. de B. *Gramática histórica catalana.* 1952.

————. *Els llinatges catalans: assaig de divulgació lingüìstica* Palma de Mallorca: Biblioteca Raixa, 1959.

————. *Gramàtica normativa per a ús dels escriptors balearics.* Palma de Mallorca: Ed. Moll, 1963.

————.*Gramàtica catalana.* Palma de Mallorca, 1968.

Montsià, B. *El valencià en vint lliçons.* Valencia, 1964.

Roca i Pons, Josep. *Introducciò a l'estudi de la llengua catalana.* Barcelona: Col. Isard, 1971.

Russell-Gebbett, P. *Medieval Catalan Linguistic Texts.* Oxford, 1965.

Sanchís, Guarner M. *Gramática valenciana.* 1950.

————. *Els parlars romanics de Valencia i Mallorca anteriors a la Reconquista.* Madrid and Valencia, 1961.

————. *Els valencians y la llengua autòctona durant els segles XVI, XVII i XVIII.* Valencia, 1964.

Sansone, G. E. *Studi di filologia catalana.* Bari, 1963.

Vallverdu, F. *L'escriptor català i el problema de la llengua.* Barcelona, 1968.

French Philology

Dictionaries

Bloch, Oscar, and Walther von Wartburg. *Dictionnaire étymologique de la langue française.* 5th ed. Paris: P.U.F., 1968.

Caillon, O. *Dictionnaire étymologique.* Chambéry: Edsco, 1962.

Clédat, L. *Dictionnaire étymologique de la langue française.* 12th ed. Paris: Hachette, 1929.

Cotton, G. *Vocabulaire raisonné latin-français, groupant les mots d'après leur parenté étymologique.* 3d ed. Leige and Paris: Dessain, 1961.

Dauzat, Albert, Jean Dubois, and Henri Mitterand. *Nouveau dictionnaire étymologique et historique.* Paris: Larousse, 1964.

Dubois, Jean, René Lagane, and André Lerond. *Dictionnaire du français classique.* Paris: Larousse, 1971.

Förster, Wendelin, *Wörterbuch zu Kristian von Troyes sämtlichen Werken.* Halle: Niemeyer, 1964.

Godefroy, Frédéric. *Dictionnaire de l'ancienne langue française et de tous les dialectes du IXᵉ au XVᵉ siècle.* 10 vols. Paris: Vieweg, 1880–1902.

————. *Lexique de l'ancien français.* Paris: Champion, 1967.

Grandsaignes d'Hauterive, R. *Dictionnarie d'ancien français: moyen âge et renaissance*. Paris: Larousse, 1947.

Greimas, A. J. *Dictionnaire de l'ancien français jusqu'au milieu du XIVᵉ siècle*. Paris: Larousse, 1969.

Hatzfeld, A., A. Darmesteter, and A. Thomas. *Dictionnaire général de la langue française, du commencement du XVIIᵉ siècle jusqu'à nos jours, précédé d'un Traité de la formation de la langue*. 2 vols. Paris: Delagrave, 1964.

Huguet, E. *Dictionnaire de la langue française du seizème siècle*. 7 vols. to date. Paris: Champion; Paris: Didier, 1925–.

Lebrun, L. and J. Toisoul. *Dictionnaire étymologique de la langue française*. Paris, 1953.

Littré, *Dictionnaire de la langue française*. 2 vols. Paris, 1932.

Picoche, Jacqueline. *Nouveau dictionnaire étymologique du français*. Paris: Hachette-Tchou, 1971.

Plate, R. *Etymologisches Wörterbuch der französichen Sprache*. Berlin and Bonn: Dümmler, 1931.

Sainte-Palaye, Jean-Baptiste de la Curne de. *Dictionnaire historique de l'ancien langage français*. 10 vols. Paris: Champion, 1875–82.

Tobler, Adolf, and Ernhard Lomatzsch. *Altfranzösisches Wörterbuch*. 9 vols. to date. Berlin: Weidmann; Wiesbaden: Franz Steiner, 1925–.

Urwin, K. *A Short Old French Dictionary for Students*. Foreword by John Orr. Oxford: Blackwell, 1963.

Wartburg, Walther von. *Französisches etymologisches Wörterbuch: eine Darstellung des Galloromanischen Sprachschatzes*. 25 vols. Bonn: Klop; Leipzig and Berlin: Teubner; Basel: Helbing und Lichtenhahn; Basel: Zbinden, 1928–(?).

Historical Grammars and Texts

Alessio, Giovanni. *Grammatica storica francese*. 2 vols. Bari: Leonardo da Vinci, 1951–55.

Angeli, A. *Storia della lingua francese*. Cuaderni di cultura linguistica 15. Milan: Marangoni, 1949.

Anglade, Joseph. *Grammaire élémentaire de l'ancien français*. 13th ed. Paris: Armand Colin, 1965.

Bartsch, Karl. *Chrestomathie de l'ancien français (VIIIᵉ-XVᵉ siècles), accompagnée: d'une grammaire et d'un glossaire*. 12th ed., rev. and corrected by Leo Wiese. New York: Hafner Publishing Co., 1968.

Batany, Jean. *Français médiéval: textes choisis, commentaires linguistiques, commentaires littéraires, chronologie phonétique*. Collection Etudes. Paris and Montreal: Bordas, 1972.

Bertoldi, V., *Grammatica storica della lingua francese: aspetti e problemi*. 2d ed. rev. Naples: Ligueri, 1951.

Bonaccorso, G. *Nozioni di fonetica francese con cenni di storia della lingua e di fonetica storica francese*. Messina: Ferrara, 1962.

Bonnard, Henri. *Synopsis de phonétique historique*. 2d ed. Paris: J. Touquet, 1968.

Bonnie, Jean-André et al. *Textes d'étude pour l'initiation à la langue de XVIIᵉ siècle.* Quebec: Presses de l'Université Laval, 1970.

Bourciez, Edouard. *Precis historique de phonétique française.* 9th ed. rev. Jean Bourciez. Paris: Klincksieck, 1967.

Bourciez, Jean. *Phonétique française: étude historique.* Collection, Tradition de l'Humanisme. Paris: Klincksieck, 1967.

Bruneau, Charles. *Petite histoire de la langue française.* 4th ed., rev. by M. Parent and G. Moignet. 2 vols. Paris: Armand Colin, 1966.

Brunot, Ferdinand. *Histoire de la langue française des origines à 1900.* Nouvelle edition. 15 vols. Paris: Armand Colin, 1966–.

———— and Charles Bruneau. *Précis de grammaire historique de la langue française.* 5th ed. Paris: Masson, 1969.

Buscherbruck, K. *Einführung in die historische Lautlehre des Französischen.* Berlin and Bonn: F. Dummler, 1931.

Caput, Jean-Pol. *La langue française: histoire d'une institution.* Collection L. Paris: Larousse, 1971.

Chaurand, Jacques. *Histoire de la langue française.* 2d ed. Collection "Que sais-je?" no. 167. Paris: P.U.F., 1972.

Clédat, Léon. *Nouvelle grammaire historique du français.* Paris: Garnier, 1889.

Cohen, Marcel. *Histoire d'une langue: le français.* 3d ed. Paris: Editions Sociales, 1967.

Colin, J. P., Delas D. Maldidier; J. B. Marcelessi; Mejean; Minard; and Zink. *Textes d'étude: XVIᵉ et XVIIᵉ siècles.* Paris: Centre de Documentation Universitaire, 1969.

Daële, H. van. *Phonétique historique du français.* Paris: Hatier, 1930.

Darmesteter, A., and L. Sudre. *Cours de grammaire historique de la langue française.* 3d ed. 4 vols. Paris: Delagrave, 1925.

Dauzat, A. *Histoire de la langue française.* Paris: Payot, 1930.

————. *Phonétique et grammaire historique de la langue française.* Paris: Larousse, 1951.

————. *Précis d'histoire de la langue et du vocabulaire français.* Paris: Larousse, 1951.

Davis, J. C. *The Use of the Subjunctive and the Conditional in the "Perlesvaus."* Chicago: Univ. of Chicago Libraries, 1938.

Ewert, Alfred. *The French Language.* Collection, The Great Languages. 2d ed. London: Faber and Faber, 1943.

Foulet, Lucien. *Petite syntaxe de l'ancien français.* 3d ed., rev. Classiques Français du Moyen Age. Paris: Honoré Champion, 1965.

Fox, John, and Robin Wood. *A Concise History of the French Language.* Oxford: Basil Blackwell, 1968.

François, A. *Histoire de la langue française cultivée dès origines à nos jours.* 2 vols. Geneva: Jullien, 1959.

Galliot, M. *Études d'ancien français.* Paris: Didier, 1967.

Gamillscheg, Ernst. *Historische französische Syntax.* Tübingen: Niemeyer, 1957.

Gardner, Rosalyn, and Marion St. Greene. *A Brief Description of Middle French Syntax.* Studies in the Romance Languages and Literatures, vol. 29. Chapel Hill: University of North Carolina Press, 1958.

Gougenheim, Georges. *Grammaire de la langue française du seizième siècle.* Collection, "Les Langues du Monde." Paris and Lyon: I.A.C., 1951.

Guiraud, Pierre. *L'ancien français.* Collection, "Que sais-je?" no. 1056. Paris: P.U.F., 1963.

————. *Le moyen français.* Collection, "Que sais-je?" no. 1086. Paris: P.U.F., 1963.

Haase, A. *Syntaxe française du XVIIᵉ siècle.* Translated by M. Obert. 7th ed. Paris: Delagrave; Munich: Max Hueber, 1969.

Haudricourt, André, and Alphonse Juilland. *Essai pour une histoire structurale du phonétisme français.* 2d ed., rev. The Hague and Paris: Mouton, 1970.

Henry, Albert. *Chrestomathie de la littérature en ancien français.* Bern: Francke, 1953.

Herman, József. *Précis d'histoire de la langue française.* Budapest: Tankönyvkaido, 1967.

Holmes, Urban Tigner, and Alexander H. Schutz. *A History of the French Language.* 2d ed. Columbus, Ohio: Harold L. Hedrick, 1948.

Ineichen, Gustav. *Repetitorium der altfranzösischen Lautlehre.* Berlin: Erich Schmidt, 1968.

James, A. Ll. *Historical Introduction to French Phonetics.* London: University of London Press, 1929.

Jordan, Leo. *Altfranzösisches Elementarbuch: Einführung in das historische Studium der französischen Sprache und ihren Mundarten.* Leipzig: Velhagen and Klasing, 1923.

Kukenheim, Louis. *Esquisse historique de la linguistique française et de ses rapports avec la linguistique générale.* 2d ed., rev. Leiden: Universitaire Pers Leiden, 1966.

————. *Grammaire Historique de la langue française: les parties du discours.* Publications de l'Universite de Leiden, vol. 13. Leiden: Presses Universitaires de Leiden, 1967.

————. *Grammaire historique de la langue française: les syntagmes.* Publications Romanes de l'Université de Leiden, vol. 14. Leiden: Universitaire Pers Leiden, 1968.

Lanly, André. *Fiches de philologie française.* Collection, Etudes. Paris and Montreal: Bordas, 1971.

Lerch, Eugen. *Historische französische Syntax.* 3 vols. Leipzig: O. Reisland, 1925–34.

Luquiens, Frederick Bliss. *An Introduction to Old French Phonology and Morphology.* Rev. and enl. New Haven: Yale University Press, 1926.

Mańczak, W. *Phonétique et morphologie historiques du français.* Lodž-Warszawa-Kraków: Państwowe Wydawnictwo Narodowe, 1962.

Marouzeau, J. *Du latin au français.* Collection d'Etudes Latines, Série Pédagogique, vol. 7. Paris: Belles-Lettres, 1957.

Ménard, Philippe. *Manuel d'ancien français.* Vol. 3, *Syntaxe.* Bordeaux: Sobodi, 1968.

Meyer-Lübke, Wilhelm. *Historische Grammatik der französischen Sprache.* 5th ed. 2 vols. Heidelberg: Carl Winter, 1934.

————. *Historische Grammatik der franzosischen Sprache.* Vol. 2, *Wortbildungslehre.* Rev. by Joseph Maria Piel. Sammlung romanischer Elementar-und Handbücher, Reihe 1, Bd. 2. Heidelberg: Winter, 1966.

Nyrop, Kristoffer. *Grammaire historique de la langue française.* Vol. 4, *Sémantique.* Copenhagen: Gyldendalske Boghandel-Nordisk Vorlag; Paris: Picard, 1913.

———. *Grammaire historique de la langue française.* Vol. 2, *Morphologie.* 2d ed. Copenhagen: Gyldendalske Boghandel-Nordisk Vorlag; Paris: Picard, 1924.

———. *Grammaire historique de la langue française.* Vols. 5–6, *Syntaxe.* Copenhagen: Gyldendalske Boghandel-Nordisk Vorlag; Paris: Picard, 1925–30.

———. *Grammaire historique de la langue française.* Vol. 3, *Formation des mots.* 2d ed. Copenhagen: Gyldendalske Boghandel-Nordisk Vorlag; Paris: Picard, 1936.

———. *Grammaire historique de la langue française.* Vol. 1, *Histoire générale de la langue française: phonétique.* 5th ed., rev. by P. Laurent. Copenhagen: Gyldendalske Boghandel-Nordisk Norlag; Paris: Picard, 1967.

Paris, Gaston, and Ernest Langlois. *Chrestomathie du moyen âge.* Paris: Hachette, 1887.

Paton, Dorothea A. *Manuel d'ancien français.* London: Nelson, 1933.

Placé, J. A. *Essai sur la phonétique historique du français, des origines à l'époque actuelle.* Vol. 1, *Dès origines au dernier quart du XIIᵉ siècle.* Paris: Chez l'auteur, 1956.

Poreck, Guy de. *Notions de grammaire historique du français et exercises philologiques.* 4th ed. 2 vols. Gent: Storey, 1962.

———. *Grammaire historique du français.* Gent: Gents Akademisch Kooperatief, Gakko, 1971.

Pope, Mildred K. *From Latin to Modern French, with Especial Consideration of Anglo-Norman: Phonology and Morphology.* 2d ed., rev. Manchester: Manchester University Press, 1952.

Porteau, P. *Deux études d'histoire de la langue.* Vol. 1, *Latin parlé, latin vulgaire et roman commun;* vol. 2, *Langue d'oc et langue d'oïl.* Paris: P.U.F., 1963.

Price, Glanville. *The French Language: Present and Past.* London: Edward Arnold, 1971.

Raynaud, de Lage, Guy. *Introduction à l'ancien français.* 3d ed. Paris: Société d'Edition d'Enseignement Superieur, 1962.

———. *Manuel pratique d'ancien français.* Collection, Connaissance des Langues. Paris: Picard, 1964.

Regula, Moritz. *Historische Grammatik der französischen Sprache.* 2 vols. Heidelberg: Winter, 1955–56.

Rheinfelder, Hans. *Altfranzösische Grammatik.* Vol. 1, *Lautlehre.* 3d ed. Munich: Max Hueber, 1963.

———. *Altfranzösische Grammatik.* Vol. 2, *Formenlehre.* Munich: Max Hueber, 1967.

Richter, Elise. *Beiträge zur Geschichte der Romanismen.* Vol. 1, *Chronologische Phonetik des Französischen bis zum Ende des 18. Jahrhunderts.* Beihefte zur Zeitschrift für romanische Philologie, vol. 82. Halle: Niemeyer, 1934.

Rickard, Peter. *La langue française au seizième siècle: étude suivie de textes.* Cambridge: Cambridge University Press, 1968.

Rohlfs, Gerhard. *Vom Vulgärlatein zum Altfranzösischen: Einführung in das Studium der altfranzösischen Sprache.* 2d ed. Sammlung kurzer Lehrbücher der romanischen Sprachen und Literaturen, vol. 15. Tübingen: Niemeyer, 1963.

_____. *From Vulgar Latin to Old French.* Translated by Vincent Almazan and Lillian McCarthy. Detroit: Wayne State University Press, 1970.

Roncaglia, Aurelio. *La lingua d'oïl: avviamento allo studio del francese antico.* Rome, 1971.

Sauro, A. *Grammatica storica della lingua francese.* 3 vols. Bari: Adriatica Editrice, 1952.

Schwan, Eduard. *Grammatik des Altfranzösischen.* Edited by Dietrich Behrens. 4th ed. 1931. Reprint. Darmstadt: Wiss. Buchgesellschaft, 1963.

Sneyders de Vogel, K. *Syntaxe historique du français.* 2d ed., rev. and enl. Gronigen: Wolters, 1927.

Studer, Paul and E. G. R. Waters. *Historical French Reader: Medieval Period.* 1924. Reprint. Oxford: Oxford University Press, 1967.

Thérive, A. *Libre histoire de la langue française.* Paris: Grasset, 1954.

Voretzsch, K. *Einführung in das Studium der altfranzösischen Sprache.* 9th ed., rev. Sammlung kurzer Lehrbücher der romanischen Sprachen und Literaturen, vol. 1. Gerhard Rohlfs. Tübingen: Niemeyer, 1966.

Vossler, Karl. *Frankreichs Kultur und Sprache: Geschichte der französischen Schriftsprache von den Anfängen bis zur Gegenwart.* 2d ed. Heidelberg: Carl Winter, 1929.

_____. *Langue et culture de la France.* Translated by Alphonse Juilland. Paris: Payot, 1953.

Wagner, Robert-Léon. *Introduction à la linguistique française.* 3d ed. Publications Romanes et Françaises, vol. 27. Geneva: Droz, 1964.

_____. *Textes d'étude (ancien et moyen français).* Geneva: Droz, 1964.

Wartburg, Walther von. *Évolution et structure de la langue française.* 9th ed. Bern: Francke, 1971.

Provençal and Franco-Provençal Philology

Dictionaries

Adams, George Cotton Smith. *A Census of French and Provençal Dialect Dictionaries in America.* Lancaster, Pa.: Lancaster Press, 1937.

Avril, J. T. *Dictionaire provençal-français.* Apt: E. Cartier, 1839.

Diez, Friedrich Christian. *Anciens glossaires romans corrigés et expliqués.* Paris: A. Frank, 1870.

Fourvières, R. R. and R. X. de. *Lou pichot trésor dictionnaire provençal-français et français-provençal.* Avignon, 1902.

Hombres, M. d' and G. Charvet. *Dictionaire languedocien-français, contenant les définitions, radicaux et étymologies des mots, les idiotismes, dictions, maximes, proverbes, leurs origines.* Alais: Brugueirolle, 1884.

Levy, Emil. *Petit dictionnaire provençal-français.* 3d ed. Heidelberg: Carl Winter, 1961.

———. *Provenzalsches Supplement-Wörterbuch.* 8 vols. 1894–1924. Reprint. Olm, 1972.

Mistral, Frédéric. *Lou trésor doù félibrige.* 1885. Reprint. Onansbauch: Biblio Verlag, 1972.

Offner, Philadelphe. *Dictionnaire incomplet des locutions grenobloises à l'usage des Français.* Grenoble: Petite Bibliothèque dauphinoise, 1894.

Puitspelu, N. du. *Dictionnaire étymologique du patois lyonnais.* Lyon: Georg, 1887.

Raynouard, François Juste-Marie. *Lexique roman ou dictionnaire de la langue des troubadours.* 6 vols. Paris: Silvestre, 1836–44.

Vocabulaire provençal-latin. Edited by Alphonse Blanc. 1891.

Historical Grammars and Texts

Aebischer, Paul. *Chrestomathie franco-provençale: recueil de textes franco-provençaux antérieurs à* 1630. Bibliotheca Romanica. Bern: A. Francke, 1950.

Anglade, Joseph. *Grammaire de l'ancien provençal ou ancienne langue d'oc: phonétique et morphologie.* Paris, 1921.

———. *Anthologie des troubadors.* 2d ed. Paris, 1953.

Appel, C. *Provenzalische Chrestomathie.* 3d ed. Leipzig, 1907.

———. *Provenzalische Lautlehre.* Leipzig, 1918.

Bartsch, Karl. *Grundriss zur Geschichte der Provenzalischen Literatur.* Elberfed, 1872.

——— and E. Koschwitz. *Chrestomathiche provençale.* 6th ed. Marburg, 1904.

Bayle, L. *Grammaire provençale.* N.p., 1967.

Bayle, Marc Antoine. *Anthologie provençale.* Aix, 1879.

Bec, Pierre. *La langue occitane.* Collection, "Que sais-je." Paris, 1963.

Berlitz, M. D. *Metode pèr l'ensignamen di lengo mouderno aplicado a la lengo prouveçalo.* Berlin: S. Cronbach, 1926.

Berry, A. *Florilège des troubadors.* Paris, 1930.

Berthaud, P. L., and J. Lesaffre. *Guide des études occitanes.* Paris, 1953.

Bertoni, G. *I trovatori d'Italia.* 1915. Reprint. Rome: Società Multigrafica Editrice SOMU. 1967.

Camproux, C. *Étude syntaxique des parlers gévaudannais.* Paris, n.d.

Compan, A. *Grammaire niçoise.* Nice, 1965.

Cremonesi, C. *Nozioni di grammatica storica provenzale.* 2d ed. Milan, 1962.

Crescini, Vincenzo. *Manuale per l'avviamento agli studi provenzali: introduzione grammaticale, crestomazia e glossario.* Milan: U. Hoepli, 1926.

Dauzat, A. *Les patois.* Paris, 1946.

Devaux, A. *Essai sur la langue vulgaire du Dauphiné septentrional au moyen âge.* Lyon: Côte, 1894.

Faidit, Uc. *Donatz proensals.* Edited by J. H. Marshall. London and New York: Oxford University Press, 1969.

Fouché, P. *Morphologie historique du rousillonnais.* Bibliothèque Meridionale. Toulouse: Privat, 1925.

_____. *Phonétique historique du roussillonnais.* Toulouse: Privat, 1925.

Fourvières, X. de. *Grammaire provençale suivie d'un guide de conversation.* Revised edition of *Éléments de Grammaire Provençale.* 1966.

Frank, István. *Répertoire métrique des troubadors.* Paris, 1957.

Garaud, L. *Essais: le latin populaire, sa transformation et sa dégradation étudiées au point de vue de la phonétique dans le dialecte languedocien de Palmiers (Ariège).* Paris V^e: Belin et fils, 1885.

Gourdan, A. *Langue et littérature d'oc.* Collection, "Que sais-je?" Paris, 1962.

Grafström, Ake. *Étude sur la graphie des plus anciennes chartes languedociennes, avec un essai d'interprétation phonétique.* Uppsala: Almqvist and Wiksell, 1958.

_____. *Étude sur la morphologie des plus anciennes chartes languedociennes.* Stockholm: Almqvist and Wiksell, 1968.

Grandgent, Charles Hall. *An Outline of the Phonology and Morphology of Old Provençal.* Boston: Heath and Co., 1905.

Grateloup, de [*sic*]. *Grammaire gasconne et françoise.* Paris: Maisonneuve et Leclerc, 1887.

Guérin, Pierre. *Le languedocien-nîmois.* Nîmes: J. Courroy, 1925.

Hamlin, Frank R., Peter T. Ricketts, and John Hathaway. *Introduction a l'étude de l'ancien provençal.* Geneva: Librarie Droz, 1967.

Haskall, D. C. *Provençal Literature and Language.* New York: New York Public Library, 1925.

Hill, Raymond Thompson, and Thomas Goddard Bergin. *Anthology of the Provençal Troubadours.* New Haven: Yale University Press, 1957.

Jeanroy, A. *La poésie lyrique des troubadours,* 2 vols. Paris, 1934.

Kitchen, Darcy Butterworth. *An Introduction to the Study of Provençal.* London: Williams and Northgate, 1887.

Koschwitz, Eduard. *Grammaire historique de la langue des Félibres.* Griefswald: J. Abel, 1894.

Lafon, Bernard (called Mary-Lafon, Jean). *Tableau historique et littéraire de la langue parlée dans le midi de la France et connue sous le nom de langue romane-provençale.* Paris: Mattre-Capin, 1842.

Lienig, Paul. *Die Grammatik der provenzalischen Leys d'amours.* Breslau: Koebner, 1890.

Mahn, Carl August Friedrich. *Etymologische Untersuchungen auf dem Gabiete romanischen Sprachen.* Bern, n.d.

Martinet, André. *La description phonologique avec application au parler franco-provençal d'Hauteville, Savoie.* Publications Romanes et Françaises, 56. Paris, 1939.

Maudet, F. *Histoire de la langue romane.* Paris, 1840.

Mila y Fontanals, Manuel. *De los trovadores en España.* Barcelona, 1889.

Moldenhaurer, G. *Introducción a la primitiva poesía provenzal.* Madrid, 1956.

Molinier, Guillem. *Las flors del gay saber.* Edited by Joseph Anglade. Barcelona, 1926.

Molyneaux, R. G. *Grammar and Vocabulary of the Language of Béarn for Beginners.* Oxford: March, 1888.

Pansier, P. *Histoire de la langue provençale à Avignon du XIIᵉ au XXVᵉ siècle.* Avignon: Aubanel Freres, 1925.

Raynouard, François Juste-Marie. *Choix des poésies originales des troubadours.* 6 vols. Paris: Didot, 1816–21.

Roncaglia, A. *La lingua dei trovatori, profilo di grammatica del provanzale antico.* Rome, 1965.

Ronjat, J. *Essai de syntaxe des parlers provençaux modernes.* Macon, 1913.

———. *Grammaire historique des parlers provençaux modernes.* 4 vols. Montpellier, 1930–41.

Sabersky, Heinrich. *Zur provenzalischen Lautlehre.* Berlin: Mayer and Müller, 1881.

Salvat, J. *La langue d'oc à l'école.* Paris: Occitania, 1925.

Saviniau. *Grammaire provençale.* Avignon: Aubanel, 1882.

Schultz-Gora, Oskar. *Altprovenzalisches Elementarbuch.* Heidelberg: Carl Winter, 1936.

Simonde de Sismundi, Jean Claude-Lionel. *De la littérature du Midi de l'Europe.* Vol. 1. Paris: Treuttel et Würtz, 1819.

Suchier, H. *Le français et le provençal.* Paris, 1891.

Vidal de Besalú, Roman. *Razos de trobar* in *Grammaires provençales de Hugues faidit et de R. Vidal de Besaudun, XIIIᵉ siécle.* Edited by F. Guessard. 2d ed. Reprint. Marseilles: Lafitte, 1972.

———. *The Razos de Trobar of Raimon Vidal and Associated Texts.* Edited by J. H. Marshall. London: Oxford University Press, 1972.

Spanish Philology

Dictionaries

Academia española. *Diccionario de autoridades.* Madrid, 1726–39. 6 vols.

Alcalá Venceslada, Antonio. *Vocabulario andaluz.* Madrid, 1951.

Boggs, Kasten et al. *Tentative Dictionary of Medieval Spanish.* 1946.

Casares, Julio. *Diccionario ideológico de la lengua española.* Barcelona, 1948.

Corominas, Joan. *Diccionario crítico etimológico de la lengua castellana.* 4 vols. Berne, Switzerland: Editorial Franke, 1954–55.

Covarrubias Orozco, Sebastián de. *Tesoro de la lengua castellana o española.* Madrid, 1611.

García de Diego, Vicente. *Diccionario etimológico español e hispánico.* Madrid, 1954.

Gili Gaya, Samuel. *Vox diccionario de americanismos.* Tercera edición. Buenos Aires: Emece Editores, 1946.

———. *Tesoro lexicográfico.* (1492–1726). Madrid, 1947.

Malaret, Augusto. *Diccionario de americanismos.* Tercera edición. Buenos Aires: Emece Editores, 1946.

Nebrija, Antonio de. *Diccionarium ex hispaniensi in latinum sermonem.* Salamanca, ca. 1493.

Real academia española. *Diccionario de la lengua española.* 19th ed. Madrid, 1970.

Richardson, Henry B. *An Etymological Vocabulary to the Libro de Buen Amor.* 1930.

Salvá y Pérez, Vicente. *Nuevo diccionario de la lengua castellana.* Paris, 1857.

Santamaría, Francisco J. *Diccionario general de americanismos.* Robredo, México, D. F.: Editorial Pedro, 1942–43.

Saubidet, Tito. *Vocabulario y refranero criollo.* 1943.

Historical Grammars, Bibliographies, and Texts

Alarcos Llorach, Emilio. *Fonología española.* Madrid, 1961.

Alonso, Amado. *Estudios lingüísticos: Temas españoles.* Madrid, 1951.

_____. *Estudios lingüísticos: Temas hispanoamericanos.* Madrid, 1953.

_____. *De la pronunciación medieval a la moderna en español.* Madrid, 1955.

Alvar, Manuel. *Textos hispánicos dialectales: Antología Histórica.* Revista de Filología Española, Anejo 63, vols. 1 and 2. Madrid, 1960.

Bello, Andrés y Rodolfo Oroz. *El español en Chile: Trabajos de Rodolfo Lenz.* Buenos Aires, 1940.

Bello, Andrés y Rufino J. Cuervo. *Gramática de la lengua castellana.* Buenos Aires, 1943.

Boyd-Bowman, Peter. *El habla de Guanajuato.* México, D. F., 1960.

_____. *Indice geobiográfico de cuarenta mil pobladores españoles de América en el siglo XVI.* 2 vols. Bogotá and México, 1964–68.

Canfield, D. Lincoln. *Spanish Literature in Mexican Languages as a Source for the Study of Spanish Pronunciation.* New York, 1934.

_____. *La pronunciación del español en América.* Bogotá: Instituto Caro y Cuervo, 1962.

_____. *Observaciones sobre el español salvadoreño.* Buenos Aires, 1962.

Carreter, Fernando Lázaro. *Diccionario de Términos Filológicos.* Madrid, 1953.

Catalán, Diego Menéndez-Pidal. *La escuela lingüística española y su concepción del lenguaje.* Madrid, 1955.

C.S.I.C. *Atlas Lingüístico de la Península Ibérica.* 1962.

Cuervo, Rufino J. *Apuntaciones críticas sobre el lenguaje bogotano.* 1939.

Entwistle, W. J. *The Spanish Language, together with Portuguese, Catalan and Basque.* London: Faber and Faber, 1936.

Espinosa, Aurelio M. *Estudios sobre el español de Nuevo México.* Vol. 1, *Fonetica;* Vol. 2, *Morfología.* Buenos Aires, 1930 and 1946.

Estrugo, José M. *Los sefardíes.* La Habana, 1958.

Florez, Luis. *La pronunciación del español en Bogotá.* Bogotá, 1951.

_____. *Habla y cultura popular en Antioquia.* Bogotá. 1957.

Ford, J. D. M. *Old Spanish Readings.* New York: Ginn, 1906, 1911. (Excellent introduction on phonology.)

Fotitch, Tatiana. *An Anthology of Old Spanish.* Washington, D.C., 1962.

Gili-Gaya, Samuel. *Curso superior de sintaxis española.* Barcelona, 1948.

Henriquez Ureña, Pedro. *Observaciones sobre el español en América.* 1931.

Kahane, Henry, and Angelina Pietrangeli. *Structural Studies on Spanish Themes.* 1959.
Kany, Charles. *American-Spanish Syntax.* Chicago, 1945.
————. *American-Spanish Euphemisms.* Berkeley, 1960.
————. *American-Spanish Semantics.* Berkeley, 1960.
————. tr. *Semántica hispanoamericana.* Madrid, 1962.
Lacayo, Heberto. *Como pronuncian el español en Nicaragua.* México, D. F., 1962.
Lapesa, R. *Historia de la lengua española.* Madrid, 1965.
Lenz, Rodolfo. *El español en Chile.* 1945.
Lope, Blanch, Juan M., *La filología hispánica en México.* Universidad Nacional Autónoma de México Ciudad Universitaria. México 20, D.F., 1969.
MacCurdy, Raymond. *The Spanish Dialect in St. Bernard Parish, Louisiana.* Albuquerque, 1950.
Matluck, Joseph. *La pronunciación en el español del valle de México.* México, D.F., 1951.
Menéndez-Pidal, R. *Manual de gramática histórica española.* Madrid, 1944.
————. *Orígenes del español: estado lingüístico de la península ibérica hasta el siglo XI.* Madrid, 1950.
————. *El dialecto leonés.* Oviedo, 1962.
Navarro Tomás, Tomás. *Cuestionario lingüístico hispanoamericano.* Buenos Aires, 1945.
————. *Manual de entonación española.* New York, 1948.
————. *Métrica española.* Syracuse, N.Y., 1956.
————. *Manual de pronunciación española.* New York, 1957.
Oroz, Rodolfo. *La lengua castellana en Chile.* Santiago, 1966.
Otero, Carlos-Peregrín. *Evolución y Revolución en Romance.* Editorial Seix Barral, S.A.: Barcelona, 1971.
Post, Anita C. *Southern Arizona Spanish Phonology.* University of Arizona Bulletin, vol. 5, no. 1. January 1934.
Ramsey, M. M., and R. K. Spaulding. *A Textbook of Modern Spanish.* New York: Holt, Rinehart and Winston, 1966.
Resnick, Melvyn. *The Coordination and Tabulation of Phonological Data in Spanish American Dialectology.* 1968.
Robe, Stanley. *The Spanish of Rural Panama.* 1960.
Saporta, Sol, and Heles Contreras. *A Phonological Grammar of Spanish.* 1962.
Spaulding, Robert. *How Spanish Grew.* Berkeley, 1943.
Toscano Mateus, Humberto. *El español en el Ecuador.* Madrid, 1953.
Zamora Vicente, Alonso. *El habla de Mérida y sus cercanías.* Revista de Filología Española, Anjeo 29. Madrid, 1943.
————. *Dialectología española.* N.p., 1960.

Rhetian Philology

Gartner, Th. *Handbuch der rätoromanischen Sprache und Literatur.* N.p., n.d.
————. *Raetoromanische Grammatik.* Heilbronn, 1883.

Oeuvre Suisse des Lectures pour la Jeunesse. (A series of booklets, stories for young people in various Rhetian dialects: Ladin, Sursilvan, Sutsilvan, Surmiran). La Ligia Romontscha, Via dalla Plessur 47, Cuera, Switzerland. (There are many other studies dealing with local dialects.)

Peer, Oscar. *Dicziunari rumantsch ladin-tudais*. Cuoira (Cuera): La Lia Rumantscha, 1962.

Schlatter, Martin. *J'apprends le romanche, quatrieme langue nationale. Grammaire abregée du romanche de la Basse-Engadine*. Translated and adapted by M. Viredaz. Lausanne, 1964.

Romanian Philology

Gaster, M. *Crestomatie română*. Leipzig: Brockhaus, 1891.

Ghetie, Ion et al. *Studii de limbă literară şi filologie*. Bucharest: Institutul de Lingvistică al Academiei Republicii Socialiste România, 1969.

Istoria limbii române. Vol 1. Bucharest: Academia Republici Populare Române, 1965.

Nandris, Grigore. *Colloquial Rumanian*. 2d ed. London: Routledge and Kegan Paul, 1953.

Pop, S. *Grammaire roumaine*. Bern, 1947.

Puşcariu, S. *Limba romană*. N.p., n.d.

Seiver, George O. *Introduction to Romanian*. New York: Hafner, 1953.

Sardinian Philology

Atzori, M. T. *Bibliografia di linguistica sarda*. Modena, 1959.

Wagner, M. L. *Dizionario Etimologico Sardo*. Heidelberg: Winter, 1957.

_____. *La lingua sarda: storia, spirito e forma*. Bern: Francke, 1951.

_____. *Lautlehre der Sudsardischen Mundarten*. Halle, 1907.

Index

Accent: shift in, 22–23; uses of acute, circumflex, 39
Accretion, 44–45, 101–2
Adjectives: demonstrative, 127–28; possessive, 147
Adverbs, 128–29
Agreement: between object and past participle, 129–30; in intransitive verbs, 130–31
Albanian, 31n13
Allomorphs, 7
Allophones, 7, 17
Analogy, 47, 50, 53, 55, 96n142, 107–9
Anticipation. See Assimilation
Apheresis, 43–44, 85n123, 93, 101–2
Arabic: basic vowel sounds, 6
Articles, definite: origin of, 126; assimilation to nouns in Sardinian, 127; use with possessive adjectives, 147
Assimilation, 26–27, 31, 40, 41, 47–48, 49, 50, 61n84, 103–5, 123n175, 127. See also Dissimilation
Augmentatives. See Diminutives and augmentatives
Auxiliaries. See Verbs

Babcock, Sandra S., 145
Back formation, 98n148
Balearic. See Catalan
Basque: influence of, 24, 68
Bimatización, 33, 35
Brazilian Portuguese, 9, 32, 53n62

Cantar de myo Cid, 54n64, 67, 99n46, 106n154
Case endings. See Latin cases
Castilian: formation of, 24; origin of Castilian [θ], 62n85
Catalan: where spoken, 10
Celtic (Keltic), 24, 25

Cervantes, Miguel de, 67n99
Classification of languages, 7
Clusters: consonant, 21–22. See also Consonants
Coda, syllable, 17
Comparison of languages, 7–8, 23–26
Conditional sentences, conditional tense. See Verbs
Confusion. See Contamination
Consonants: classification of, 56; initial, 57–71; medial, 72–95; voicing and loss, 72–78, 82; double consonants and groups, 82–92; palatalized combinations, 85–88, 90–91; final, 95–100
— use as spelling device: h, 66, 81; n, 83n120, 96; c, 94
Contamination (crossing), 47, 100, 101, 108, 125
Creole, creolized languages. See Haiti
Crossing. See Contamination
Culture: language and culture, 1–2

Dalmation: where spoken, 13–15
Developments: learned, semilearned, popular, 28, 36, 39, 46, 51–52, 58, 71, 84 and n122, 87 and n129
Diachronic studies, 4
Dialects, 23
Diez, Friedrich, 85n125, 109n158
Diminutives and augmentatives, 120–22
Diphthongization: in general, 31–38; in Portuguese, 124–25
Dissimilation, 40, 49, 55, 78, 79, 104–5. See also Assimilation
Doublets, 51–52, 57nn69,70
Doubling (double consonants), 77, 80–81, 82–83, 123–24

Elcock, W. D., 13n2, 15
Enclitic. See Consonants

201